ACCOUNTING ESSENTIALS FOR CAREER SECRETARIES

THIRD EDITION

A. B. CARSON, PhD, CPA

Professor of Accounting
University of California
Los Angeles

ARTHUR E. CARLSON, PhD

Professor of Accounting
Washington University
St. Louis

MARY E. BURNET, MBA, CPA

Associate Professor
Rochester Institute of Technology
Rochester, New York

 Published by

A15 **SOUTH-WESTERN PUBLISHING CO.**

Cincinnati   Chicago   Dallas   New Rochelle, N.Y.   Burlingame, Calif.   Brighton, England

Printed in the United States of America

preface

As the world of business and the professions continually grows larger and more complicated, a knowledge of accounting becomes more and more essential. More opportunities are thus created for those persons who are proficient in secretarial skills and who also have an understanding of the accounting process. *Accounting Essentials for Career Secretaries* presents a system of accounting which can be used in any business office. In addition, special attention is paid to accounting problems and situations encountered by attorneys and physicians.

The accounting cycle and the income statement and balance sheet are presented early in the course. The remaining chapters in the book are an elaboration of the basic material presented earlier. The student is thus continually building upon and reinforcing his or her knowledge of the underlying structure of accounting. Chapter 3 is devoted to accounting for cash and includes a discussion of banking procedure. Chapter 4 covers payroll accounting. The latter chapters of the book which follow those on accounting for attorneys and physicians take up the end-of-the-period activities. Because of the widespread use of various data processing procedures, the text material concludes with an appendix, "Automated Accounting Systems and Procedures."

In order to provide supplementary learning aids, each chapter consists of one or more study assignments. A workbook containing practice assignments is available. Additional accounting problems which may be used for additional work are included in the text following Chapters 4 and 8. In order to provide ready access to the meaning of the technical terms used in the book, a glossary of these terms follows the appendix.

Two new practice sets are available for use with the text. One of the sets covers one month's transactions in the office of an attorney (Wesley R. Baker, Attorney at Law). This set can be effectively started upon the completion of Chapter 5. A second set (Ebersold and Watkins, Physicians and Surgeons) provides practice in recording a month's transactions in a physician's office. This set is designed to be started upon the completion of Chapter 6. For those teachers who wish to emphasize the record keeping of a general business, a third set (Howard C. Miller, Architect), designed to correlate with *College Accounting*, is available for use after Chapter 5 or 6. All three sets are designed to give the student a review of the complete accounting cycle.

Tests are available for use following the completion of Chapters 4 and 8. Upon completion of each practice set, a test is used to determine the student's ability to interpret the records and financial statements intelligently.

The authors acknowledge with gratitude the assistance received from the Rochester, New York, professional and business community. Among those persons deserving mention are Mr. Robert H. Marlette, of Haskins & Sells; Mr. Robert J. Symon, of Arthur Andersen & Co.; Mr. Paul Cimicata, of Ernst & Ernst; Mr. Joseph M. Kostiw; and Mr. R. E. Nichols, of Accounting Forms, Inc. Special thanks are due Mr. Thomas E. Byrne, Jr., of Price Waterhouse & Co., who read Chapters 5 and 6 and who made a number of helpful suggestions.

A. B. C.
A. E. C.
M. E. B.

contents

chapter one

the nature of business accounting

The purpose of business accounting is to provide information about the financial affairs of an enterprise to the individuals, agencies, and organizations who have the need and the right to be so informed. These interested parties normally include the following:

(a) The **owners** of the business — both existing and prospective.

(b) The **managers** of the business. (Often, but not always, the owners and the managers are the same persons.)

(c) The **creditors** of the business — both existing and prospective. (*Creditors* are those who furnish or supply products and services "on credit" — meaning that payment need not be made immediately. The creditor category also includes banks and individuals who loan money to the business.)

(d) **Government agencies** — local, state, and national. (For purposes of either regulation or taxation — sometimes both — various government agencies must be given certain financial information.)

The preceding list of four classes of users of financial information applies to virtually every business enterprise. In connection with many businesses, some or all of the following also make use of relevant information: customers or clients, labor unions, competitors, trade associations, stock exchanges, commodity exchanges, financial analysts, and financial journalists.

The information needed by all of the users is not identical, though most want data regarding either results of operations — net income or loss — for a recent period, or financial status as of a recent date, or both. In addition to these requirements, a variety of other financial information may be wanted. The exact requirement depends upon who wants it and for what purpose. As might be expected, the demand for the most and greatest variety of financial information comes from the managers of the business. They constantly need up-to-the-minute information about many things.

The accountant has the task of accumulating and dispensing needed financial information. Since his activities touch upon nearly every phase of business operation and financial information is communicated in accounting terms, accounting is said to be the "language of business." Anyone intending to engage in any type of business activity is well advised to learn this language.

Since accounting relates to so many phases of business, it is not surprising that there are several fields of specialization in accounting. Some major fields are tax work, cost accounting, system design and installation, and budget preparation. Many accountants have but one employer; whereas, others become qualified as public accountants and offer their services as independent contractors or consultants. Some states license individuals as *Public Accountants* or *Registered Accountants*. All states grant the designation *Certified Public Accountant* (CPA) to those who meet various prescribed requirements, including the passing of a uniform examination prepared by the American Institute of Certified Public Accountants. Public accountants perform various functions. One of their major activities is *auditing*. This involves testing and checking the records of an enterprise to be certain that acceptable policies and practices have been consistently followed. In recent years, public accountants have been extending their activities into what is called "management services" — a term that covers a variety of consulting assignments. Specialization is common among members of the accounting profession. Tax work is one important specialty.

All of the foregoing comments have related to accounting and accountants in connection with profit-seeking organizations. Since there are thousands of nonprofit organizations (such as governments, educational institutions, churches, and hospitals) that also need to accumulate financial information, thousands of accountants are in their employ. These organizations also engage public accountants. While the "rules of the game" are somewhat different for nonprofit organizations, much of the record keeping is identical with that found in business.

the accounting process

Accounting Defined

A widely quoted definition of accounting is

> . . . the art of recording, classifying, and summarizing in a significant manner and in terms of money, transactions and events which are, in part at least, of a financial character, and interpreting the results thereof.[1]

Recording traditionally has meant writing something by hand. Much of the record keeping in accounting still is manual, but for years typewriters and many varieties of so-called "bookkeeping machines" (which, typically, combine the major attributes of typewriters and adding machines or desk calculators) have been in use. Today the recording sometimes takes the form of holes punched in certain places on a card or a paper tape, or of invisible magnetized spots on a special type of tape used to feed information into an electronic computer.

Classifying relates to the process of sorting or grouping like things together rather than merely keeping a simple, diary-like narrative record of numerous and varied transactions and events.

Summarizing is the process of bringing together various items of information to determine or explain a result.

Interpretation refers to the steps taken to direct attention to the significance of various matters and relationships. Percentage analyses and ratios often are used to help explain the meaning of certain related bits of information.

---

[1]*Accounting Research and Terminology Bulletins, Final Edition,* "No. 1 — Review and Résumé" (New York: American Institute of Certified Public Accountants, 1961), p. 9.

Accounting and Bookkeeping

Accounting involves records design, policy making, data analysis, report preparation, and report interpretation. A person involved with or responsible for these functions may be referred to as an accountant. Bookkeeping is the recording phase of the accounting process. The person who records the information in the books of account may be referred to as a bookkeeper. Sometimes the accountant also serves as the bookkeeper, an experience that may be of great value to him.

Accounting Elements

If complete accounting records are to be maintained, all transactions and events that affect the accounting elements must be recorded. The accounting elements are *assets, liabilities,* and *owner's equity.*

Assets. Properties of value that are owned by a business are called assets. Properties such as money, accounts receivable, notes receivable, merchandise, furniture, fixtures, machinery, buildings, and land are common examples of business assets. *Accounts receivable* are unwritten promises by customers to pay for goods purchased on credit or for services rendered. *Notes receivable* are formal written promises by debtors to pay specified sums of money at some future time.

It is possible to conduct a business or a professional practice with very few assets. A dentist, for example, may have relatively few assets, such as money, instruments, laboratory equipment, and office equipment. But in many cases, a variety of assets is necessary. A merchant must have merchandise to sell and store equipment on which to display the merchandise, in addition to other assets. A manufacturer must have materials, tools, and various sorts of machinery, in addition to other assets.

Liabilities. An obligation of a business to pay a debt is a business liability. The most common liabilities are accounts payable and notes payable. *Accounts payable* are unwritten promises to pay creditors for property, such as merchandise, supplies, and equipment purchased on credit, or for services rendered. *Notes payable* are formal written promises to pay creditors or lenders specified sums of money at some future time. A business also may have one or more types of *taxes payable.*

Owner's Equity. The amount by which the business assets exceed the business liabilities is termed the owner's equity in the business. The word *equity* used in this sense means "interest in" or "claim of." It would be quite reasonable to call liabilities "creditors' equity," but this is not customary. The terms *proprietorship, net worth,* or *capital* are sometimes used as synonyms for owner's equity. If there are no business liabilities, the owner's equity in the business is equal to the total amount of the assets of the business.

In visualizing a business that is owned and operated by one person (traditionally called the proprietor), it is essential to realize that a distinction must be made between his *business* assets and liabilities and any *nonbusiness* assets and liabilities that he may have. The proprietor will certainly have various types of personal property, such as clothing; it is probable that he will have a home, furniture, and a car. He may own a wide variety of other valuable properties quite apart from his business. Likewise the proprietor may owe money for reasons that do not pertain to his business. Amounts owed to merchants from whom food and clothing have been purchased and amounts owed to doctors and dentists for services received are common examples. Legally there is no distinction between his business and nonbusiness assets nor between his business and nonbusiness liabilities; but since it is to be expected that the formal accounting records for the enterprise will relate to the business only, any nonbusiness assets and liabilities should be excluded. While the term "owner's equity" can be used in a very broad sense, its use in accounting is nearly always limited to the meaning: business assets minus business liabilities.

Frequent reference will be made to the owner's investing money or other property in the business, or to his withdrawal of money or other property from the business. All that is involved in either case is that some property is changed from the category of a nonbusiness asset to a business asset or vice versa. It should be apparent that these distinctions are important if the owner is to be able to judge the financial condition and results of the operations of his business apart from his nonbusiness affairs.

The Accounting Equation

The relationship between the three accounting elements can be expressed in the form of a simple equation:

$$\text{ASSETS} = \text{LIABILITIES} + \text{OWNER'S EQUITY}$$

When the amounts of any two of these elements are known, the third can always be calculated. For example, C. J. Wilson has assets in his business on December 31 in the sum of $21,800. His business debts on that date consist of $300 owed for supplies purchased on credit and $400 owed to a bank on a note. The owner's equity element of his business may be calculated by subtraction ($21,800 − $700 = $21,100). These facts about his business can be expressed in equation form as follows:

$$\begin{array}{ccc} \text{ASSETS} & = \text{LIABILITIES} + & \text{OWNER'S EQUITY} \\ \$21,800 & \$700 & \$21,100 \end{array}$$

For Mr. Wilson to increase his equity in the business, he must either increase the assets without increasing the liabilities, or decrease the liabilities without decreasing the assets. For him to increase the assets and owner's equity without investing more money or other property in the business, he will have to operate the business at a profit.

For example, if one year later the assets amount to $32,900 and the liabilities to $1,300, the status of the business would be as follows:

$$\text{ASSETS} = \text{LIABILITIES} + \text{OWNER'S EQUITY}$$
$$\$32,900 \qquad \$1,300 \qquad\qquad \$31,600$$

However, the fact that Mr. Wilson's equity in the business increased by $10,500 (from $21,100 to $31,600) does not prove that he made a profit (often called *net income*) equal to the increase. He might have invested additional money or other property in the business. Suppose, for example, that he invested additional money during the year in the amount of $4,000. In that event the remainder of the increase in his equity ($6,500) would have been due to profit (net income).

Another possibility could be that he had a very profitable year and withdrew assets in an amount less than the amount of profit. For example, his equity might have been increased by $15,000 as a result of profitable operation, and during the year he might have withdrawn a total of $4,500 in cash for personal use. This series of events could account for the $10,500 increase. It is essential that the business records show the extent to which the change in owner's equity is due to the regular operation of the business and the extent to which increases and decreases in owner's equity are due to the owner's investing and withdrawing assets.

Transactions

The activities of an enterprise which involve the exchange of values are usually referred to as *transactions*. These values are expressed in terms of money. Buying and selling property and services are common transactions. The following typical transactions are analyzed to show that each one represents an exchange of values.

TYPICAL TRANSACTIONS	ANALYSIS OF TRANSACTIONS
(a) Purchased equipment for cash, $250.	Money is exchanged for equipment.
(b) Received cash in payment of professional fees, $125.	Professional service is rendered in exchange for money.
(c) Paid office rent, $100.	Money is exchanged for the right to use property.
(d) Paid a debt owed to a creditor, $300.	Money is given in settlement of a debt that may have resulted from the purchase of property on credit or from services rendered by a creditor.
(e) Paid wages in cash, $90.	Money is exchanged for services rendered.

(f) Borrowed $1,000 at a bank giving a 6 percent interest-bearing note due in 30 days.

A liability known as a note payable is incurred in exchange for money.

(g) Purchased office equipment on credit, $200.

A liability known as an account payable is incurred in exchange for office equipment.

Effect of Transactions on the Accounting Equation

Each transaction affects one or more of the three accounting elements. For example, the purchase of equipment for cash represents both an increase and a decrease in assets. The assets are increased because equipment is acquired; the assets are decreased because cash is disbursed. If the equipment were purchased on credit, thereby incurring a liability, the transaction would result in an increase in assets (equipment) with a corresponding increase in liabilities (accounts payable). Neither of these transactions has any effect upon the owner's equity element of the equation.

The effect of any transaction on the accounting elements may be indicated by addition and subtraction. To illustrate: assume that David Bennett, an engineer, decided to go into business for himself. During the first month of this venture (May, 1971), the following transactions relating to his business took place:

An Increase in an Asset Offset by an Increase in Owner's Equity

Transaction (a). Mr. Bennett opened a bank account with a deposit of $3,000. This transaction caused his new business to receive the asset cash, and since no business liabilities were involved, the owner's equity element was increased by the same amount. As a result of this transaction, the equation for the business appears as follows:

$$\left. \begin{array}{c} \underline{\text{ASSETS}} \\ \text{Cash} \\ \text{(a) } 3{,}000 \end{array} \right\} = \left\{ \begin{array}{c} \underline{\text{LIABILITIES} + \text{ OWNER'S EQUITY}} \\ \text{David Bennett, Capital} \\ 3{,}000 \end{array} \right.$$

An Increase in an Asset Offset by an Increase in a Liability

Transaction (b). Mr. Bennett purchased office equipment (desk, chairs, file cabinet, etc.) for $2,600 on 30 days' credit. This transaction caused the asset office equipment to increase by $2,600 and resulted in an equal increase in the liability accounts payable. Amending the foregoing equation by this (b) transaction gives the following result:

ASSETS		LIABILITIES	+ OWNER'S EQUITY
Cash + Office Equipment		Accounts Payable	David Bennett, Capital
Bal. 3,000			3,000
(b) +2,600		+2,600	
Bal. 3,000 2,600		2,600	3,000

An Increase in One Asset Offset by a Decrease in Another Asset

Transaction (c). Mr. Bennett purchased office supplies (stationery, carbon paper, pencils, etc.) for cash, $350. This transaction caused a $350 increase in the asset office supplies that exactly offset the $350 decrease in the asset cash. The effect on the equation is as follows:

ASSETS				LIABILITIES + OWNER'S EQUITY	
	Office	Office		Accounts	David Bennett,
Cash +	Equipment +	Supplies		Payable	Capital
Bal. 3,000	2,600		=	2,600	3,000
(c) − 350		+350			
Bal. 2,650	2,600	350		2,600	3,000

A Decrease in an Asset Offset by a Decrease in a Liability

Transaction (d). Mr. Bennett paid $1,000 on account to the company from which the office equipment was purchased. (See Transaction (b).) This payment caused the asset cash and the liability accounts payable both to decrease $1,000. The effect on the equation is as follows:

ASSETS				LIABILITIES + OWNER'S EQUITY	
	Office	Office		Accounts	David Bennett,
Cash +	Equipment +	Supplies		Payable	Capital
Bal. 2,650	2,600	350	=	2,600	3,000
(d) −1,000				−1,000	
Bal. 1,650	2,600	350		1,600	3,000

An Increase in an Asset Offset by an Increase in Owner's Equity Resulting from Revenue

Transaction (e). Mr. Bennett received $900 cash from a client for professional services. This transaction caused the asset cash to increase $900, and since the liabilities were not affected, the owner's equity increased by the same amount. The effect on the equation is as follows:

ASSETS				LIABILITIES + OWNER'S EQUITY	
	Office	Office		Accounts	David Bennett,
Cash +	Equipment +	Supplies		Payable	Capital
Bal. 1,650	2,600	350	=	1,600	3,000
(e) + 900					+ 900
Bal. 2,550	2,600	350		1,600	3,900

A Decrease in an Asset Offset by a Decrease in Owner's Equity Resulting from Expense

Transaction (f). Mr. Bennett paid $200 for office rent for May. This transaction caused the asset cash to be reduced by $200 with an equal reduction in owner's equity. The effect on the equation is as follows:

ASSETS				LIABILITIES + OWNER'S EQUITY	
	Office	Office		Accounts	David Bennett,
Cash +	Equipment +	Supplies		Payable	Capital
Bal. 2,550	2,600	350	=	1,600	3,900
(f) − 200					− 200
Bal. 2,350	2,600	350		1,600	3,700

Transaction (g). Mr. Bennett paid a bill for telephone service, $21. This transaction, like the previous one, caused a decrease in the asset cash with an equal decrease in owner's equity. The effect on the equation is as follows:

ASSETS				LIABILITIES + OWNER'S EQUITY	
	Office	Office		Accounts	David Bennett,
Cash +	Equipment +	Supplies		Payable	Capital
Bal. 2,350	2,600	350	=	1,600	3,700
(g) − 21					− 21
Bal. 2,329	2,600	350		1,600	3,679

The Financial Statements

A set of accounting records is maintained to fill a variety of needs. Foremost is its use as source data in preparing various reports including those referred to as *financial statements*. The two most important of these are the *income statement* and the *balance sheet*.

The Income Statement. The income statement, sometimes called a *profit and loss statement* or *operating statement*, shows the *net income* (*net profit*) or *net loss* for a specified period of time and how it was calculated. A very simple income statement relating to the business of David Bennett for the first month's operation, May, 1971, is shown below. The information it contains was obtained by analysis of the changes in the owner's equity element of the business for the month. This element went from zero to $3,679. Part of this increase, $3,000, was due to the investment of Mr. Bennett. The remainder of the increase, $679, must have been due to net income, since Mr. Bennett had made no withdrawals. Transaction (e) involved revenue of $900; transactions (f) and (g) involved expenses of $200 and $21, respectively. Taken together, these three transactions explain the net income of $679.

DAVID BENNETT, ENGINEER
Income Statement
For the Month of May, 1971

Professional fees.........................		$900
Expenses:		
Rent expense........................	$200	
Telephone expense....................	21	221
Net income for month....................		$679

The Balance Sheet. The balance sheet, sometimes called a *statement of financial condition* or *statement of financial position*, shows the assets, liabilities, and owner's equity of a business at a specified date. A balance sheet for Mr. Bennett's business as of May 31, 1971, is shown below. The information it contains was obtained from the accounting equation after the last (g) transaction.

DAVID BENNETT, ENGINEER
Balance Sheet
May 31, 1971

Assets		Liabilities	
Cash........................	$2,329	Accounts payable..........	$1,600
Office supplies.............	350	**Owner's Equity**	
Office equipment..........	2,600	David Bennett, capital.......	3,679
	$5,279		$5,279

NOTE: In order to keep the illustrations of transaction analysis, the income statement, and the balance sheet as simple as possible at this point, two expenses were ignored; namely, office supplies used and depreciation of office equipment.

Report No. 1

A workbook is provided for use with this textbook. Each practice assignment in the workbook is referred to as a report. The work involved in completing Report No. 1 requires a knowledge of the principles developed in the preceding study assignment. Before proceeding with the following assignment, complete Report No. 1 in accordance with the instructions given in the workbook.

the double-entry mechanism

The meanings of the terms asset, liability, and owner's equity were explained in the preceding pages. Examples were given to show how each business transaction causes a change in one or more of the three accounting elements. The first transaction (a) shown on page 7 involved an increase in an asset with a corresponding increase in owner's equity. In the second transaction (b), an increase in an asset caused an equal increase in a liability. In the third transaction (c), an increase in one asset was offset by a decrease in another. In each of the transactions illustrated, there was this *dual effect*. This is always true. A change (increase or decrease) in any asset, any liability, or in owner's equity is always accompanied by an offsetting change within the accounting elements.

The fact that each transaction has two aspects — a dual effect upon the accounting elements — provides the basis for what is called *double-entry bookkeeping*. This phrase describes a recording system that involves the making of a record of each of the two aspects that are involved in every transaction. Double entry does not mean that a transaction is recorded twice; instead, it means that both of the two aspects of each transaction are recorded.

The technique of double entry is described and illustrated in the following pages. This method of recording transactions is not new. Double entry is known to have been practiced for at least 500 years. This long popularity is easily explained since the method has several virtues. It is orderly, fairly simple, and very flexible. There is no transaction that cannot be recorded in a double-entry manner. Double entry promotes accuracy. Its use makes it impossible for certain types of errors to remain undetected for very long. For example, if one aspect of a transaction is properly recorded but the other part is overlooked, it will soon be found that the records are "out of balance." The bookkeeper then knows that something is wrong and can check his work to discover the trouble and can make the needed correction.

The Account

It has been explained previously that the assets of a business may consist of a number of items, such as money, accounts receivable, notes receivable, merchandise, equipment, buildings, and land. The liabilities may consist of one or more items, such as accounts payable and notes payable. A separate record should be kept of each asset and of each liability. Later it will be shown that a separate record should also be kept of the increases and decreases in owner's equity. The form of record kept for each item is known as an *account*. There are many types of account forms in general use. They may be ruled on sheets of paper and bound in book form or kept in a loose-leaf binder, or they may be ruled on cards and kept in a file of some sort. Following is an illustration of a standard form of account that is widely used:

ACCOUNT									ACCOUNT NO.
DATE	ITEMS	POST. REF.	✓	DEBITS	DATE	ITEMS	POST. REF.	✓	CREDITS

Standard Form of Account

This account form is designed to facilitate the recording of the essential information regarding each transaction that affects the account. Before any entries are recorded in an account, the title and number of the account should be written on the horizontal line at the top of the form. Each account should be given an appropriate title that will indicate whether it is an asset, a liability, or an owner's equity account. The standard account form is divided into two equal parts or sections which are ruled identically to facilitate recording increases and decreases. The left side is called the debit side, while the right side is called the credit side. The columnar arrangement and headings of the columns on both sides are the same except that the amount column on the left is headed "Debits" while that on the right is headed "Credits." The Date columns are used for recording the dates of transactions. The Items columns may be used for writing a brief description of a transaction when deemed necessary. The Posting Reference columns and the (√) columns will be discussed later. The Debits and Credits columns are used for recording the amounts of transactions.

The three major parts of the standard account form are **(1)** the title (and, usually, the account number), **(2)** the debit side, and **(3)** the credit side. To determine the balance of an account at any time, it is necessary only to total the amounts in the Debits and Credits columns, and calculate the difference between the two totals. To save time, a "T" form of account is commonly used for instructional purposes. It consists of a two-line drawing resembling the capital letter T and is sometimes referred to as a skeleton form of account.

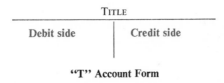

TITLE

| Debit side | Credit side |

"T" Account Form

Debits and Credits

To debit an account means to record an amount on the left or debit side of the account. To credit an account means to record an amount on the right or credit side of the account. The abbreviation for debit is Dr. and for credit Cr. Sometimes the word *charge* is used as a substitute for debit. Increases in assets are recorded on the left side of the accounts; increases in liabilities and in owner's equity are recorded on the right side of the accounts. Decreases in assets are recorded on the right side of the accounts; decreases in liabilities and in owner's equity are recorded on the left side of the accounts. Recording increases and decreases in the accounts in this manner will reflect the basic equality of assets to liabilities plus owner's equity; at the same time it will maintain equality between the total amounts debited to all accounts and the total amounts credited to all accounts. These basic relationships may be illustrated in the following manner:

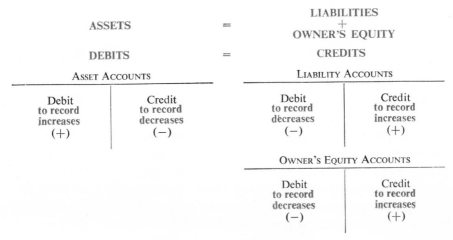

		LIABILITIES
ASSETS	=	+ OWNER'S EQUITY
DEBITS	=	CREDITS

ASSET ACCOUNTS

| Debit to record increases (+) | Credit to record decreases (−) |

LIABILITY ACCOUNTS

| Debit to record decreases (−) | Credit to record increases (+) |

OWNER'S EQUITY ACCOUNTS

| Debit to record decreases (−) | Credit to record increases (+) |

Use of Asset, Liability, and Owner's Equity Accounts

To illustrate the application of the double-entry process, the transactions discussed on pages 7–9 will be analyzed and their effect on the accounting elements will be indicated by showing the proper entries in "T" accounts. As before, the transactions are identified by letters; dates are omitted intentionally.

An Increase in an Asset Offset by an Increase in Owner's Equity

Transaction (a). David Bennett, an engineer, started a business of his own and invested $3,000 in cash.

CASH		DAVID BENNETT, CAPITAL	
(a) 3,000			(a) 3,000

Analysis: As a result of this transaction the business acquired an asset, cash. The amount of money invested by Mr. Bennett represents his equity in the business; thus the amount of the asset cash is equal to the owner's equity in the business. Separate accounts are kept for the asset cash and for the owner. To record the transaction properly, the cash account was debited and David Bennett's capital account was credited for $3,000.

An Increase in an Asset Offset by an Increase in a Liability

Transaction (b). Purchased office equipment (desk, chairs, file cabinet, etc.) for $2,600 on 30 days' credit.

OFFICE EQUIPMENT		ACCOUNTS PAYABLE	
(b) 2,600			(b) 2,600

Analysis: As a result of this transaction the business acquired a new asset, office equipment. The debt incurred as a result of purchasing the office equipment on 30 days' credit is a liability, accounts payable. Separate accounts are kept for office equipment and for accounts payable. The purchase of office equipment caused an increase in the assets of the business. Therefore, the asset account Office Equipment was debited for $2,600. The purchase also caused an increase in a liability. Therefore, the liability account Accounts Payable was credited for $2,600.

An Increase in One Asset Offset by a Decrease in Another Asset

Transaction (c). Purchased office and drawing supplies (stationery, carbon paper, pencils, etc.) for cash, $350.

CASH				OFFICE SUPPLIES	
(a)	3,000	(c)	350	(c)	350

Analysis: As a result of this transaction the business acquired a new asset, office supplies. However, the addition of this asset was offset by a decrease in the asset cash. To record the transaction properly, Office Supplies was debited and Cash was credited for $350. (It will be noted that this is the second entry in the cash account; the account was previously debited for $3,000 when Transaction (a) was recorded.)

It is proper to record office supplies as an asset at time of purchase even though they will become an expense when consumed. The procedure in accounting for supplies consumed will be discussed later.

A Decrease in an Asset Offset by a Decrease in a Liability

Transaction (d). Paid $1,000 "on account" to the company from which the office equipment was purchased. (See Transaction (b).)

CASH				ACCOUNTS PAYABLE			
(a)	3,000	(c)	350	(d)	1,000	(b)	2,600
		(d)	1,000				

Analysis: This transaction resulted in a decrease in the liability accounts payable with a corresponding decrease in the asset cash; hence, it was recorded by debiting Accounts Payable and by crediting Cash for $1,000. (It will be noted that this is the second entry in the accounts payable account and the third entry in the cash account.)

Revenue and Expense

The owner's equity element of a business or professional enterprise may be increased in two ways as follows:

(a) The owner may invest additional money or other property in the enterprise. Such investments result in an increase in both the assets of the enterprise and in the owner's equity, but they do not further enrich the owner; he merely has more property invested in the enterprise and less property outside of the enterprise.

(b) Revenue may be derived from sales of goods or services, or from other sources.

As used in accounting, the term *revenue* refers to an increase in the owner's equity in a business resulting from transactions of any kind except the investment of assets in the business by its owner. In most cases, the increase in owner's equity due to revenue results from an addition to the assets without any change in the liabilities. Often it is cash that is increased. However, an increase in cash and other assets can occur in connection with several types of transactions that do not involve revenue. For this reason, revenue is defined in terms of the change in owner's equity rather than the change in assets. Any transaction that causes owner's equity to increase, except investments in the business by its owner, involves revenue.

The owner's equity element of a business or professional enterprise may be decreased in two ways as follows:

(a) The owner may withdraw assets (cash or other property) from the enterprise.

(b) Expenses may be incurred in operating the enterprise.

As used in accounting, the term *expense* means a decrease in the owner's equity in a business caused by a transaction other than a withdrawal by the owner. When an expense is incurred, either the assets are reduced or the liabilities are increased. In either event, owner's equity is reduced. If the transaction causing the reduction was not a withdrawal of assets by the owner, an expense was incurred. Common examples of expense are rent of office or store, salaries of employees, telephone service, supplies consumed, and many types of taxes.

If, during a specified period of time, the total increases in owner's equity resulting from revenue exceed the total decreases resulting from expenses, it may be said that the excess represents the *net income* or net profit for the period. On the other hand, if the expenses of the period exceed the revenue, such excess represents a *net loss* for the period. The time interval used in the measurement of net income or net loss can be chosen by the owner. It may be a month, a quarter (three months), a year, or some other period of time. If the accounting period is a year, it is usually referred to as a *fiscal year*. The fiscal year frequently coincides with the *calendar year*.

Transactions involving revenue and expense always cause a change in the owner's equity element of an enterprise. Such changes could be recorded by debiting the owner's equity account for expenses and crediting it for revenue. If this practice were followed, however, the credit side of the owner's equity account would contain a mixture of increases due to revenue and to the investment of assets in the business by the owner, while the debit side would contain a mixture of decreases due to expenses and to the withdrawal of assets from the business by the owner. In order to calculate the net income or the net loss for each accounting period, a careful analysis of the owner's equity account would be required. It is, therefore, better practice to record revenue and expenses in separate accounts. These are called *temporary* owner's equity accounts because it is customary to close them at the end of each accounting period by transferring their balances to a *summary* account. The balance of this summary account then represents the net income or net loss for the period. The summary account is also a temporary account which is closed by transferring its balance to the owner's equity account.

A separate account should be kept for each type of revenue and for each type of expense. When a transaction produces revenue, the amount of the revenue should be credited to an appropriate revenue account. When a transaction involves expense, the amount of the expense should be debited to an appropriate expense account. The relationship of these temporary accounts to the owner's equity account and the application of the debit and credit theory to the accounts are indicated in the following diagram:

OWNER'S EQUITY ACCOUNT

Debit to record decreases (−)	Credit to record increases (+)

EXPENSE ACCOUNTS		REVENUE ACCOUNTS	
Debit to record increases (+)	Credit to record decreases (−)	Debit to record decreases (−)	Credit to record increases (+)

It is important to recognize that the credit side of each revenue account is serving temporarily as a part of the credit side of the owner's equity account. Increases in owner's equity are recorded as credits. Thus, increases in owner's equity resulting from revenue should be credited to revenue accounts. The debit side of each expense account is serving temporarily as a part of the debit side of the owner's equity account. Decreases in owner's equity are recorded as debits. Thus, decreases in owner's equity resulting from expense should be debited to expense accounts.

Use of Revenue and Expense Accounts

To illustrate the application of the double-entry process in recording transactions that affect revenue and expense accounts, the additional transactions completed by David Bennett, an engineer, will be analyzed and their effect on the accounting elements will be indicated by showing the proper entries in "T" accounts. These transactions represent a continuation of the transactions completed by David Bennett in the conduct of his business. (See pages 14 and 15 for Transactions (a) to (d).)

An Increase in an Asset Offset by an Increase in Owner's Equity Resulting from Revenue

Transaction (e). Received $900 in cash from a client for professional services rendered.

CASH				PROFESSIONAL FEES	
(a)	3,000	(c)	350	(e)	900
(e)	900	(d)	1,000		

Analysis: This transaction resulted in an increase in the asset cash with a corresponding increase in owner's equity because of revenue from professional fees. To record the transaction properly, Cash was debited and an appropriate account for the revenue was credited for $900. Accounts should always be given a descriptive title that will aid in classifying them in relation to the accounting elements. In this case the revenue account was given the title Professional Fees. (It will be noted that this is the fourth entry in the cash account and the first entry in the account Professional Fees.)

A Decrease in an Asset Offset by a Decrease in Owner's Equity Resulting from Expense

Transaction (f). Paid $200 for office rent for one month.

CASH				RENT EXPENSE	
(a)	3,000	(c)	350	(f)	200
(e)	900	(d)	1,000		
		(f)	200		

Analysis: This transaction resulted in a decrease in the asset cash with a corresponding decrease in owner's equity because of expense. To record the transaction properly, Rent Expense was debited and Cash was credited for $200. (This is the first entry in the rent expense account and the fifth entry in the cash account.)

Transaction (g). Paid bill for telephone service, $21.

CASH				TELEPHONE EXPENSE	
(a)	3,000	(c)	350	(g)	21
(e)	900	(d)	1,000		
		(f)	200		
		(g)	21		

Analysis: This transaction is identical with the previous one except that telephone expense rather than rent expense was the reason for the decrease in owner's equity. To record the transaction properly, Telephone Expense was debited and Cash was credited for $21.

The Trial Balance

It is a fundamental principle of double-entry bookkeeping that the amount of the assets is always equal to the sum of the liabilities and owner's equity. In order to maintain this equality in recording transactions, the sum of the debit entries must always be equal to the sum of the credit entries. To determine whether this equality has been maintained, it is customary to take a trial balance periodically. A *trial balance* is a list of all of the accounts showing the title and balance of each account. The balance of any account is the difference between the total debits and the total credits to the account. Preliminary to taking a trial balance, the debit and credit amounts in each account should be totaled. This is called *footing* the amount columns. If there is only one item entered in a column, no footing is necessary. To find the balance of an account it is necessary only to determine the difference between the footings by subtraction. Since asset and expense accounts are debited for increases, these accounts normally have *debit balances*. Since liability, owner's equity, and revenue accounts are credited to record increases, these accounts normally have *credit balances*. The balance of an account should be entered on the side of the account that has the larger total. The footings and balances of accounts should be written in small figures just below the last entry. A pencil is generally used for this purpose. If the footings of an account are equal in amount the account is said to be *in balance*.

The accounts of David Bennett are reproduced below. To show the relationship to the fundamental accounting equation, the accounts are arranged in three columns under the headings of Assets, Liabilities, and Owner's Equity. It will be noted that the cash account has been footed and the balance inserted on the left side. The footings and the balance are printed in italics. It was not necessary to foot any of the other accounts

ASSETS	=	LIABILITIES	+	OWNER'S EQUITY

CASH

(a)	3,000	(c)	350
(e)	900	(d)	1,000
2,329	*3,900*	(f)	200
		(g)	21
			1,571

OFFICE SUPPLIES

| (c) | 350 |

OFFICE EQUIPMENT

| (b) | 2,600 |

ACCOUNTS PAYABLE

| (d) | 1,000 | (b) | 2,600 |
| | | *1,600* | |

DAVID BENNETT, CAPITAL

| | | (a) | 3,000 |

PROFESSIONAL FEES

| | | (e) | 900 |

RENT EXPENSE

| (f) | 200 |

TELEPHONE EXPENSE

| (g) | 21 |

because none of them contained more than one entry on either side. The balance of the accounts payable account is shown on the credit side in italics. It was not necessary to enter the balances of the other accounts because there were entries on only one side of the accounts.

A trial balance of these accounts is shown below. The trial balance was taken on May 31, 1971; therefore, this date is shown in the third line of the heading. The trial balance reveals that the debit and credit totals are equal in amount. This is proof that in recording Transactions (a) to (g) inclusive the total of the debits was equal to the total of the credits.

David Bennett, Engineer
Trial Balance
May 31, 1971

Account	Dr. Balance	Cr. Balance
Cash	2329 00	
Office Supplies	350 00	
Office Equipment	2600 00	
Accounts Payable		1600 00
David Bennett, Capital		3000 00
Professional Fees		900 00
Rent Expense	200 00	
Telephone Expense	21 00	
	5500 00	5500 00

A trial balance is not a formal statement or report. Normally, it is never seen by anyone except the accountant or bookkeeper. It is used to aid in preparing the income statement and the balance sheet. If the above trial balance is studied in conjunction with the income statement and balance sheet shown on pages 9 and 10, it will be seen that those statements could have been prepared quite easily from the information that this trial balance provides.

Report No. 2

Refer to the workbook and complete Report No. 2 in accordance with the instructions given therein. The work involved in completing the assignment requires a knowledge of the principles developed in the preceding discussion. Any difficulty experienced in completing the report will indicate a lack of understanding of these principles. In such event further study should be helpful. After completing the report, you may continue with the textbook discussion in Chapter 2 until the next report is required.

chapter two

accounting procedure

The principles of double-entry bookkeeping were explained and illustrated in the preceding pages. To avoid distraction from the fundamentals, the mechanics of collecting and classifying information about business transactions were ignored. In actual practice the first record of a transaction (sometimes called the "immediate record") is made in the form of a business paper, such as a check stub, receipt, cash register tape, sales ticket, or purchase invoice. The information supplied by business papers is an aid in analyzing transactions to determine their effect upon the accounts.

journalizing transactions

The first formal double-entry record of a transaction is usually made in a record called a *journal* (frequently in book form). The act of recording transactions in a journal is called *journalizing*. It is necessary to analyze each transaction before it can be journalized properly. The purpose of the journal entries is to provide a chronological record of all transactions completed showing the date of each transaction, titles of accounts to be debited and credited, and amounts of the debits and credits. The journal then provides all the information needed to record the debits and credits in the proper accounts. The flow of data concerning transactions can be illustrated in the following manner:

Transactions are evidenced by various BUSINESS PAPERS——►The business papers provide the information needed to record the transactions in a JOURNAL——►The journal provides the information needed to record the debits and credits in the accounts which collectively comprise a LEDGER

Business Papers

The term business papers covers a wide variety of forms and documents. Almost any document that provides information about a business transaction can be called a business paper.

BUSINESS PAPERS

Examples:	Provide Information about:
(a) Check stubs or carbon copies of checks	Cash disbursements
(b) Receipt stubs, or carbon copies of receipts, cash register tapes, or memos of cash register totals	Cash receipts
(c) Copies of sales tickets or sales invoices issued to customers or clients	Sales of goods or services
(d) Purchase invoices received from vendors	Purchases of goods or services

The Journal

While the original record of a transaction usually is a business paper as explained above, the first formal double-entry record of a transaction is made in a journal. For this reason a journal is commonly referred to as a *book of original entry*. The ruling of the pages of a journal varies with the type and size of an enterprise and the nature of its operations. The simplest form of journal is a two-column journal. A standard form of such a journal is illustrated on page 23. It is referred to as a two-column journal because it has only two amount columns, one for debits and one for credits. In the illustration the columns have been numbered as a means of identification in connection with the following discussion.

DATE	DESCRIPTION	POST. REF.	DEBITS	CREDITS
①	②	③	④	⑤

Standard Two-Column Journal

Column No. 1 is a date column. The year should be written in small figures at the top of the column immediately below the column heading and need only be repeated at the top of each new page unless an entry for a new year is made farther down on the page. The date column is a double column, the perpendicular single rule being used to separate the month from the day. Thus in writing June 20, the name of the month should be written to the left of the single line and the number designating the day of the month should be written to the right of this line. The name of the month need only be shown for the first entry on a page unless an entry for a new month is made farther down on the page.

Column No. 2 is generally referred to as a description or an explanation column. It is used to record the titles of the accounts affected by each transaction, together with a description of the transaction. Two or more accounts are affected by each transaction, and the titles of all accounts affected must be recorded. Normally the titles of the accounts debited are written first and then the titles of the accounts credited. A separate line should be used for each account title. The titles of the accounts to be debited are generally written at the extreme left of the column, while the titles of the accounts to be credited are usually indented about one-half inch. The description should be written immediately following the credit entry, and usually is indented an additional one-half inch. Reference to the journal reproduced on pages 29 and 30 will help to visualize the arrangement of the copy in the Description column. An orderly arrangement is desirable.

Column No. 3 is a posting reference column — sometimes referred to as a folio column. No entries are made in this column at the time of journalizing the transactions; such entries are made only at the time of posting (which is the process of entering the debits and credits in the proper accounts in the ledger). This procedure will be explained in detail later in this chapter.

Column No. 4 is an amount column in which the amount that is to be debited to any account should be written on the line on which the title of the account appears. In other words, the name of the account to be debited should be written in the Description column and the amount of the debit entry should be written on the same line in the Debits column.

Column No. 5 is an amount column in which the amount that is to be credited to any account should be written on the line on which the title of the account appears. In other words, the name of the account to be credited should be written in the Description column and the amount of the credit entry should be written on the same line in the Credits column.

Journalizing

Journalizing involves recording the desired information concerning each transaction either (1) at the time the transaction occurs or (2) subsequently, but in the chronological order in which the transactions occurred. For every transaction the entry should record the date, the title of each account affected, the amount, and a brief description. The only effect a transaction can have on any account is either to increase or to decrease the balance of the account. Before a transaction can be recorded properly, therefore, it must be analyzed in order to determine:

(a) Which accounts are affected by the transaction.
(b) What effect the transaction has upon each of the accounts involved; that is, whether the balance of each affected account is increased or decreased.

The Chart of Accounts

In analyzing a transaction preparatory to journalizing it, the accountant or bookkeeper must know which accounts are being kept. When an accounting system is being established for a new business, the first step is to decide which accounts are required. The accounts used will depend upon the information needed or desired. Ordinarily it will be found desirable to keep a separate account for each type of asset and each type of liability, since it is certain that information will be desired in regard to what is owned and what is owed. A permanent owner's equity or capital account should be kept in order that information may be available as to the owner's interest or equity in the business. Furthermore, it is advisable to keep separate accounts for each type of revenue and each kind of expense. The revenue and expense accounts are the temporary accounts that are used in recording increases and decreases in owner's equity apart from changes caused by the owner's investments and withdrawals. The specific accounts to be kept for recording the increases and the decreases in owner's equity depend upon the nature and the sources of the revenue and of the expenses incurred in earning the revenue.

A professional man or an individual engaged in operating a small enterprise may need to keep relatively few accounts. On the other hand, a large manufacturing enterprise, a public utility, or any large business may need to keep a great many accounts in order that the information required or desired may be available. Regardless of the number of accounts kept, they can be segregated into the three general classes and should be grouped according to these classes in the ledger. The usual custom is to place the asset accounts first, the liability accounts second, and the owner's equity accounts, including the revenue and the expense accounts, last. It is common practice to prepare a list of the accounts that are to be kept. This list, often in the form of an outline, is called a *chart of accounts*. It has become a general practice to give each account a number and to keep the accounts in numerical order. The numbering usually follows a consistent pattern and becomes a *code*. For example, asset accounts may be assigned numbers that always start with "1," liability accounts with "2," owner's equity accounts with "3," revenue accounts with "4," and expense accounts with "5."

To illustrate: Suppose that on November 30, 1971, C. D. Whitman engages in the advertising business under the name of The Whitman Advertising Agency. He decides to keep his accounts on the calendar year basis; therefore, his first accounting period will be for one month only; that is, the month of December. It is decided that a two-column journal and a ledger with standard form of account will be used. Mr. Whitman realizes that he will not need many accounts at present because the business is new. He also realizes that additional accounts may be added as the need arises. Following is a chart of the accounts to be kept at the start:

THE WHITMAN ADVERTISING AGENCY

CHART OF ACCOUNTS

*Assets**
11 Cash
12 Office Supplies
13 Office Equipment

Liabilities
21 Accounts Payable

Owner's Equity
31 C. D. Whitman, Capital
32 C. D. Whitman, Drawing

Revenue
41 Advertising Fees

Expenses
51 Rent Expense
52 Salary Expense
53 Traveling Expense
54 Telephone Expense
55 Office Supplies Expense
56 Miscellaneous Expense

*Words in italics represent headings and not account titles.

Journalizing Procedure Illustrated

To illustrate journalizing procedure, the transactions completed by The Whitman Advertising Agency through December 31, 1971, will be journalized. A *narrative* of the transactions follows. It provides all of the information that is needed in journalizing the transactions. Some of the transactions are analyzed to explain their effect upon the accounts, with the journal entry immediately following the explanation of the entry. The journal of The Whitman Advertising Agency with all of the entries recorded is reproduced on pages 29 and 30.

THE WHITMAN ADVERTISING AGENCY

NARRATIVE OF TRANSACTIONS

Tuesday, November 30, 1971

Mr. Whitman invested $1,500 cash in a business enterprise to be known as The Whitman Advertising Agency.

As a result of this transaction, the business acquired the asset cash in the amount of $1,500. Since neither a decrease in any other asset nor an increase in any liability was involved, the transaction caused an increase of $1,500 in owner's equity. Accordingly, the entry to record the transaction is a debit to Cash and a credit to C. D. Whitman, Capital, for $1,500.

	JOURNAL			PAGE 1
DATE	DESCRIPTION	POST. REF.	DEBITS	CREDITS
1971 Nov. 30	Cash		1 50 0 00	
	C. D. Whitman, Capital			1 50 0 00
	Original investment in			
	advertising agency.			

Note that the following steps were involved:

(a) Since this was the first entry on the journal page, the year was written at the top of the Date column.

(b) The month and day were written on the first line in the Date column.

(c) The title of the account to be debited, Cash, was written on the first line at the extreme left of the Description column. The amount of the debit, $1,500, was written on the same line in the Debits column.

(d) The title of the account to be credited, C. D. Whitman, Capital, was written on the second line indented one-half inch from the left side of the Description column. The amount of the credit, $1,500, was written on the same line in the Credits column.

(e) The explanation of the entry was started on the next line indented an additional one-half inch. The second line of the explanation was also indented the same distance as the first.

Wednesday, December 1

Paid office rent for December in advance, $200.

This transaction resulted in a decrease in owner's equity because of expense, with a corresponding decrease in the asset cash. The transaction is recorded by debiting Rent Expense and by crediting Cash for $200.

Dec 1	Rent Expense		2 0 0 00	
	Cash			2 0 0 00
	Paid December rent.			

Note: Mr. Whitman ordered several pieces of office equipment. Since the dealer did not have in stock what Mr. Whitman wanted, the articles were ordered from the factory. Delivery is not expected until the latter part of the month. Pending their arrival, the dealer loaned Mr. Whitman some used office equipment. No entry is required until the new equipment is received.

Thursday, December 2

Purchased office supplies from the Central Supply Co. on account, $183.14.

In this transaction the business acquired a new asset which represented an increase in the total assets. A liability was also incurred because of the purchase on account. The transaction is recorded by debiting Office Supplies and by crediting Accounts Payable for $183.14. As these supplies are consumed, they will become an expense of the business.

2	Office Supplies		1 8 3 14	
	Accounts Payable			1 8 3 14
	Central Supply Co.			

Friday, December 3

Paid the City Telephone Co. $22.50 covering the cost of installing a telephone in the office, together with the first month's service charges payable in advance.

This transaction caused a decrease in owner's equity because of expense and a corresponding decrease in the asset cash. The transaction is recorded by debiting Telephone Expense and by crediting Cash for $22.50.

3	Telephone Expense		2 2 50	
	Cash			2 2 50
	Paid telephone bill.			

Monday, December 6

Paid $6 for a subscription to a trade journal.

This transaction resulted in a decrease in owner's equity due to expense and a corresponding decrease in the asset cash. The transaction is recorded by debiting Miscellaneous Expense and by crediting Cash for $6.

6	Miscellaneous Expense		6 00	
	Cash			6 00
	Trade journal subscription.			

Tuesday, December 7

Received $125 from the City Hardware Co. for services rendered.

This transaction resulted in an increase in the asset cash with a corresponding increase in owner's equity because of revenue from advertising fees. The transaction is recorded by debiting Cash and by crediting Advertising Fees for $125. In keeping his accounts Mr. Whitman follows the practice of not recording revenue until it is received in cash. This practice is common to professional and personal service enterprises.

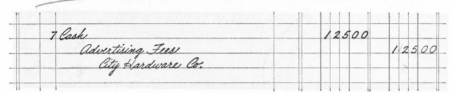

Note: The Posting Reference column has been left blank in the six foregoing journal entry illustrations. This is because the column is not used until the amounts are posted to the accounts in the ledger, a process to be described starting on page 31. Account numbers are shown in the Posting Reference column of the journal illustrated on pages 29–30, since the illustration shows how the journal appears *after* the posting has been completed.

The journal entries for the following transactions are illustrated on pages 29–30.

Thursday, December 9

Paid the Brown Travel Service $128.30 for a plane ticket to be used the next week for a business trip.

Wednesday, December 15

Paid Mary Bergstrom $175 covering her salary for the first half of the month.

Miss Bergstrom is employed by Mr. Whitman as his secretary and bookkeeper at a salary of $350 a month. The transaction resulted in a decrease in owner's equity because of salary expense with a corresponding decrease in the asset cash. The transaction is recorded by debiting Salary Expense and by crediting Cash for $175. (The matter of payroll taxes is purposely ignored at this point. These taxes will be discussed in detail in Chapter 4.)

Thursday, December 16

Received $365 from The Morton Manufacturing Co. in payment for services rendered.

Monday, December 20

Mr. Whitman withdrew $300 for personal use.

Amounts of cash withdrawn for personal use by the owner of a business enterprise represent a decrease in owner's equity. Although amounts withdrawn might be recorded as debits to the owner's capital account, it is better practice to record withdrawals in a separate account. Doing it in this way makes it a little easier to summarize the decreases in owner's equity caused by the owner's withdrawals. This transaction is recorded in the journal by debiting C. D. Whitman, Drawing, and by crediting Cash for $300.

Wednesday, December 22

Received $520 from Mid-Town Sales Co. for services rendered.

DATE	DESCRIPTION	POST. REF.	DEBITS	CREDITS
1971 Nov. 30	Cash	11	150000	
	C. D. Whitman, Capital	31		150000
	Original investment in			
	advertising agency.			
Dec. 1	Rent Expense	51	20000	
	Cash	11		20000
	Paid December rent.			
2	Office Supplies	12	18314	
	Accounts Payable	21		18314
	Central Supply Co.			
3	Telephone Expense	54	2250	
	Cash	11		2250
	Paid telephone bill.			
6	Miscellaneous Expense	56	600	
	Cash	11		600
	Trade journal subscription.			
7	Cash	11	12500	
	Advertising Fees	41		12500
	City Hardware Co.			
9	Traveling Expense	53	12830	
	Cash	11		12830
	Plane fare - business trip.			
15	Salary Expense	52	17500	
	Cash	11		17500
	Paid secretary's salary.			
16	Cash	11	36500	
	Advertising Fees	41		36500
	The Morton Mfg. Co.			
20	C. D. Whitman, Drawing	32	30000	
	Cash	11		30000
	Withdrawn for personal use.			
22	Cash	11	52000	
	Advertising Fees	41		52000
	Mid-Town Sales Co.			
23	Miscellaneous Expense	56	3000	
	Cash	11		3000
	N.A.A.A. dues.			
27	Office Equipment	13	237221	
	Accounts Payable	21		237221
	Acme Office Equipment Co.		592715	592715

The Whitman Advertising Agency Journal

DATE	DESCRIPTION	POST. REF.	DEBITS	CREDITS
1971 Dec. 28	Accounts Payable	21	18314	
	Cash	11		18314
	Central Supply Co.			
28	Cash	11	35000	
	Advertising Fees	41		35000
	Gordon Downey.			
31	Salary Expense	52	17500	
	Cash	11		17500
	Paid secretary's salary.			
31	Office Supplies Expense	55	2000	
	Office Supplies	12		2000
	Cost of supplies used			
	during December.		72814	72814

The Whitman Advertising Agency Journal

Note: Some bookkeepers leave a blank line after the explanation of each entry.

Thursday, December 23

Paid $30 membership dues in the National Association of Advertising Agencies.

Monday, December 27

Received the office equipment ordered December 1. These items were purchased on account from the Acme Office Equipment Co. Cost: $2,372.21. The dealer removed the used equipment that had been loaned to Mr. Whitman.

Tuesday, December 28

Paid the Central Supply Co. $183.14 for the office supplies purchased on December 2.

> This transaction caused a decrease in the liability accounts payable with a corresponding decrease in the asset cash. The transaction was recorded by debiting Accounts Payable and by crediting Cash for $183.14.

Received $350 from Gordon Downey for services rendered.

Friday, December 31

Paid Mary Bergstrom $175 covering her salary for the second half of the month.

Office supplies used during the month, $20.

> By referring to the transaction of December 2 it will be noted that office supplies amounting to $183.14 were purchased and were recorded as an asset. By taking an

inventory, counting the supplies in stock at the end of the month, Mr. Whitman was able to determine that the cost of supplies used during the month amounted to $20. The expenses for the month of December would not be reflected properly in the accounts if the supplies used during the month were not taken into consideration. Therefore, the cost of supplies used was recorded by debiting the expense account, Office Supplies Expense, and by crediting the asset account, Office Supplies, for $20.

Proving the Journal

Because a double entry is made for each transaction, the equality of debit and credit entries on each page of the journal may be proved merely by totaling the amount columns. The total of each column is usually entered as a footing immediately under the last entry. When a page of the journal is filled, the footings may be entered just under the last single horizontal ruled line at the bottom of the page as shown in the illustration on page 29. When the page is not filled, the footings should be entered immediately under the last entry as shown in the illustration on page 30.

Report No. 3

Refer to the workbook and complete Report No. 3. To complete this assignment correctly, the principles developed in the preceding discussion must be understood. Review the text assignment if necessary. After completing the report, continue with the following study assignment until the next report is required.

posting to the ledger; the trial balance

The purpose of a journal is to provide a chronological record of financial transactions expressed as debits and credits to accounts. These accounts are kept to supply desired information. Collectively the accounts are described as the *general ledger* or, often, simply as "the ledger." The account forms may be on sheets of paper or on cards. When on sheets of paper, the sheets may be bound in book form or they may be kept in a loose-leaf binder. Usually a separate page or card is used for each account. The accounts should be classified properly in the ledger; that is, the asset accounts should be grouped together, the liability accounts together, and the owner's equity accounts together. A proper grouping of the accounts in the ledger is an aid in preparing the various reports desired by the owner. Mr. Whitman decided to keep all of the accounts for The Whitman Advertising Agency in a loose-leaf ledger. The numbers shown in the agency's chart of accounts on page 25 were used as a guide in arranging the accounts in the ledger. The ledger of The Whitman Advertising Agency is reproduced on pages 34 and 35. Note that the accounts are in numerical order.

Since Mr. Whitman makes few purchases on account, he does not keep a separate account for each creditor. When invoices are received for items purchased on account, the invoices are checked and recorded in the journal by debiting the proper accounts and by crediting Accounts Payable. The credit balance of Accounts Payable indicates the total amount owed to creditors. After each invoice is recorded, it is filed in an unpaid invoice file, where it remains until it is paid in full. When an invoice is paid in full, it is removed from the unpaid invoice file and is then filed under the name of the creditor for future reference. The balance of the accounts payable account may be proved at any time by determining the total of the unpaid amounts of the invoices.

Posting

The process of recording information in the ledger is known as *posting*. All amounts entered in the journal should be posted to the accounts kept in the ledger in order to summarize the results. Such posting may be done daily or at frequent intervals. The ledger is not a reliable source of information until all the transactions recorded in the journal have been posted.

Since the accounts provide the information needed in preparing financial statements, a posting procedure that will insure accuracy in maintaining the accounts must necessarily be followed. Posting from the journal to the ledger involves recording the following information in the accounts:

(a) The date of each transaction.
(b) The amount of each transaction.
(c) The page of the journal from which each transaction is posted.

As each amount in the journal is posted to the proper account in the ledger, the number of that account should be entered in the *Posting Reference* column in the journal so as to provide a cross-reference between the journal and the ledger. The first entry to be posted from the journal (a segment of which is reproduced below) required a debit to Cash of $1,500. This was accomplished by entering the year, "1971," the month, abbreviated "Nov.," and the day, "30," in the Date column of the cash account (reproduced below); the number "1" in the Posting Reference column (since the posting came from Page 1 of the journal); and the amount, "1,500.00," in the Debits column. Inasmuch as the number of the cash account is 11, that number was entered in the Posting Reference column of the journal on the same line as the debit of 1,500.00 that was just posted to Cash. The same pattern was followed in posting the credit part of the entry — $1,500 to C. D. Whitman, Capital, Account No. 31 (reproduced below).

Reference to the journal of The Whitman Advertising Agency (reproduced on pages 29 and 30) and its ledger (reproduced on pages 34 and 35) will indicate that a similar procedure was followed in posting every amount from the journal. Note also that in the ledger, the year "1971" was entered only at the top of each Date column, and that (with the exception of the first posting to Cash and the first posting to C. D. Whitman, Capital, where the month "Nov." was entered) the month "Dec." was entered only with the first posting to an account.

ACCOUNT *Cash*   ACCOUNT NO. 11

DATE	ITEMS	POST. REF.	✓	DEBITS	DATE	ITEMS	POST. REF.	✓	CREDITS
1971 Nov. 30		1		1 5 0 0 0 0	1971 Dec. 1		1		2 0 0 0
Dec. 7		1		1 2 5 0 0	3		1		2 2 5 0
16		1		3 6 5 0 0	6		1		6 0 0
22		1		5 2 0 0 0	9		1		1 2 8 3 0
28	1,640.06	2		3 5 0 0 0	15		1		1 7 5 0 0
				2 7 6 0 0 0	20		1		3 0 0 0 0
					23		1		3 0 0
					28		2		1 8 3 1 4
					31		2		1 7 5 0 0
									1 2 1 9 9 4

ACCOUNT *Office Supplies*   ACCOUNT NO. 12

DATE	ITEMS	POST. REF.	✓	DEBITS	DATE	ITEMS	POST. REF.	✓	CREDITS
1971 Dec. 2	163.14	1		1 8 3 1 4	1971 Dec. 31		2		2 0 0 0

ACCOUNT *Office Equipment*   ACCOUNT NO. 13

DATE	ITEMS	POST. REF.	✓	DEBITS	DATE	ITEMS	POST. REF.	✓	CREDITS
1971 Dec. 27		1		2 3 7 2 2 1						

ACCOUNT *Accounts Payable*   ACCOUNT NO. 21

DATE	ITEMS	POST. REF.	✓	DEBITS	DATE	ITEMS	POST. REF.	✓	CREDITS
1971 Dec. 28		2		1 8 3 1 4	1971 Dec. 2		1		1 8 3 1 4
					27	2,372.21	1		2 3 7 2 2 1
									2 5 5 5 3 5

ACCOUNT *C. D. Whitman, Capital*   ACCOUNT NO. 31

DATE	ITEMS	POST. REF.	✓	DEBITS	DATE	ITEMS	POST. REF.	✓	CREDITS
					1971 Nov. 30		1		1 5 0 0 0 0

ACCOUNT *C. D. Whitman, Drawing*   ACCOUNT NO. 32

DATE	ITEMS	POST. REF.	✓	DEBITS	DATE	ITEMS	POST. REF.	✓	CREDITS
1971 Dec. 20		1		3 0 0 0 0						

The Whitman Advertising Agency Ledger

ACCOUNT *Advertising Fees*   **ACCOUNT NO.** 41

DATE	ITEMS	POST. REF.	✓	DEBITS	DATE	ITEMS	POST. REF.	✓	CREDITS
					1971 Dec. 7		1		1 2500
					16		1		3 6500
					22		1		5 2000
					28		2		3 5000
									1 3 6 0 0 0

ACCOUNT *Rent Expense*   **ACCOUNT NO.** 51

DATE	ITEMS	POST. REF.	✓	DEBITS	DATE	ITEMS	POST. REF.	✓	CREDITS
1971 Dec. 1		1		2 0000					

ACCOUNT *Salary Expense*   **ACCOUNT NO.** 52

DATE	ITEMS	POST. REF.	✓	DEBITS	DATE	ITEMS	POST. REF.	✓	CREDITS
1971 Dec. 15		1		1 7500					
31		2		1 7500					
				3 5 0 0 0					

ACCOUNT *Traveling Expense*   **ACCOUNT NO.** 53

DATE	ITEMS	POST. REF.	✓	DEBITS	DATE	ITEMS	POST. REF.	✓	CREDITS
1971 Dec. 9		1		1 2830					

ACCOUNT *Telephone Expense*   **ACCOUNT NO.** 54

DATE	ITEMS	POST. REF.	✓	DEBITS	DATE	ITEMS	POST. REF.	✓	CREDITS
1971 Dec. 3		1		2250					

ACCOUNT *Office Supplies Expense*   **ACCOUNT NO.** 55

DATE	ITEMS	POST. REF.	✓	DEBITS	DATE	ITEMS	POST. REF.	✓	CREDITS
1971 Dec. 31		2		2000					

ACCOUNT *Miscellaneous Expense*   **ACCOUNT NO.** 56

DATE	ITEMS	POST. REF.	✓	DEBITS	DATE	ITEMS	POST. REF.	✓	CREDITS
1971 Dec. 6		1		600					
23		1		3000					
				3 6 0 0					

The Whitman Advertising Agency Ledger

It will be seen from the foregoing discussion that there are four steps involved in posting — three involving information to be recorded in the ledger and one involving information to be recorded in the journal. The date, the amount, and the effect of each transaction are first recorded in the journal. The same information is later posted to the ledger. Posting does not involve an analysis of each transaction to determine its effect upon the accounts. Such an analysis is made at the time of recording the transaction in the journal, and posting is merely transcribing the information in the ledger. In posting, care should be used to record each debit and each credit entry in the proper columns so that the entries will reflect correctly the effects of the transactions on the accounts.

When the posting is completed, the same information is provided in both the journal and the ledger as to the date, the amount, and the effect of each transaction. A cross-reference from each book to the other book is also provided. This cross-reference makes it possible to trace the entry of November 30 on the debit side of the cash account in the ledger to the journal by referring to the page indicated in the Posting Reference column. The entry of November 30 on the credit side of the account for C. D. Whitman, Capital, may also be traced to the journal by referring to the page indicated in the Posting Reference column. Each entry in the journal may be traced to the ledger by referring to the account numbers indicated in the Posting Reference column of the journal. By referring to pages 29 and 30, it will be seen that the account numbers were inserted in the Posting Reference column. This was done as the posting was completed.

The Trial Balance

The purpose of a trial balance is to prove that the totals of the debit and credit balances in the ledger are equal. In double-entry bookkeeping, equality of debit and credit balances in the ledger must be maintained. A trial balance may be taken daily, weekly, monthly, or whenever desired. Before taking a trial balance, all transactions previously completed should be journalized and the posting should be completed in order that the effect of all transactions will be reflected in the ledger accounts.

Footing Accounts. When an account form similar to the one illustrated on page 35 is used, it is necessary to foot or add the amounts recorded in each account preparatory to taking a trial balance. The footings should be recorded immediately below the last item in both the debit and credit amount columns of the account. The footings should be written in small figures close to the preceding line so that they will not interfere with the recording of an item on the next ruled line. At the same time, the balance, the difference between the footings, should be computed and recorded in small figures in the Items column of the account on the side with the larger footing. In other words, if an account has a debit balance, the balance should be written in the Items column on the debit or left side of the account. If the account has a credit balance, the balance should be written in the Items column on the credit or right side of the account. The balance or difference between the footings should be recorded in the Items column just below the line on which the last regular entry appears and in line with the footing.

Reference to the accounts kept in the ledger shown on pages 34 and 35 will reveal that the accounts have been footed and will show how the footings and the balances are recorded. When only one item has been posted to an account, regardless of whether it is a debit or a credit amount, no footing is necessary.

Care should be used in computing the balances of the accounts. If an error is made in adding the columns or in determining the difference between the footings, the error will be carried to the trial balance, and considerable time may be required to locate the mistake. Most accounting errors result from carelessness. For example, a careless bookkeeper may write an account balance on the wrong side of an account or may enter figures so illegibly that they may be misread later. Neatness in writing the amounts is just as important as accuracy in determining the footings and the balances.

Preparing the Trial Balance. It is important that the following procedure be followed in preparing a trial balance:

(a) Head the trial balance, being certain to show the name of the individual, firm, or organization, and the date. (The date shown is the day of the last transaction that is included in the accounts — usually the last day of a month. Actually, the trial balance might be prepared on January 3, but if the accounts reflected only transactions through December 31, this is the date that should be used.)

(b) List the account titles in order, showing each account number.

(c) Record the account balances in parallel columns, entering debit balances in the left amount column and credit balances in the right amount column.

(d) Add the columns and record the totals, ruling a single line across the amount columns above the totals and a double line below the totals in the manner shown in the illustration on page 38.

Even though the trial balance indicates that the ledger is in balance, there may be errors in the ledger. For example, if a journal entry has been made in which the wrong accounts are debited or credited, or if an item has been posted to the wrong account, the ledger will still be in balance. It is important, therefore, that extreme care be used in preparing the journal entries and in posting them to the ledger accounts.

A trial balance is usually prepared on ruled paper (though it can be typewritten on plain paper if desired). An illustration of the trial balance, as of December 31, 1971, of the ledger of The Whitman Advertising Agency is shown below.

Account	No.	Dr. Balance	Cr. Balance
The Whitman Advertising Agency			
Trial Balance			
December 31, 1971			
Cash	11	1 640 06	
Office Supplies	12	1 63 14	
Office Equipment	13	2 372 21	
Accounts Payable	21		2 372 21
C. D. Whitman, Capital	31		1 500 00
C. D. Whitman, Drawing	32	300 00	
Advertising Fees	41		1 360 00
Rent Expense	51	200 00	
Salary Expense	52	350 00	
Traveling Expense	53	128 30	
Telephone Expense	54	22 50	
Office Supplies Expense	55	20 00	
Miscellaneous Expense	56	36 00	
		5 232 21	5 232 21

Model Trial Balance

Report No. 4

Refer to the workbook and complete Report No. 4. To complete this assignment correctly, the principles developed in the preceding discussion must be understood. Review the text assignment if necessary. After completing the report, continue with the following study assignment until the next report is required.

the financial statements

The transactions completed by The Whitman Advertising Agency during the month of December were recorded in a two-column journal (see pages 29 and 30). The debits and credits were subsequently posted to the proper accounts in a ledger (see pages 34 and 35). At the end of the month a trial balance was taken as a means of proving that the equality of debits and credits had been maintained throughout the journalizing and posting procedures (see page 38).

Although a trial balance may provide much of the information that the owner of a business may desire, it is primarily a device used by the bookkeeper for the purpose of proving the equality of the debit and credit account balances. Although the trial balance of The Whitman Advertising Agency taken as of December 31 contains a list of all of the accounts showing the amounts of the debit and credit balances, it does not present all of the information that Mr. Whitman may need or desire regarding either the results of operations during the month or the status of his business at the end of the month. To meet these needs it is customary to prepare two types of *financial statements*. One is known as an income statement and the other as a balance sheet or statement of financial position.

The Income Statement

The purpose of an *income statement* is to provide information regarding the results of operations *during a specified period of time*. It is an itemized statement of the changes in owner's equity resulting from the revenue and expenses of the period. Such changes are recorded in temporary owner's equity accounts known as revenue and expense accounts. Changes in owner's equity resulting from investments or withdrawals of assets by the owner are not included in the income statement as they involve neither revenue nor expense.

A model income statement for The Whitman Advertising Agency showing the results of operations for the month ended December 31, 1971, is reproduced on page 40. The heading of an income statement consists of the following:

    (a) The name of the business.
    (b) The title of the statement.
    (c) The period of time covered by the statement.

The body of an income statement consists of **(1)** an itemized list of the sources and amounts of revenue for the period and **(2)** an itemized list of the various expenses incurred during the period.

The financial statements are usually first prepared on ruled paper. Such handwritten copies may then be typed so that a number of copies will be available for those who are interested in examining the statements. Since the typewritten copies are not on ruled paper, dollar signs are included in the handwritten copy so that the typist will understand just where they are to be inserted. Note that a dollar sign is placed beside the first amount in each column and the first amount below a ruling in each column. The income statement illustrated below is shown on two-column ruled paper; however, the columns do not have any debit-credit significance.

The Whitman Advertising Agency		
Income Statement		
For the Month Ended December 31, 1971		
Revenue:		
Advertising fees		$1360.00
Expenses:		
Rent expense	$200.00	
Salary expense	350.00	
Traveling expense	128.30	
Telephone expense	22.50	
Office supplies expense	20.00	
Miscellaneous expense	36.00	
Total expenses		756.80
Net income		$ 603.20

Model Income Statement

In the case of The Whitman Advertising Agency the only source of revenue was advertising fees that amounted to $1,360. The total expenses for the month amounted to $756.80. The revenue exceeded the expenses by $603.20. This represents the amount of the net income for the month. If the total expenses had exceeded the total revenue, the excess would have represented a net loss for the month.

The trial balance supplied the information needed in preparing the income statement. However, it can be seen readily that the income statement provides more information concerning the results of the month's operations than is supplied by the trial balance.

The Balance Sheet

The purpose of a *balance sheet* is to provide information regarding the financial condition of a business enterprise *as of a specified time or date*. It is an itemized statement of the assets, liabilities, and owner's equity at the close of business on the date indicated in the heading.

A model balance sheet for The Whitman Advertising Agency showing the status of the business as of December 31, 1971, is reproduced on pages 42 and 43. The heading of a balance sheet contains the following:

(a) The name of the business.
(b) The title of the statement.
(c) The date of the statement.

The body of a balance sheet consists of an itemized list of the assets, the liabilities, and the owner's equity, the latter being the difference between the total amount of the assets and the total amount of the liabilities. The balance sheet illustrated is arranged in account form. Note the similarity of this form of balance sheet to the standard account form illustrated on page 12. The assets are listed on the left side and the liabilities and owner's equity are listed on the right side. The information provided by the balance sheet of The Whitman Advertising Agency may be summarized in equation form as follows:

$$\text{ASSETS} = \text{LIABILITIES} + \text{OWNER'S EQUITY}$$
$$\$4,175.41 \qquad \$2,372.21 \qquad \$1,803.20$$

The trial balance was the source of the information needed in listing the assets and the liabilities in the balance sheet. The amount of the owner's equity may be calculated by subtracting the total liabilities from the total assets. Thus, the amount of Mr. Whitman's equity in The Whitman Advertising Agency as of December 31 was computed in the following manner:

Total assets	$4,175.41
Less total liabilities	2,372.21
Owner's equity	$1,803.20

Proof of the amount of the owner's equity as calculated above may be determined by taking into consideration the following factors:

(a) The amount invested in the enterprise by Mr. Whitman on November 30 as shown by his capital account.
(b) The amount of the net income of The Whitman Advertising Agency for December as shown by the income statement.
(c) The total amount withdrawn for personal use during December as shown by Mr. Whitman's drawing account.

Assets													
Cash	$	1	6	4	0	0	6						
Office supplies			1	6	3	1	4						
Office equipment		2	3	7	2	2	1						
Total assets								$	4	1	7	5	4	1

Model Balance Sheet — Account Form (Left Page)

The trial balance on page 38 shows that Mr. Whitman's equity in The Whitman Advertising Agency on November 30 amounted to $1,500. This is indicated by the credit balance of his capital account. The income statement shows that the net income of The Whitman Advertising Agency for December amounted to $603.20. The trial balance on page 38 shows that the amount withdrawn by Mr. Whitman for personal use during the month amounted to $300. This is indicated by the debit balance of his drawing account. On the basis of this information, Mr. Whitman's equity in the Whitman Advertising Agency as of December 31, 1971, may be computed as follows:

Amount of capital November 30		$1,500.00
Net income for December	$603.20	
Less amount withdrawn for personal use during the month.	300.00	303.20
Capital at end of December		$1,803.20

Liabilities											
Accounts payable			$ 2 3 7 2 2 1								
Total liabilities						$ 2 3 7 2 2 1					
Owner's Equity											
C. D. Whitman, capital											
Capital, Nov. 30, 1971				1 5 0 0 0 0							
Net income	$ 603.20										
Less withdrawals	300.00										
Net increase				3 0 3 2 0							
Capital, Dec. 31, 1971						1 8 0 3 2 0					
Total liabilities and owner's equity						$ 4 1 7 5 4 1					

Model Balance Sheet — Account Form (Right Page)

Report No. 5

Refer to the workbook and complete Report No. 5. This assignment provides a test of your ability to apply the principles developed in Chapters 1 and 2 of this textbook. The textbook and the workbook go hand in hand, each serving a definite purpose in the learning process. Inability to solve correctly any problem included in the report indicates that you have failed to master the principles developed in the textbook. After completing the report, you may proceed with the textbook discussion in Chapter 3 until the next report is required.

chapter three

accounting for cash

In the preceding chapters the purpose and nature of business accounting, transaction analysis, and the mechanics of double-entry bookkeeping were introduced. Explanations and illustrations were given of **(1)** *journalizing* (recording transactions in a *general journal* — a "book of original entry"), **(2)** *posting* (transcribing the entries to the accounts that, all together, comprise the *general ledger*), **(3)** taking a *trial balance*, and **(4)** using the latter to aid in preparing an *income statement* and a *balance sheet* (two basic and important *financial statements*). This chapter is devoted to a discussion of the handling of and accounting for cash receipts and disbursements, including various considerations that are involved when cash is kept in a commercial bank. (The use of bank "checking accounts" is a near-universal business practice.)

records of cash receipts and disbursements; petty cash

The term *cash* has different, though not totally dissimilar, meanings. In a very narrow sense, cash means currency and coin. In a broader sense, cash includes checks, drafts, and money orders. All of these, as well as currency and coin, are sometimes called "cash items." Usually any reference to the *cash receipts* of a business relates to the receipt of checks, drafts, and money orders payable to the business, as well as to the receipt of currency and coin. The amount of the balance of the cash account, as well as the amount shown for cash in a balance sheet, normally includes cash and cash items on hand plus the amount on deposit in a checking account in a bank. In some cases the balance sheet figure for cash includes amounts on deposit in more than one bank. In accounting for cash, it is rather rare to make a distinction between "cash on hand" and "cash in bank," but sometimes this is done.

The Cash Account

This account is debited when cash is increased and credited when cash is decreased. This means that the cash account has a debit balance unless the business has no cash. In the latter case, the account will be *in balance* — meaning that the account has no balance since the total of the debits is equal to the total of the credits.

Cash Receipts. It is vital that an accurate and timely record be kept of cash receipts. When the volume of the receipts is large in both number and amount, a practice designed to reduce the danger of mistake and embezzlement may be followed. In order to segregate the functions of **(1)** handling money and cash items and **(2)** keeping the records, some one other than the bookkeeper prepares, in duplicate, a list of all receipts. One copy is kept with the receipts until a deposit ticket has been prepared and checked against the actual receipts. The other copy goes to the bookkeeper for recording purposes. An example of such a list is presented at the top of page 46.

When numerous cash receipts are involved, the amounts received are usually recorded in a cash register. The cash register tape provides a list of the receipts. If a cash register is not used, some form of receipt in duplicate should be used for each cash transaction. The customer should

DATE	FROM WHOM RECEIVED	NATURE OF REMITTANCE	AMOUNT
1971			
Jan. 2	Emerson Colaw	Check	$ 21.40
	Leland Rincker	Postal Money Order	53.07
	Harold Templeton	Currency	30.00
	Mrs. Verne Carroll	Express Money Order	42.16
	James Sargent	Bank Draft	28.75
	Delbert Stoddard	Cashier's Check	19.25
Total Cash Receipts..			$194.63

be given a copy and another copy should be retained for accounting purposes. Under such a plan the bookkeeper does not actually handle any cash; instead he records cash receipts from lists prepared by other persons. The procedure of having transactions involving cash handled by two or more persons reduces the danger of fraud and is one of the important features of a system of internal control.

Cash Disbursements. Disbursements may be made in cash or by bank check. When a disbursement is made in cash, a receipt or a receipted voucher should be obtained as evidence of the payment. When a disbursement is made by bank check, it is not necessary to obtain a receipt since the canceled check that is returned by the bank on which it was drawn serves as a receipt.

Recording Cash Receipts and Disbursements. In the preceding chapter, transactions involving the receipt and disbursement of cash were recorded in a two-column general journal along with other transactions. If the number of cash transactions is relatively small, the manner of recording that was illustrated is quite satisfactory. If, however, the number of such transactions is large, the repetition entailed in making numerous debit postings or credit postings to the cash account is time-consuming, tedious, and burdensome. Reference to the cash account at the top of page 34 discloses that even the brief illustration presented in that chapter involved fourteen postings to Cash (five debits and nine credits) out of a total of thirty-four postings required to record the seventeen transactions. It clearly would be more efficient to reduce the number of postings to the debit side of the cash account by summarizing the cash receipts for the month and posting the total. A similar observation applies to the transactions that involve cash disbursements.

The Four-Column Journal. One means of reducing the number of postings, as well as conserving space and effort in journalizing, is to use a journal that has four amount columns. An illustration of this form is reproduced on page 47. Note that it is the same as the journal used in the preceding chapter except that two additional amount columns have been added. (In this case the additional columns are placed at the left of the date column; however, such placement is not essential.) The two amount columns at the left are used exclusively for debits and credits to Cash; the two amount columns at the right, headed "General," are used for the amounts to be debited or credited to all other accounts. The De-

JOURNAL   PAGE

CASH		DATE	DESCRIPTION	POST. REF.	GENERAL	
DEBITS	CREDITS				DEBITS	CREDITS

Four-Column Journal

scription column is used primarily to record the titles of the accounts that are to be debited or credited with the amount entered in one of the columns at the right. Sometimes, a brief explanatory note is also included in the Description column.

Journalizing Procedure Illustrated. To illustrate the use of the four-column journal and to contrast it with the two-column type, the transactions of the Whitman Advertising Agency that were given in Chapter 2 (starting on page 26) are recorded in a four-column journal reproduced on page 48. Several features of this journal should be noted:

   (a) In the case of each entry that involves either a debit or a credit to Cash, the title of the account to receive the related credit or debit is written starting at the extreme left of the Description column. No indentation is made. However, in the case of any entry that does not involve cash, the title of the account to be debited is written at the extreme left, and the title of the account to be credited is indented about one-half inch. Note the entries of December 2 and 27, and the second entry of December 31. These entries appear just as they did in the two-column journal.

   (b) Usually a separate line is not used for an explanation of each entry. While this could be done, it is not customary because it is desirable to save space. Furthermore, in most instances, the entries explain themselves. Consider the first entry: It is evident that Mr. Whitman invested $1,500 in the business. In other cases, an appropriate notation is made following the title of the account. For example, when a debit or a credit to Accounts Payable is involved, the name of the creditor is noted. (See entries of December 2, 27, and 28.) In all entries involving a credit to Advertising Fees, the name of the client is noted. (See entries of December 7, 16, 22, and 28.) A word or two of explanation should be given whenever appropriate. (Note the entries of December 15 and 31 where the word "[Secretary]" was included.) Occasionally an explanation will be of such a length that an additional line will be required. When a cash disbursement is made by check, the check number should be noted. It is quite common to have a narrow column headed "Check Number" placed next to the Cash Credits column to use in noting the number of each check issued. (In Chapter 2, no mention was made of the manner of cash payments; therefore, no check numbers were given and there is no need for a check number column in the illustration below.)

(c) The numbers shown in the Posting Reference column were not entered at the time of journalizing the transactions; they were entered later when the amounts were posted to the accounts in the ledger.

CASH		DATE	DESCRIPTION	POST. REF.	GENERAL	
DEBITS	CREDITS				DEBITS	CREDITS
150000		Nov. 30	C.D. Whitman, Capital	31		150000
	20000	Dec. 1	Rent Expense	51	20000	
		2	Office Supplies	12	18314	
			Accounts Payable (Central Supply Co.)	21		18314
	2250	3	Telephone Expense	54	2250	
	600	6	Miscellaneous Expense	56	600	
12500		7	Advertising Fees (City Hardware Co.)	41		12500
	12830	9	Traveling Expense	53	12830	
	17500	15	Salary Expense (Secretary)	52	17500	
36500		16	Advertising Fees (Morton Mfg. Co.)	41		36500
	30000	20	C.D. Whitman, Drawing	32	30000	
52000		22	Advertising Fees (Mid-Town Sales Co.)	41		52000
	3000	23	Miscellaneous Expense	56	3000	
		27	Office Equipment	13	237221	
			Accounts Payable (Acme Office Equip Co.)	21		237221
	18314	28	Accounts Payable (Central Supply Co.)	21	18314	
35000		28	Advertising Fees (Gordon Downey)	41		35000
	17500	31	Salary Expense (Secretary)	52	17500	
		31	Office Supplies Expense	55	2000	
			Office Supplies	12		2000
286000	121994		1,640.06		379529	543535
286000	121994				379529	543535
(11)	(11)				(✓)	(✓)

The Whitman Advertising Agency Four-Column Journal

Proving the Four-Column Journal. In order to be sure that the debits recorded in the journal are equal to the credits, the journal must be *proved*. Each amount column should be footed and the sum of the footings of the debit columns and the sum of the footings of the credit columns compared. The footings should be recorded in small pencil figures immediately below the last regular entry. If these sums are not the same, the journal entries must be checked to discover and correct any errors that are found. The footings should be proved frequently; when the transactions are numerous it may be advisable to prove the footings daily. The footings must be proved when a page of the journal is filled to be sure that no error is carried forward to a new page. Proof of the footings is essential at the end of the month before the journal is ruled or any column totals are posted. The following is a proof of the footings of the four-column journal of The Whitman Advertising Agency at the end of December:

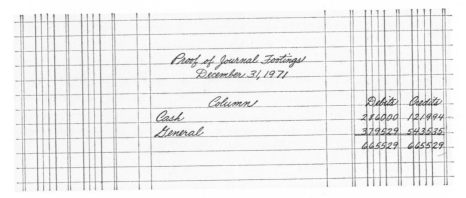

Four-Column Journal — Proof of Journal Footings

Footing and Ruling the Four-Column Journal. Normally, the journal should be footed and ruled at the end of each month. (In the illustration of The Whitman Advertising Agency, the business was started on November 30, and the single transaction on that date was included with the entries for December.) As previously stated, the footings should be recorded in small pencil figures immediately below the last regular entry. After being proved, the figures should be recorded in ink on the next horizontal line. A single rule should be drawn across all of the amount columns just above the totals and a double rule should be drawn across all of the columns except the Description column just below the totals. A practice often followed when journals of this type are used is to make a notation of the cash balance at the end of the month. This amount should be equal to the balance at the end of the previous month, plus the receipts and minus the disbursements of the month just ended. This balance may be noted in small figures (in pencil, if preferred) in the Description column just below the line on which the last regular entry was made. It is common practice to start the entries for a new month on a fresh page. When this practice is followed, the cash balance at the start of the month (the balance at the end of the month just past) is entered in small figures in the Description column at the top of the new page.

When it is necessary to use more than one journal page for the transactions of a month, no regular entry should be made on the last line of a page. That line is used to show the column totals. These should not be recorded in ink until the equality of the footings has been proved. The words "Carried Forward" should be written in the Description column on the last line. The amount-column totals are entered on the top line of the new page with the words "Amounts Forwarded" written in the Description column.

Posting the Four-Column Journal. Posting from a four-column journal involves both individual posting and summary (column total) posting. The individual amounts in the two General columns are posted. This may be done daily or as often as convenient, but it should be done by the end of each month. The totals of the Cash Debits and Cash Credits columns cannot be posted until the end of the month when the journal has been proved and the column totals recorded. As the individual amounts in the General columns are posted, the numbers of the accounts to which the postings were made are entered in the Posting Reference column of the journal. (Entering the journal page from which an amount has come is a part of the process of posting to the ledger.) When the totals of the Cash Debits and Cash Credits columns are posted, the number of the cash account (No. 11 in the illustration) is shown in parentheses just below the column totals. In order to indicate that the totals of the General Debits and General Credits columns are not to be posted, a check mark is shown in parentheses ($\sqrt{}$) below each of those totals.

The general ledger of The Whitman Advertising Agency after completion of postings from the two-column journal is illustrated on pages 34 and 35. If these postings had come from the four-column journal instead, the ledger accounts would appear exactly the same except for the fact that some of the postings came from page 2 of the two-column journal, whereas all of the postings came from page 1 of the four-column journal. Furthermore, the cash account, instead of containing five debits and nine credits, would contain only one debit and one credit as illustrated below.

ACCOUNT Cash								ACCOUNT NO. 11	
DATE	ITEMS	POST. REF.	✓	DEBITS	DATE	ITEMS	POST. REF.	✓	CREDITS
1971 Dec. 31	1,640.06	1		2 8 6 0 0 0	1971 Dec. 31			1	1 2 1 9 9 4

Comparison of the two-column journal illustrated on pages 29 and 30 and the four-column journal shown on page 48 reveals that the former required thirty-four postings, while the latter needed only twenty-two. If there had been 100 transactions, of which ninety involved either a debit or a credit to Cash, 200 postings would have been required if the transactions had been recorded in a two-column journal. If the same transactions had been recorded in a four-column journal of the type illustrated, only 112 postings would have been required. These savings in the number of postings roughly reflect comparable savings in space required, words to be written, and time needed.

The four-column journal discussed and illustrated might be called a "junior version" of a book of original entry known as a *combined cash journal*. This designation arises from the fact that such a book combines the features of a two-column general journal and a *cashbook* — the latter being a book in which only transactions involving cash receipts and disbursements are recorded. The fundamental characteristics of a combined cash journal are that it provides columns for debits to cash, credits to cash, debits and credits to be posted individually ("general" columns), and as many other "special" columns as circumstances require. These "special" columns are used to record like debits or credits so that the totals of amounts destined for the same place can be summary posted. Thus, in addition to the four columns whose use has already been explained and illustrated, there may be one, two, three, or even a dozen other "special" columns if needed. The Whitman Advertising Agency example included four transactions requiring a credit to Advertising Fees, Account No. 41. This circumstance suggests that a special column for "Advertising Fees Credit" would have been in order.

Other Types of Cash Journals. In many businesses, transactions involving the receipt or the disbursement of cash are so numerous that it is desirable to keep the original journal record of such transactions separate from the record of noncash transactions. When a separate record is kept of cash receipts, it is usually referred to as a *cash receipts journal*. When a separate record is kept of cash payments or disbursements, it is usually referred to as a *cash payments journal* or a *cash disbursements journal*. When all disbursements are made by check, the journal is sometimes called a *check register*. When cash receipts and cash payments are both recorded in the same book of account, the book is usually referred to as a cashbook. This type of record typically has a facing-page arrangement. Receipts are recorded on the left-hand page; disbursements on the right-hand page.

All original entry books (journals) relating to cash have the same characteristics regardless of whether there are separate books for receipts and disbursements or whether they are combined and called a cashbook. For cash receipts, there is one debit column in which the amounts of all receipts are recorded. At the end of a month, the total of this column is posted as a debit to Cash. Some or all of the individual credit amounts are separately posted as credits to the proper accounts. If there are numerous credits to the same account, a column may be provided in which to record the amounts of these credits so that their sum can be posted at the end of the month. Within limits, there may be as many "special" columns as needed. A comparable set of observations relates to the cash disbursements: The major column in this case, of course, is the credit column that assembles all of the decreases in cash so that one summary credit to Cash can be posted each month. The debits may all be posted individually or, if needed, special columns may be used to reduce the number of postings.

In each instance, all of the fundamental qualities of any journal are present: (1) space is provided to show the date of the transaction, (2) provision is made to indicate the titles of the accounts that are affected, (3) space is provided for any needed explanation or description, (4) the amount of each transaction is shown, and (5) space is provided to indicate the number of the account to which each posting was made. If cash disbursements are made by check, the cash disbursements record will probably have a column in which to note the check numbers. It is not uncommon for there to be a memo column in which to note the bank balance after each deposit and each check written. It is possible to "prove" any of these journals at any time by determining whether the total debits recorded are equal to the total credits.

It must be understood that cash journals do not completely eliminate the need for a general journal, unless every transaction of the business involves cash — an unlikely circumstance. In almost every business there is need for a general journal — either separate or combined with another journal — in which to record unusual, infrequent transactions.

Proving Cash. The process of determining whether the amount of cash (on hand and in the bank) is the amount that should be there according to the records is called *proving cash*. Cash should be proved at least once a week and, perhaps, more often if the volume of cash transactions is large. The first step is to determine from the records what amount of cash should be on hand. The cash balance should be calculated by adding the total of the receipts to the opening balance and subtracting the total of the payments. The result should be equal to the amount of cash on deposit in the bank plus the total of currency, coins, checks, and money orders on hand. Normally, an up-to-date record of cash in bank is maintained — often by using stubs in a checkbook for this purpose. There is space provided on the stubs to show deposits as well as the record of checks drawn, and the resulting balance after each deposit made or check drawn. (See check stubs illustrated on page 67.) The amount of cash and cash items on hand must be determined by actual count.

Cash Short and Over. If the effort to prove cash is not successful, it means that either (1) the records of receipts, disbursements, and cash on deposit contain one or more errors, **(2)** the count of cash and cash items was incorrect, or **(3)** a "shortage" or an "overage" exists. If a verification of the records and the cash count does not uncover any error, it is evident that due to some mistake in handling cash, either not enough or too much cash is on hand.

Finding that cash is slightly short or over is not unusual. If there are numerous cash transactions, it is difficult to avoid occasional errors in making change. (There is always the danger of shortages due to dishonesty, but most discrepancies are the result of mistakes.) Many businesses have a ledger account entitled *Cash Short and Over*. If, in the effort to prove cash, it is found that a shortage exists, its amount is treated as a cash disbursement transaction involving a debit to Cash Short and Over. Any overage discovered is regarded as a cash receipt transaction involving a credit to Cash Short and Over. By the end of the fiscal year it is not unlikely that the cash short and over account will have both debits and credits. If the total of the debits exceeds the total of the credits, the balance represents an expense or loss; if the reverse is the case, the balance represents revenue.

The Petty Cash Fund

A good policy for a business enterprise to adopt is one which requires that all cash and cash items which it receives shall be deposited in a bank. When this is done, its total cash receipts will equal its total deposits in the bank. It is also a good policy to make arrangements with the bank so that all checks and other cash items received by the business from customers or others in the usual course of business will be accepted by the bank for deposit only. This will cause the records of cash receipts and disbursements of the business to agree exactly with the bank's record of deposits and withdrawals. Arrangements may also be made with the bank so that no item will be charged to the depositor's account until a check from the depositor for the proper amount is obtained. For example, an arrangement can be made to have dishonored checks (defined on page 62) presented to the depositor for payment instead of having them charged to the depositor's account. Service charges also may be paid by check.

When all cash and cash items received are deposited in a bank, an office fund or *petty cash fund* may be established for paying small items. ("Petty" means small or little.) Such a fund eliminates the necessity of writing checks for small amounts.

Operating a Petty Cash Fund. To establish a petty cash fund, a check should be drawn for the amount that is to be set aside in the fund. The amount may be $25, $50, $100, or any amount considered necessary. The check is usually made payable to "Cash," "Petty Cash," or "Office

Fund." When the check is cashed by the bank, the money is placed in a cash drawer, a cash register, or a safe at the depositor's place of business, and a designated individual in the office is authorized to make payments from the fund. The one who is responsible for the fund should be able to account for the amount of the fund at any time. Disbursements from the fund should not be made without obtaining a voucher or a receipt. A form of petty cash voucher is shown below. Such a voucher should be used for each expenditure unless a receipt or receipted invoice is obtained.

Petty Cash Voucher

The check drawn to establish the petty cash fund may be recorded in the journal by debiting Petty Cash Fund and by crediting Cash. When it is necessary to replenish the fund, the petty cashier usually prepares a statement of the expenditures, properly classified. A check is then drawn for the exact amount of the total expenditures. This check is recorded in the journal by debiting the proper accounts indicated in the statement and by crediting Cash.

The petty cash fund is a revolving fund that does not change in amount unless the fund is increased or decreased. The actual amount of cash in the fund plus the total of the petty cash vouchers or receipts should always be equal to the amount originally charged to the petty cash fund.

Petty Cash Disbursements Record. When a petty cash fund is maintained, it is good practice to keep a formal record of all disbursements from the fund. Various types of records have been designed for this purpose. One of the standard forms is illustrated on pages 56 and 57. The headings of the Distribution columns may vary with each enterprise, depending upon the desired classification of the expenditures. It should be remembered that the headings represent accounts that eventually are to be charged for the expenditures. The desired headings may either be printed on the form or they may be written in. Often the account numbers instead of account titles are used in the headings to indicate the accounts to be charged.

The petty cashier should have a document for each disbursement made from the petty cash fund. Unless a receipt or receipted invoice is obtained, the petty cashier should prepare a voucher. The vouchers should be numbered consecutively.

A model petty cash disbursements record is reproduced on pages 56 and 57. It is a part of the records of J. K. Jenkins, a business consultant. Since Mr. Jenkins is out of the office much of the time, he considers it advisable to provide a petty cash fund from which his secretary is authorized to make petty cash disbursements not to exceed $15 each. A narrative of the petty cash transactions completed by Mr. Jenkins' secretary, during the month of December, follows:

J. K. JENKINS

NARRATIVE OF PETTY CASH TRANSACTIONS

Dec. 1. Issued check for $100 payable to Petty Cash, cashed the check, and placed the proceeds in a petty cash fund.

> This transaction was recorded in the journal by debiting Petty Cash Fund and by crediting Cash. A memorandum entry was also made in the Description column of the petty cash disbursements record reproduced on pages 56 and 57.

During the month of December the following disbursements were made from the petty cash fund:

3. Paid $4 for polishing office furniture. Petty Cash Voucher No. 1.
6. Gave Mr. Jenkins $9 to reimburse him for the amount spent in having his automobile repaired. Petty Cash Voucher No. 2.
6. Gave Mr. Jenkins $7 to reimburse him for the amount spent in entertaining a client at luncheon. Petty Cash Voucher No. 3.
7. Paid $5 for messenger fees. Petty Cash Voucher No. 4.
10. Paid $4 for an ad in local newspaper. Petty Cash Voucher No. 5.
10. Gave Mr. Jenkins $10 for personal use. Petty Cash Voucher No. 6.

> This item was entered in the Amount column provided at the extreme right of the petty cash disbursements record since no special distribution column had been provided for recording amounts withdrawn by the owner for personal use.

13. Gave the Red Cross a $5 donation. Petty Cash Voucher No. 7.
15. Paid $7.50 for typewriter repairs. Petty Cash Voucher No. 8.
17. Gave Mr. Jenkins $3.75 to reimburse him for traveling expenses. Petty Cash Voucher No. 9.
20. Gave Mr. Jenkins $3 to reimburse him for the amount spent in having his automobile washed. Petty Cash Voucher No. 10.
20. Paid $8 for cleaning office. Petty Cash Voucher No. 11.
22. Paid $1.25 for collect telegram. Petty Cash Voucher No. 12.
23. Donated $5 to the Salvation Army. Petty Cash Voucher No. 13.

DAY	DESCRIPTION		VOU. NO.	TOTAL AMOUNT	J. & T. Exp.	Auto Exp.
	AMOUNTS FORWARDED					
1	Received in fund	100.00	✓			
3	Polishing office furniture		1	4 00		
6	Automobile repairs		2	9 00		9 00
6	Client luncheon		3	7 00		
7	Messenger		4	5 00		
10	Advertising expense		5	4 00		
10	J. K. Jenkins, personal use		6	10 00		
13	Red Cross		7	5 00		
15	Typewriter repairs		8	7 50		
17	Traveling expense		9	3 75		
20	Washing automobile		10	3 00		3 00
20	Cleaning office		11	8 00		
22	Collect telegram		12	1 25	1 25	
23	Salvation Army		13	5 00		
27	Postage stamps		14	5 00		
27	Long distance call		15	3 20	3 20	
28	Polishing office furniture		16	4 00		
				84 70	4 45	12 00
				84 70	4 45	12 00
31	Balance	15.30				
31	Received in fund	84.70				
	Total	100.00				

J. K. Jenkins' Petty Cash Disbursements Record (Left Page)

27. Paid $5 for postage stamps. Petty Cash Voucher No. 14.
27. Gave Mr. Jenkins $3.20 to reimburse him for a long distance telephone call made from a booth. Petty Cash Voucher No. 15.
28. Paid $4 for polishing office furniture. Petty Cash Voucher No. 16.
31. Issued check for $84.70 to replenish the petty cash fund.

This transaction was recorded in the journal by debiting the proper accounts and by crediting Cash for the total amount of the expenditures.

Proving the Petty Cash Disbursements Record. To prove the petty cash disbursements record, it is first necessary to foot all of the amount columns. The sum of the footings of the Distribution columns should equal the footing of the Total Amount column. After proving the footings, the totals should be recorded and the record should be ruled as shown in the illustration. The illustration shows that a total of $84.70 was paid out during December. Since it was desired to replenish the petty cash fund at this time, the following statement of the disbursements for December was prepared:

		DISTRIBUTION OF CHARGES				
Post. Exp.	Don. Exp.	Adv. Exp.	Travel Exp.	Misc. Exp.	ACCOUNT	AMOUNT
				4 00		
				7 00		
				5 00		
		4 00				
					J. K. Jenkins, Drawing	10 00
	5 00					
				7 50		
			3 75			
				8 00		
	5 00					
5 00						
				4 00		
5 00	10 00	4 00	3 75	35 50		10 00
5 00	10 00	4 00	3 75	35 50		10 00

J. K. Jenkins' Petty Cash Disbursements Record (Right Page)

STATEMENT OF PETTY CASH DISBURSEMENTS
For December

Telephone and telegraph expense.........................	$ 4.45
Automobile expense....................................	12.00
Postage expense.......................................	5.00
Donations expense.....................................	10.00
Advertising expense....................................	4.00
Traveling expense.....................................	3.75
Miscellaneous expense.................................	35.50
J. K. Jenkins, drawing.................................	10.00
Total disbursements.................................	$84.70

The statement of disbursements provides the information for the issuance of a check for $84.70 to replenish the petty cash fund. After footing and ruling the petty cash disbursements record, the balance in the fund and the amount received to replenish the fund may be recorded in the

Description column below the ruling as shown in the illustration. It is customary to carry the balance forward to the top of a new page before recording any of the transactions for the following month.

The petty cash disbursements record reproduced on pages 56 and 57 is an *auxiliary record* that supplements the regular accounting records. No posting is done from this auxiliary record. The total amount of the expenditures from the petty cash fund is entered in the journal at the time of replenishing the fund by debiting the proper accounts and by crediting Cash. A *compound entry* (one that affects more than two accounts, though the sum of the debits is equal to the sum of the credits) is usually required. The statement of petty cash disbursements provides the information needed in recording the check issued to replenish the petty cash fund. The posting is done from the journal.

The method of recording the check issued by J. K. Jenkins on December 31 to replenish the fund is illustrated below. It is assumed that Mr. Jenkins uses a four-column journal similar to the one illustrated on page 47.

JOURNAL   PAGE 15

| CASH | | DATE | DESCRIPTION | POST. REF. | GENERAL | |
DEBITS	CREDITS				DEBITS	CREDITS
	84 70	1971 Dec. 31	Telephone and Telegraph Expense		4 45	
			Automobile Expense		12 00	
			Postage Expense		5 00	
			Donations Expense		10 00	
			Advertising Expense		4 00	
			Traveling Expense		3 75	
			Miscellaneous Expense		35 50	
			J. K. Jenkins, Drawing		10 00	

J. K. Jenkins' Four-Column Journal

The method of handling a petty cash fund just described is sometimes referred to as the *imprest method*. It is the method most commonly used.

Report No. 6

Refer to the workbook and complete Report No. 6. After completing the report, proceed with the textbook discussion until the next report is required.

banking procedure

A bank is a financial institution that receives deposits, lends money, makes collections, and renders other services, such as providing vaults for the safekeeping of valuables and handling trust funds for its customers. Most banks offer facilities for both checking accounts and savings accounts.

Checking Account

A checking account is sometimes referred to as a commercial account. Important factors in connection with a checking account are **(1)** opening the account, **(2)** making deposits, **(3)** making withdrawals, and **(4)** reconciling the bank statement.

Opening a Checking Account. To open a checking account with a bank, it is necessary to obtain the approval of an official of the bank and to make an initial deposit. Money, checks, bank drafts, money orders, and other cash items usually will be accepted for deposit. Cash is accepted for deposit subject to verification as to its amount and validity. Cash items are accepted for deposit subject to their being paid by their makers when presented for payment by the bank or its agent.

Signature Card. Banks usually require a new depositor to sign his name on a card or form as an aid in verifying the depositor's signature on checks that he may issue, on cash items that he may endorse for deposit, and on other business papers that he may present to the bank. The form a depositor signs to give the bank a sample of his signature is called a *signature card*. If desired, a depositor may authorize others to sign his name to checks and to other business forms. Each person who is so authorized is required to sign the depositor's name along with his own signature on a signature card. A signature card is one of the safeguards that a bank uses to protect its own interests as well as the interests of its depositors.

Deposit Ticket. Banks provide depositors with a printed form to use for a detailed listing of items being deposited. This form is called a *deposit ticket*. A model filled-in deposit ticket is reproduced on page 60. This illustration is typical of the type of ticket that most banks provide. Note that the number of the depositor's account is preprinted at the bottom in so-called "MICR" numbers (meaning *magnetic ink character recognition*) that can be "read" by a type of electronic equipment used by banks. This

CHECKING ACCOUNT DEPOSIT TICKET			
THE P. G. THOMAS CO.	CASH	CURRENCY	486	00
12 PIKE STREET		COIN	20	73
	CHECKS	420-1	141	50
		420-22	600	00
DATE October 29 19 71		420-3	250	00

13- 3
420

TOTAL FROM OTHER SIDE

TOTAL 1498 | 23

LESS CASH RECEIVED

NET DEPOSIT

USE OTHER SIDE FOR ADDITIONAL LISTING

Checks and other items
are received for deposit
subject to the terms and
conditions of this bank's
collection agreement.

BE SURE EACH ITEM
IS PROPERLY ENDORSED

BELLEVUE TRUST CO.
CINCINNATI, OHIO

⑆0420⑈0003⑆   136⑈92146⑈

Deposit Ticket

series of digits (which also is preprinted at the bottom of all of the depositor's checks) is actually a code used in sorting and routing deposit slips and checks. In the first set of digits, 0420-003, the "4" indicates that the bank is in the Fourth Federal Reserve District. The "20" is what is called a "routing" number. The "3" is a number assigned to the Bellevue Trust Co. This numbering method was established by the American Bankers Association (ABA). The second set of digits, 136–92146, is the number assigned by the Bellevue Trust Co. to the P. G. Thomas Co.'s account.

Deposit tickets may be prepared in duplicate or a receipt may be obtained from the bank teller. In preparing a deposit ticket, the date should be written in the space provided. Currency (paper money) should be arranged in the order of the denominations, the smaller denominations being placed on top. The bills should all be faced up and top up. Coins (pennies, nickels, dimes, quarters, half dollars, and silver dollars) that are to be deposited in considerable quantities should be wrapped in coin wrappers, which the bank will provide. The name of the depositor should be written on the outside of each coin wrapper as a means of identification in the event that a mistake has been made in counting the coins. The amounts of cash represented by currency and by coins should be entered in the amount column of the deposit ticket on the lines provided for these items.

Each additional item to be deposited should be listed on a separate line of the deposit ticket as shown in the illustration above. In listing checks on the deposit ticket, the instructions of the bank should be observed in describing the checks for identification purposes. It was once common practice to list local checks by name of bank and out-of-town checks by name of city. Another practice widely followed at one time was to show the name of the maker (drawer) of each check being deposited. Still another procedure that is used by some depositors is to attach to the deposit slip an adding machine tape listing the amount of each check and the total. For many years, banks preferred to have the checks identified on the deposit slip by showing the ABA "transit number" of each check (the numerator of a fraction-type bank identification that was, and almost always still is, printed on each check). Today, some banks ask their depositors to identify checks being deposited by showing the numbers contained in the first set of MICR digits that appears to the left at the bottom of each check. Any zeros ("0") that lie to the left of a group of digits may be omitted.

Endorsements. The signature or stamp of a depositor on the back of a check is called an *endorsement*. Negotiable instruments (checks, notes, and drafts) made payable to the depositor either directly or by prior endorsement, must be endorsed by him before a bank will accept them for deposit. One purpose of such endorsement is to transfer the title of the instrument to the bank. By means of his endorsement the depositor also guarantees the payment of the instrument. Checks and other items submitted for deposit that require endorsements on the back may be endorsed as shown in the illustration on page 62. In endorsing a check, the name of the payee should be written exactly as it appears on the face of the check. Note that the endorsement is written near the left end of the check. An endorsement that limits the holder of the check as to the use to be made of the amount collected is known as a *restrictive endorsement*. The check reproduced on the next page has a restrictive endorsement. This type of endorsement makes it unlikely that the check will be cashed by anyone other than the bank or person to whom it is endorsed. Businesses commonly use a rubber stamp to endorse checks for deposit.

The total of the cash and other items deposited should be entered on the deposit ticket. The deposit ticket, together with the cash and the other items to be deposited, should be delivered to the receiving teller of the bank together with a *passbook* that the bank will have provided for use by receiving tellers in acknowledging the receipt of deposits. The date, amount of deposit, and the initial of the teller are entered in the passbook. Instead of using a passbook, many depositors submit the deposit ticket in duplicate. The teller receipts the duplicate copy and returns it to the depositor.

Instead of providing the depositor with either a passbook or duplicate deposit tickets, the bank may provide him with a machine-printed receipt for each deposit. Some banks use *automatic teller machines* in preparing the receipts. The use of such machines saves the time required to make manual entries in a passbook and eliminates the need for making duplicate copies of deposit tickets. Such machines are not only timesaving, but they

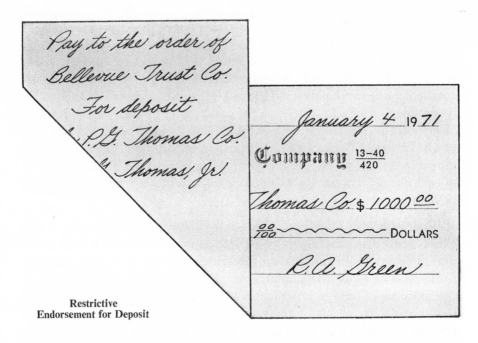

Restrictive
Endorsement for Deposit

also promote accuracy in the handling of deposits. The deposits handled by each teller during the day may be accumulated so that at the end of the day the total amount of the deposits received by a teller is automatically recorded by the machine. This amount may be proved by counting the cash and cash items accepted by a teller for deposit during the day.

Dishonored Checks. A check that a bank refuses to pay is described as a *dishonored check*. A depositor guarantees all items that he deposits and is liable to the bank for the amount involved if, for any reason, any item is not honored when presented for payment. When a check or other cash item is deposited with a bank and is not honored upon presentation to the bank upon which it is drawn, the depositor's bank may charge the amount of the dishonored item to the depositor's account or may present it to the depositor for reimbursement. It is not uncommon for checks that have been deposited to be returned to the depositor for various reasons, as indicated on the return notice reproduced on page 63. The most common reason for checks being returned unpaid is "not sufficient funds" (NSF).

Under the laws of most states, it is illegal for anyone to issue a check on a bank without having sufficient funds on deposit with that bank to cover the check when it is presented for payment. When a dishonored check is charged to the depositor's account, or is replaced by a check issued by the depositor, an entry should be made in the depositor's records debiting the issuer of the dishonored check and crediting Cash. If the dishonored check is charged to the depositor's account by the bank, the depositor

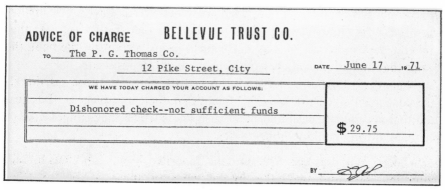

ADVICE OF CHARGE   BELLEVUE TRUST CO.

TO   The P. G. Thomas Co.

           12 Pike Street, City   DATE   June 17   19 71

WE HAVE TODAY CHARGED YOUR ACCOUNT AS FOLLOWS:

Dishonored check--not sufficient funds

$ 29.75

BY

Debit Advice

should deduct the amount from the balance shown on his checkbook stub, even though he did not issue a check.

Postdated Checks. Checks dated subsequent to the date of issue are known as *postdated checks*. For example, a check that is issued on March 1 may be dated March 15. The recipient of a postdated check should not deposit it before the date specified on the check. One reason for issuing a postdated check may be that the maker does not have sufficient funds in his bank at the time of issuance to pay it, but he may expect to have a sufficient amount on deposit by the time the check is presented for payment on or after the date of the check. When a postdated check is presented to the bank on which it is drawn and payment is not made, it is handled by the bank in the same manner as any other dishonored check and the payee should treat it as a dishonored check. Generally, it is not considered good practice to issue postdated checks.

Making Deposits by Mail. Bank deposits may be made either over the counter or by mail. The over-the-counter method of making deposits is generally used. It may not always be convenient, however, for a depositor to make his deposits over the counter, especially if he lives at a great distance from the bank. In such a case it may be more convenient for him to make his deposits by mail. When a depositor makes his deposits by mail, the bank may provide him with a special form of deposit ticket.

Night Deposits. A depositor may find it convenient to use the night deposit safe of his bank. The opening to the night deposit safe usually is on the exterior of the bank building. Upon signing a night depository contract, the bank supplies the depositor with a key to the outside door of the safe, together with a bag that has an identifying number and in which valuables may be placed, and two keys to the bag itself. Once the depositor places his bag in the night deposit safe it cannot be retrieved because it moves to a vault in the bank that is accessible to bank employees only.

Since only the depositor is provided with keys to his bag, he or his authorized representative must go to the bank to unlock the bag. At that time the depositor may or may not deposit in his account in the bank the funds that he had placed previously in the night deposit safe.

Night deposit banking service is especially valuable to those individuals and concerns that do not have safe facilities in their own places of business and that accumulate cash and other cash items which they cannot take to the bank during banking hours.

Making Withdrawals. The amount deposited in a bank checking account may be withdrawn either by the depositor himself or by any other person who has been properly authorized to make withdrawals from the depositor's account. Such withdrawals are accomplished by the use of checks signed by the depositor or by others having the authority to sign checks drawn on the account.

Checkbook. Banks provide printed forms known as checks for the convenience of their depositors. Such checks are used by depositors to authorize the bank to pay out specified amounts from the funds credited to their accounts. Special forms of checks may be used for payrolls, dividends, or other purposes. It is estimated that roughly 85 percent of all money payments in the United States are made by check.

Blank checks are often bound in a book with one or more checks to a page. Each check usually contains spaces for recording the following information:

    (a) The number of the check.
    (b) The date of the check.
    (c) The name of the payee.
    (d) The amount the bank is authorized to pay the payee.
    (e) The signature of the drawer — the depositor or his authorized agent.

Very often, each blank check is attached (usually along its left side) to what is called a *check stub*. The stubs usually contain blank spaces for recording the same information as is recorded on the checks so that the completed stubs will provide the depositor with a complete record of all checks issued. Sometimes space is also provided on the stub for recording the title of the account to be debited. In any event, sufficient data should be entered on the stub of each check to provide all information needed for recording purposes.

Checks should be numbered consecutively, and their stubs should bear identical numbers. The numbers may be entered manually or a numbering machine may be used. It is a good plan to number all stubs and checks before any checks are written. This makes it easier to keep track of all blank checks. Frequently businesses have a quantity of blank checks printed with their name and address shown. Usually such checks are prenumbered.

Some firms prepare carbon copies of checks instead of using check stubs. The copy itself is not a check; very often it is only a blank sheet except for the carbon-paper imprint of the check number, name of payee, amount, and any notations that were made on the check as to what it pays. Checks with carbon copies usually are prepared on a typewriter.

Writing a Check. If the check has a stub, the latter should be filled in before the check is written. This plan insures that the drawer will retain a record of each check issued.

When a depositor withdraws funds personally, the payee of the check is usually "Cash." If the money is to go into a petty cash fund, the check may be made payable to "Petty Cash."

When a depositor desires the bank to pay the money to a third party, he writes the name of that party, referred to as the payee, on the stub and on the check. When the payee presents the check to the bank for payment, he may be required by the bank to identify himself.

The purpose for which a check is drawn is usually recorded on the stub below the name of the payee. The purpose may also be indicated in some appropriate area of the check itself. Indicating the purpose on the check provides information for the benefit of the payee and provides a specific receipt for the drawer.

The amount of the check is stated on the stub in figures and is stated on the check in both figures and words. If the amount shown on the check in figures does not agree with the amount shown in words, the bank usually will contact the drawer for the correct amount or will return the check unpaid.

Care must be used in writing the amount on the check in order to avoid any possibility that the payee or a subsequent holder may change the amount. If the instructions given below are followed in the preparation of a check, it will be difficult to change the amount.

(a) The amount shown in figures should be written so that there is no space between the dollar sign and the first digit of the amount.

(b) The amount stated in words should be written beginning at the extreme left on the line provided for this information. The cents should be written in the form of a common fraction; if the check is for an even number of dollars, use two ciphers or the word "no" as the numerator of the fraction. If a vacant space remains, a line should be drawn from the amount stated in words to the word "Dollars" on the same line with it, as illustrated on page 67.

A machine frequently used to write the amount of a check in figures and in words is known as a *checkwriter*. The use of a checkwriter is desirable because it practically eliminates the possibility of a change in the amount of a check.

Each check issued by a depositor will be returned to him by the bank on which it is drawn after the check has been paid. Canceled checks are returned to the depositor with the bank statement, which is usually rendered each month. Canceled checks will have been endorsed by the payee and any subsequent holders. They constitute receipts that the depositor should retain for future reference. They may be attached to the stubs from which they were removed originally or they may be filed.

Overdraft. As stated previously, it is illegal in most states for a depositor to issue a check against a bank in excess of the amount on deposit. However, it may happen that through an oversight or an error in calculation a depositor will overdraw his checking account. Should this happen the bank may refuse to honor the check or it may honor the check and notify the depositor by mail that he has overdrawn his account. Sometimes an official of the bank will telephone the depositor instead of notifying him by mail. Overdrawing a bank checking account is considered a serious matter, and the depositor is expected to make the necessary adjustment without delay. Some banks impose a small charge against a depositor who has overdrawn his account.

Electronic Processing of Checks. It has already been mentioned that nearly all banks furnish their depositors with a special type of check that can be processed by MICR (magnetic ink character recognition) equipment. The unique characteristic of such checks is that there is imprinted in magnetic ink along the lower margin of the check a series of numbers or digits in the form of a code that indicates **(1)** the identity of the Federal Reserve District in which the bank is located and a routing number, **(2)** the identity of the bank, and **(3)** the account number assigned to the depositor. In processing checks with electronic equipment, the first bank that handles a check will imprint its amount in magnetic ink characters to further aid in the processing of the check. The amount will be printed directly below the signature line in the lower right-hand corner of the check.

Checks imprinted with the bank's number and the depositor's number can be fed into MICR machines which will "read" the numbers and cause the checks to be sorted in the desired fashion. If the amounts of the checks are printed thereon in magnetic ink, such amounts can be totaled, and each check can be posted electronically to the customer's account. This process can be carried on at extremely high speed with almost no danger of error.

Shown on the next page is a reproduction of two checks which illustrates the appearance of the magnetic ink characters that have been printed at the bottom, as well as check stubs properly completed. (For a further discussion of electronic processing of checks, see Appendix, pages A-11 and A-12.)

Recording Bank Transactions. A depositor should keep a record of the transactions he completes with his bank. The usual plan is to keep this record on the checkbook stubs as shown in the illustration below. It will be noted that the record consists of detailed information concerning each check written and an amount column in which should be recorded (1) the balance brought forward or carried down, (2) the amount of deposits to be added, and (3) the amount of checks to be subtracted. The purpose is to

NO. 92		$75 00	BELLEVUE TRUST CO.		No. 92	13-3 / 420
DATE April 2 19 71			Cincinnati, Ohio			
TO Brandon Bros					April 2	19 71
FOR Rent						
Rent Expense ✓			PAY TO THE ORDER OF Brandon Bros.		$75 00	
	DOLLARS	CENTS	Seventy-five 00/100			DOLLARS
BAL. BRO'T FOR'D	4198	72				
AMT. DEPOSITED			THE P. G. THOMAS CO.			
TOTAL			P. G. Thomas, Jr.			
AMT. THIS CHECK	75	00				
BAL. CAR'D FOR'D	4123	72	⑆0420⑈0003⑆ 136⑈92146⑈			

NO. 93		$531 37	BELLEVUE TRUST CO.		No. 93	13-3 / 420
DATE April 5 19 71			Cincinnati, Ohio			
TO Glenview Mfg. Co.					April 5	19 71
FOR Inv. Mar. 31						
Accounts Pay. ✓			PAY TO THE ORDER OF Glenview Manufacturing Co. $531 37			
	DOLLARS	CENTS	Five hundred thirty-one 37/100			DOLLARS
BAL. BRO'T FOR'D	4123	72				
AMT. DEPOSITED	625	00	THE P. G. THOMAS CO.			
TOTAL	4,748	72	P. G. Thomas, Jr.			
AMT. THIS CHECK	531	37				
BAL. CAR'D FOR'D	4217	35	⑆0420⑈0003⑆ 136⑈92146⑈			

Checks and Stubs

keep a detailed record of deposits made and checks issued and to indicate the balance in the checking account after each check is drawn.

As the amount of each check is recorded in the journal, a check mark may be placed immediately after the account title written on the stub to indicate that it has been recorded. When the canceled check is subsequently received from the bank, the amount shown on the stub may be checked to indicate that the canceled check has been received.

Records Kept by a Bank. The usual transactions completed by a bank with a depositor are listed at the top of the next page.

(a) Accepting deposits made by the depositor.

(b) Paying checks issued by the depositor.

(c) Lending money to the depositor.

(d) Discounting commercial paper for the depositor (another type of lending).

(e) Collecting the amounts of various kinds of commercial paper, such as notes and drafts, for the account of the depositor.

The bank keeps an account for each depositor. Each transaction affecting a depositor's account is recorded by debiting or crediting his account, depending upon the effect of the transaction. When a bank accepts a deposit, the account of the depositor is credited for the amount of the deposit. The deposit increases the bank's liability to the depositor.

When the bank pays a check that has been drawn on the bank, it debits the account of the depositor for the amount of the check. If the bank makes a collection for a depositor, the net amount of the collection is credited to his account. At the same time the bank notifies the depositor on a form similar to the one shown below that the collection has been made.

ADVICE OF CREDIT   **BELLEVUE TRUST CO.**

OFFSETTING DR.   April 16 ₁₉ 71

WE CREDIT YOUR ACCOUNT AS FOLLOWS:

R. L. Morgan's note $250.00

Less collection charge   5.00

$ 245.00

To____The P. G. Thomas Co._____

____12 Pike Street, City____   APPROVED___E M D___

Credit Advice

Bank Statement. Once each month a bank renders a statement of account to each depositor similar to that shown on the next page. This statement is a report showing **(1)** the balance on deposit at the beginning of the period, **(2)** the amounts of deposits made during the period, **(3)** the amounts of checks honored during the period, **(4)** other items charged to the depositor's account during the period, and **(5)** the balance on deposit at the end of the period. With his bank statement, the depositor also receives all checks paid by the bank during the period, together with any other vouchers representing items charged to his account.

Reconciling the Bank Statement. When a bank statement is received, the depositor should check it immediately with the bank balance record

BELLEVUE TRUST CO.

STATEMENT OF ACCOUNT

PERIOD ENDING
May 19, 1971

ACCOUNT NO.
136-92146

The P. G. Thomas Co.
12 Pike Street
City

CHECKS - LISTED IN ORDER OF PAYMENT - READ ACROSS			DEPOSITS	DATE	NEW BALANCE
3 74				4 21 71	5346 69
5 00				4 23 71	5341 69
25 00			719 36	4 26 71	6036 05
29 49				4 26 71	6006 56
			41 55	4 27 71	6048 11
5 00				4 28 71	6043 11
17 17				5 03 71	6025 94
3740 40			1079 70	5 03 71	3365 24
2 00				5 05 71	3363 24
5 00	121 00			5 06 71	3237 24
500 00				5 06 71	2737 24
16 00	60 00			5 10 71	2661 24
150 00				5 10 71	2511 24
10 94				5 10 71	2500 30
16 79	21 05		249 00	5 12 71	2711 46
18 82		75S		5 14 71	2691 89

SUMMARY OF ACTIVITY

BALANCE FORWARD	DEBITS		CREDITS		SERVICE CHARGE		NEW BALANCE
	NUMBER	AMOUNT	NUMBER	AMOUNT	ITEMS	AMOUNT	
5350 43	18	4747 40	4	2089 61	1	75	2691 89

Please examine this statement at once. If no error is reported in ten days the account will be considered correct.
All items are credited subject to final payment.

EXPLANATION OF SYMBOLS

PLEASE ADVISE US OF
ANY CHANGE IN ADDRESS

S SERVICE CHARGE   R REVERSING ENTRY
T TENPLAN CHARGE   M MISCELLANEOUS ENTRY   F FOLLOW SHEET
A AUTOMATIC PAYROLL ENTRY N NO TICKET ENTRY   OD OVERDRAFT

Bank Statement

kept on his check stubs. This procedure is known as *reconciling the bank statement*. The balance shown on the bank statement may not be the same as the amount shown on the check stubs for one or more of the following reasons:

    (a) Some of the checks issued during the period may not have been presented to the bank for payment before the statement was prepared. These are known as *outstanding checks*.

(b) Deposits made by mail may have been in transit, or a deposit placed in the night depository may not have been recorded by the bank until the day following the date of the statement.

(c) Service charges or other charges may appear on the bank statement that the depositor has not recorded on his check stubs.

(d) The depositor may have erred in keeping his bank record.

(e) The bank may have erred in keeping its account with the depositor.

If a depositor is unable to reconcile his bank statement, he should report the matter to his bank immediately.

A suggested procedure in reconciling the bank statement is enumerated below.

(a) The amount of each deposit recorded on the bank statement should be checked with the amount recorded on the check stubs.

(b) The amount of each canceled check should be compared both with the amount recorded on the bank statement and with the amount recorded on the depositor's check stubs. When making this comparison it is a good plan to place a check mark by the amount recorded on each check stub to indicate that the canceled check has been returned by the bank and its amount verified.

(c) The amounts of any items listed on a bank statement that represent charges to a depositor's account which have not been entered on the check stubs should be deducted from the balance on the check stubs and should be recorded in the journal that is being used to record cash disbursements.

(d) A list of the outstanding checks should be prepared. The information needed for this list may be obtained by examining the check stubs and noting the amounts that have not been check marked.

After completing the foregoing steps, the balance shown on the check stubs should equal the balance shown in the bank statement less the total amount of the checks outstanding. A common error on the part of depositors is failure to record the amount of *counter checks* issued. Banks usually provide counter checks for the convenience of their depositors in withdrawing funds for personal use. Such checks are canceled and returned to the depositor with the bank statement so that it is an easy matter for the depositor to detect if he has failed to record such checks.

On the following page is a reconciliation of the bank balance shown in the statement reproduced on page 69. In making this reconciliation it was assumed that the depositor's check stub indicated a balance of $2,903.51 on May 19, that Checks Nos. 112, 115, and 117 had not been presented for payment and thus were not returned with the bank statement, and that a deposit of $465.92 placed in the night depository on May 19 is not shown on the statement.

Service Charges. A service charge may be made by a bank for the handling of checks and other items. The basis and the amount of such charges vary with different banks in different localities.

When a bank statement indicates that a service charge has been made, the depositor should record the amount of the service charge by debiting an expense account, such as Miscellaneous Expense, and by crediting Cash. He should also deduct the amount of such charges from the check stub balance.

Keeping a Ledger Account with the Bank. As explained previously, a memorandum account with the bank may be kept on the depositor's checkbook stub. The depositor may also keep a ledger account with the bank if desired. The title of such an account usually is the name of the

THE P. G. THOMAS CO.
Reconciliation of Bank Statement
May 19, 1971

Balance, May 19, per bank statement..........		$2,691.89
Add: Deposit, May 19.....................		465.92
		$3,157.81
Less: Checks outstanding, May 19:		
No. 112...............................	$ 75.00	
No. 115...............................	19.50	
No. 117...............................	160.55	255.05
Corrected bank balance, May 19.............		$2,902.76
Check stub balance, May 19.................		$2,903.51
Less: Bank service charge..................		.75
Corrected check stub balance, May 19........		$2,902.76

bank. Sometimes more than one account is kept with a bank in which case each account should be correctly labeled. Such terms as "commercial," "executive," and "payroll" are used to identify the accounts.

The bank account should be debited for the amount of each deposit and should be credited for the amount of each check written. The account should also be credited for any other items that may be charged to the account by the bank, including service charges.

When both a cash account and a bank account are kept in the ledger, certain procedures, as illustrated on the next page, should be observed in recording transactions affecting these accounts.

Under this method of accounting for cash and banking transactions, the cash account will be in balance when all cash on hand has been deposited in the bank. To prove the balance of the cash account at any time,

CASH		BELLEVUE TRUST COMPANY	
Debit	Credit	Debit	Credit
For all receipts of cash and cash items.	(a) For all payments in cash. (b) For all bank deposits.	For all deposits.	(a) For all checks written. (b) For all service charges. (c) For all other charges, such as for dishonored checks.

it is necessary only to count the cash and cash items on hand and to compare the total with the cash account balance. To prove the bank account balance, it will be necessary to reconcile the bank balance in the same manner in which it is reconciled when only a memorandum record of bank transactions is kept on the check stubs.

The cash account can be dispensed with when a bank account is kept in the ledger and all cash receipts are deposited in the bank. When this is done, all disbursements (except small expenditures made from a petty cash fund) are made by check.

Under this method of accounting, the Cash Debits and the Cash Credits columns of the journal may be headed as follows:

BANK	
DEPOSITS DEBIT	CHECKS CREDIT

When this form of journal is used, all cash receipts should be entered in the Bank Deposits Debit column and all checks issued should be entered in the Bank Checks Credit column. Daily, or at frequent intervals, the receipts are deposited in the bank. If all cash received during the month has been deposited before the books are closed at the end of the month, the total amount of the bank deposits will equal the total cash receipts for the month. If all disbursements during the month are made by check, the total amount of checks issued will be the total disbursements for the month.

Time Deposits

Time deposits are interest bearing deposits which are expected to remain in the bank for a period of time. Thirty days' notice for withdrawal may be required by the bank but this rule is almost never enforced. Savings accounts are a type of time deposit, but savings accounts may be held only by individuals and nonprofit organizations and usually may not exceed a certain amount. Time deposits, unlimited in amount, may be held by business firms as well as individuals.

When a time deposit is opened in a bank, a signature card must be signed by the depositor. He may be given a passbook that he must present at the bank when making deposits or when making withdrawals. By signing the signature card, the depositor agrees to abide by the rules and the regulations of the bank. These rules and regulations vary with different banks and may be altered and amended from time to time. The principal differences between a time deposit and a checking account are that interest is paid by the bank on the time deposit and withdrawals from a time deposit must be made at the bank or by mail by the depositor or his authorized agent. Checks cannot be written on time deposits. Interest is usually computed on a semiannual basis, although it may be computed more often. If a passbook is used, it must be presented along with a withdrawal slip when money is drawn from the account. Banks do not pay interest on the balances in checking accounts. Depositors use checking accounts primarily as a convenient means of making payments, while time deposits are used primarily as a means of accumulating funds with interest.

If the assets of a business include money in a bank time deposit, there should be a separate account in the ledger with a title and a number that indicate the nature of the deposit. Sometimes the name of the bank is in the title, as for example, "Bellevue Trust Co.-Time Deposit." When the bank credits interest to the account, the depositor should record the amount in his accounts by a debit to the time deposit account and by a credit to Interest Earned. The interest is revenue whether withdrawn or not.

Report No. 7

Refer to the workbook and complete Report No. 7. This assignment provides a test of your ability to apply the principles developed in the first three chapters of the textbook. After completing the report, you may proceed with the textbook discussion in Chapter 4 until the next report is required.

chapter four

payroll accounting

Employers need to maintain detailed and accurate payroll accounting records. Accurate accounting for employees' earnings preserves the legal and moral right of each employee to be paid according to his employment contract and the laws governing such contracts.

Payroll accounting records also provide information useful in the analysis and classification of labor costs. At the same time, payroll accounting information is invaluable in contract discussions with labor unions, in the settlement of company-union grievances, and in other forms of collective bargaining. Clearly, there is virtually no margin for error in payroll accounting.

earnings and deductions

The first step in determining the amount to be paid to an employee is to calculate the amount of his total or gross earnings for the pay period. The second step is to determine the amounts of any deductions that are required either by law or by agreement. Depending upon a variety of circumstances, either or both of these steps may be relatively simple or quite complicated. An examination of the factors that are involved follows.

Employer-Employee Relationships

Not every individual who performs services for a business is considered to be an employee. A public accountant, lawyer, or management consultant who sells his services to a business does not become its employee. Neither does a plumber nor an electrician who is hired to make specific repairs or installations on business property. These people are told what to do, but not how to do it, and the compensation that they receive for their services is called a *fee*. Any person who agrees to perform a service for a fee and is not subject to the control of those whom he serves is called an *independent contractor.*

In contrast, an employee is one who is under the control and direction of his employer with regard to the performance of services. The difference between an independent contractor and an employee is an important legal distinction. The nature and extent of the responsibilities of a contractor and a client to each other and to third parties are quite different from the mutual obligations of an employer and his employee.

Types of Compensation

Compensation for managerial or administrative services usually is called *salary*. A salary normally is expressed in terms of a month or a year. Compensation either for skilled or for unskilled labor usually is referred to as *wages*. Wages ordinarily are expressed in terms of hours, weeks, or pieces of accomplishment. The terms salary and wages often are used interchangeably in practice.

Supplements to basic salaries or wages of employees include bonuses, commissions, cost-of-living adjustments, pensions, and profit-sharing plans. Compensation also may take the form of goods, lodging, meals, or other property, and as such is measured by the fair value of the property or service given in payment for the employee's efforts.

Determination of Total Earnings

An employee's earnings commonly are based on the time worked during the payroll period. Sometimes earnings are based on units of output or of sales during the period. Compensation based on time requires a record of the time worked by each employee. Where there are only a few employees, a record of times worked kept in a memorandum book may suffice. Where there are many employees, time clocks commonly are used to record time spent on the job each day. With time clocks, a clock card is provided for each employee and the clock is used to record arrival and departure times. Whatever method is used, the total time worked during the payroll period must be computed.

Employees often are entitled to compensation at more than their regular rate of pay for work during certain hours or on certain days. If the employer is engaged in Interstate Commerce, the Federal Fair Labor Standards Act (commonly known as the Wages and Hours Law) provides that all employees covered by the Act must be paid one and one-half times the regular rate for all hours worked in excess of 40 per week. Labor-management agreements often require extra pay for certain hours or days. In such cases, hours worked in excess of eight per day or work on Sundays and specified holidays may be paid for at higher rates.

To illustrate, assume that the company which employs George Hempel pays time and a half for all hours worked in excess of 40 per week and double time for work on Sunday. Hempel's regular rate is $3 per hour, and during the week ended April 17, he worked nine hours each day Monday through Friday, six hours on Saturday, and four on Sunday. Hempel's total earnings for the week ended April 17 would be computed as follows:

40 hours @ $3.00	$120.00
11 hours @ $4.50	49.50
(Hempel worked 9 hours each day Monday through Friday and 6 hours on Saturday — a total of 51 hours. Forty hours would be paid for at the regular rate and 11 hours at time and a half.)	
4 hours (on Sunday) @ $6.00	24.00
Total earnings for the week	$193.50

An employee who is paid a regular salary may be entitled to premium pay for any overtime. If this is the case, it is necessary to compute the regular hourly rate of pay before computing the overtime rate. To illustrate, assume that Robert Virgil receives a regular salary of $500 a month. Virgil is entitled to overtime pay at the rate of one and one-half times his regular hourly rate for any time worked in excess of 40 hours per week. His overtime pay may be computed as follows:

$500 × 12 months = $6,000 annual pay
$6,000 ÷ 52 weeks = $115.38 per week
$115.38 ÷ 40 hours = $2.88 per regular hour
$2.88 × 1½ = $4.32 per overtime hour

Deductions from Total Earnings

With few exceptions employers are required to withhold portions of each employee's total earnings both for federal income taxes and for social security taxes. Certain states and cities also require tax withholding on the part of employers. Besides these deductions, an agreement between the employer and the employee may call for amounts to be withheld for any one or more of the following reasons:

(a) To purchase United States savings bonds for the employee.
(b) To pay a life, accident, or health insurance premium for the employee.
(c) To pay the employee's union dues.
(d) To add to a pension fund or profit sharing fund.
(e) To pay to some charitable organization.
(f) To repay a loan from the company or from the company credit union.

Social Security and Tax Account Number

Each employee is required to have a social security account and tax account number for payroll accounting purposes. A completed Form SS-5, the official form to be used in applying for an account number, follows:

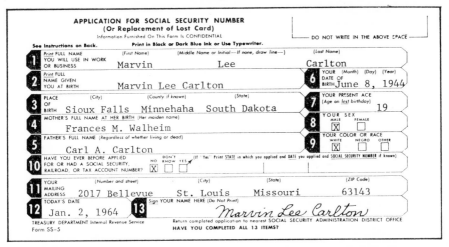

Completed Application for Social Security and Tax Account Number (Form SS-5)

Employees' Income Taxes Withheld

Under federal law employers are required to withhold certain amounts from the total earnings of each employee to be applied toward the payment of the employee's federal income tax. The amount to be withheld is governed by **(1)** the total earnings of the employee, **(2)** the number of *withholding exemptions* claimed by the employee, **(3)** the marital status of the employee, and **(4)** the length of the employee's pay period.

Each federal income taxpayer is entitled to one exemption for himself or for herself and one each for certain other qualified relatives whom he or she supports. The law specifies the relationship that must exist, the extent of support required, and how much the *dependent* may earn in order that an exemption may be claimed. A taxpayer and spouse each get an extra exemption for age over 65 years and still another exemption for blindness.

An employed taxpayer must furnish his employer with an Employee's Withholding Exemption Certificate (Form W-4) showing the number of exemptions claimed. The exemption certificate completed by Marvin Lee Carlton is shown below.

FORM W-4 (Rev. July 1970)
Department of the Treasury
Internal Revenue Service
Employee's Withholding Exemption Certificate

Type or print full name: Marvin Lee Carlton   Social Security Number 504-38-8340

Home address 2017 Bellevue   City St. Louis   State Missouri   ZIP code 63143

EMPLOYEE:	HOW TO CLAIM YOUR WITHHOLDING EXEMPTIONS	
File this form with your employer. Otherwise, he must withhold U.S. income tax from your wages without exemption.	1. If SINGLE (or if married and wish withholding as single person), write "1." If you claim no exemptions, write "0" . . .	
	2. If MARRIED, one exemption each is allowable for husband and wife if not claimed on another certificate.	
	(a) If you claim both of these exemptions, write "2"; (b) If you claim one of these exemptions, write "1"; (c) If you claim neither of these exemptions, write "0"	2
EMPLOYER: Keep this certificate with your records. If you believe the employee claimed too many exemptions advise your District Director.	3. Exemptions for age and blindness (applicable only to you and your wife but not to dependents): (a) If you or your wife will be 65 years of age or older at the end of the year, and you claim this exemption, write "1"; if both will be 65 or older, and you claim both of these exemptions, write "2" . . . . (b) If you or your wife are blind, and you claim this exemption, write "1"; if both are blind, and you claim both of these exemptions, write "2"	
	4. If you claim exemptions for one or more dependents, write the number of such exemptions. (Do not claim exemption for a dependent unless you are qualified under Instruction 4 on other side.)	1
	5. If you claim additional withholding allowances for itemized deductions attach Schedule A (Form W-4) and enter the number of allowances claimed (if claimed you must file a new Form W-4 each year)	
	6. Add the exemptions and allowances (if any) which you have claimed above and enter total	3
	7. Additional withholding per pay period under agreement with employer. (See Instruction 1.) . . . . $	

Under the penalties of perjury, I certify that the number of withholding exemptions and allowances claimed on this certificate does not exceed the number to which I am entitled.

(Date) January 4, 19 71   (Signed) *Marvin Lee Carlton*

Completed Withholding Exemption Certificate (Form W-4)

Employees with large itemized deductions are permitted to claim additional withholding exemptions called *withholding allowances.* Any employee desiring to claim one or more withholding allowances must estimate his expected total earnings and itemized deductions for the coming year. The number of additional withholding allowances to be claimed is then determined by referring to one of three tables provided by the Internal Revenue Service. Use of the proper table is required. Each withholding allowance will give the taxpayer an additional exemption, but the employed taxpayer will have to file a new Withholding Exemption Certificate (Form W-4) each year to claim one or more such allowances.

Most employers use the *wage-bracket method* of determining the amount of tax to be withheld. This method involves the use of income tax withholding tables provided by the Internal Revenue Service. Such tables cover monthly, semimonthly, biweekly, weekly, and daily or miscellaneous periods. There are two types of tables: **(1)** single persons and unmarried heads of households, and **(2)** married persons. Copies may be obtained from any District Director of Internal Revenue. A portion of a weekly income tax wage-bracket withholding table for married persons is illustrated on page 79. As an example of the use of this table, assume that

Marvin Lee Carlton (who claims 3 exemptions) had gross earnings of $215 for the week ending December 18, 1971. On the line showing the tax on wages of "at least $210 but less than $220," in the column headed "3 withholding exemptions," $26.90 is given as the amount to be withheld.

MARRIED Persons — **WEEKLY** Payroll Period

And the wages are—		And the number of withholding exemptions claimed is—										
At least	But less than	0	1	2	3	4	5	6	7	8	9	10 or more
		The amount of income tax to be withheld shall be—										
$100	$105	$14.10	$12.00	$10.10	$8.20	$6.30	$4.00	$1.30	$0	$0	$0	$0
105	110	14.90	12.80	10.80	8.90	7.10	5.00	2.40	0	0	0	0
110	115	15.80	13.70	11.60	9.70	7.80	5.90	3.40	.80	0	0	0
115	120	16.60	14.50	12.40	10.40	8.60	6.70	4.50	1.90	0	0	0
120	125	17.50	15.40	13.20	11.20	9.30	7.40	5.50	2.90	.30	0	0
125	130	18.30	16.20	14.10	12.00	10.10	8.20	6.30	4.00	1.30	0	0
130	135	19.20	17.10	14.90	12.80	10.80	8.90	7.10	5.00	2.40	0	0
135	140	20.00	17.90	15.80	13.70	11.60	9.70	7.80	5.90	3.40	.80	0
140	145	20.90	18.80	16.60	14.50	12.40	10.40	8.60	6.70	4.50	1.90	0
145	150	21.70	19.60	17.50	15.40	13.20	11.20	9.30	7.40	5.50	2.90	.30
150	160	23.00	20.90	18.80	16.60	14.50	12.40	10.40	8.60	6.70	4.50	1.90
160	170	24.70	22.60	20.50	18.30	16.20	14.10	12.00	10.10	8.20	6.30	4.00
170	180	26.40	24.30	22.20	20.00	17.90	15.80	13.70	11.60	9.70	7.80	5.90
180	190	28.40	26.00	23.90	21.70	19.60	17.50	15.40	13.20	11.20	9.30	7.40
190	200	30.40	27.90	25.60	23.40	21.30	19.20	17.10	14.90	12.80	10.80	8.90
200	210	32.40	29.90	27.40	25.10	23.00	20.90	18.80	16.60	14.50	12.40	10.40
210	220	34.40	31.90	29.40	26.90	24.70	22.60	20.50	18.30	16.20	14.10	12.00
220	230	36.40	33.90	31.40	28.90	26.40	24.30	22.20	20.00	17.90	15.80	13.70
230	240	38.40	35.90	33.40	30.90	28.40	26.00	23.90	21.70	19.60	17.50	15.40
240	250	40.40	37.90	35.40	32.90	30.40	27.90	25.60	23.40	21.30	19.20	17.10

Portion of Married Persons Weekly Federal Income Tax Withholding Table

Whether the wage-bracket method or some other method is used in computing the amount of tax to be withheld, the employee is given full benefit for all exemptions claimed plus a standard deduction of approximately 10 percent. In any event, the sum of the taxes withheld from an employee's wages only approximates the tax on his actual income derived solely from wages up to $5,000 a year. An employee may be liable for a tax larger than the amount withheld. On the other hand, the amount of the taxes withheld by the employer may be greater than the employee's actual tax liability. In such an event, the employee will be entitled to a refund of the excess taxes withheld, or he may elect to apply the excess to his tax liability for the following year.

Several of the states have adopted state income tax withholding procedures. Some of these states supply employers with withholding exemption certificate forms and income tax withholding tables that are similar in appearance to those used by the federal Internal Revenue Service. Note, however, that each state that has an income tax law uses the specific tax rates and dollar amounts for exemptions as required by its law. Some states determine the amount to be withheld merely by applying a fixed percentage to the federal withholding amount.

Employees' FICA Taxes Withheld

Payroll taxes are imposed on almost all employers and employees for old-age, survivors, and disability insurance (OASDI) benefits and health insurance for the aged (HIP), both under the Federal Insurance Contributions Act (FICA). The base of the tax and the tax rate have been changed several times since the law was first enacted and are subject to change by Congress at any time in the future. For purposes of this chapter, the rate is assumed to be 4.6 percent of the taxable wages paid during the calendar year for OASDI and 0.6 percent for HIP. Only the first $9,000 of the wages paid to each employee in any calendar year is taxable. Any amount of compensation paid in excess of $9,000 is assumed to be exempt from the tax. The employees' portion of the FICA tax must be withheld from their wages by the employer. Although it is true that the base and rate of the tax may be changed at the pleasure of Congress, the accounting principles or methods of recording payroll transactions are not affected.

A few states require employers to withhold a percentage of the employees' wages for unemployment compensation benefits or for disability benefits. In some states and cities, employers are required to withhold a percentage of the employees' wages for other types of payroll taxes. The withholding of income taxes at the state and city level has already been mentioned. Despite the number of withholdings required, each employer must comply with the proper laws in withholding any taxes based on payrolls and in keeping his payroll accounting records.

Payroll Records

The needs of management and the requirements of various federal and state laws make it necessary for employers to keep records that will provide or make it possible to determine the following information:

PAYROLL REGISTER

NO.	NAME	EXEMP.	MARITAL STATUS	Earnings: REGULAR	Earnings: OVERTIME	GROSS	FICA	FEDERAL INC. TAX
1	Brown, Harold D.	2	M	120 00		120 00	6 24	13 20
2	Carlton, Marvin L.	3	M	200 00	15 00	215 00		26 90
3	Geckler, Dorene L.	1	S	95 00		95 00	4 94	12 40
4	Heath, William L.	4	M	160 00	15 00	175 00	9 10	17 90
5	Johnson, Oscar E.	3	M	125 00	15 00	140 00	7 28	14 50
6	Myers, Kent J.	3	M	105 00		105 00	5 46	8 90
7	Nichols, Joseph E.	2	M	115 00	10 00	125 00	6 50	14 10
8	Roberts, John H.	1	S	100 00		100 00	5 20	13 80
				1020 00	55 00	1075 00	44 72	121 70
				1020 00	55 00	1075 00	44 72	121 70

Payroll Register — Manually Prepared (Left Side)

(a) The name, address, and social security number of each employee.

(b) The gross amount of each employee's earnings, the date of payment, and the period of employment covered by each payroll.

(c) The total amount of gross earnings accumulated since the first of the year.

(d) The amount of any taxes or other items withheld from each employee's earnings.

Regardless of the number of employees or type of business, three types of payroll records usually need to be prepared for or by the employer. They are: (1) the payroll register or payroll journal; (2) the payroll check with earnings statement attached; and (3) the earnings record of the individual employee (on a weekly, monthly, quarterly, or annual basis). These records can be prepared either by *manual* or by *automated* methods.

Payroll Register. A manually prepared payroll register used by Central States Paper & Bag Company for the payroll period ended December 18, 1971, is illustrated on pages 80 and 81. The usual source of information for preparing a payroll register is the time memorandum book or the time clock cards. Central States Paper & Bag Company has eight employees, as the illustration shows. Regular deductions are made from the earnings of employees for FICA taxes, federal income taxes, and city earnings tax. In addition, for the pay period ending nearest to the middle of the month, deductions are made for life insurance, private hospital insurance, the company credit union, and (if desired) for the purchase of United States savings bonds. Note that the deduction column labeled "Other" is used for recording bond purchases, and may be used for other infrequent deductions as well.

Marvin L. Carlton and William L. Heath have each authorized Central States Paper & Bag Company to withhold $5 on the payday nearest to the middle of each month for United States savings bonds. When the

FOR PERIOD ENDED *December 18* 19 71

| | | DEDUCTIONS | | | | | NET PAY | |
CITY TAX	LIFE INSURANCE	PRIVATE HOSP. INS.	CREDIT UNION	OTHER		CHECK NO.	AMOUNT	
1 20	4 00		2 00			203	93 36	
2 15	5 00	2 50	2 00	*Savings Bonds*	5 00	204	171 45	
95		2 00				205	74 71	
1 75			2 00	*Savings Bond*	5 00	206	139 25	
1 40	5 00	2 50	2 00			207	107 32	
1 05	3 00					208	86 59	
1 25			2 00			209	101 15	
1 00	3 00	2 00				210	75 00	
10 75	20 00	9 00	10 00		10 00		848 53	
10 75	20 00	9 00	10 00		10 00		848 83	

Payroll Register — Manually Prepared (Right Side)

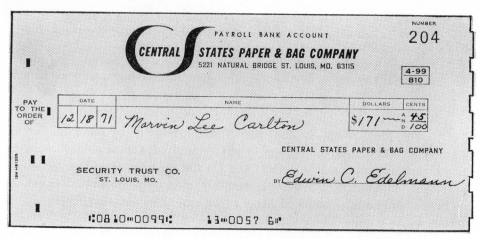

Completed Paycheck — Manually Prepared

amount withheld reaches the sum of $37.50, a $50 Series E, United States savings bond is purchased at the bank for each of the two employees and delivered to them.

Only the first $9,000 of earnings received in any calendar year is subject to FICA taxes. Mr. Carlton's earnings for the week ending December 18 are exempt from the FICA tax because he has already been taxed on earnings totaling $9,000.

After the payroll register has been completed the amount columns should be footed and the footings proved as follows:

Regular earnings..		$1,020.00
Overtime earnings.......................................		55.00
Gross earnings		$1,075.00
Deductions:		
FICA taxes..	$ 44.72	
Federal income taxes...................................	121.70	
City earnings taxes	10.75	
Life insurance premiums	20.00	
Private hospital insurance premiums	9.00	
Credit union...	10.00	
United States savings bonds............................	10.00	226.17
Net amount of payroll....................................		$848.83

After proving the footings, the totals should be entered in ink and the record should be ruled with single and double lines as shown in the illustration. Employees may be paid in cash or by check. Many businesses prepare a check for the net amount of the payroll and deposit it in a special Payroll Bank Account. The Central States Paper & Bag Co. decided to open a payroll bank account in June, 1971. Individual paychecks are then drawn on that account for the amount due each employee. The employer usually furnishes a statement of payroll deductions to the employee along

and Deduction Stub

with each wage payment. Paychecks with detachable stubs, like the one for Marvin L. Carlton illustrated above, are widely used. The stub should be detached before the check is cashed, and the stub should be retained by the employee as a permanent record of his earnings and payroll deductions.

Employee's Earnings Record. An auxiliary record of each employee's earnings usually is kept in order to provide the information needed in preparing the various federal, state, and local reports required of employers. A manually prepared employee's earnings record used by Central States Paper & Bag Company for Marvin Lee Carlton during the last two quarters of the current calendar year is illustrated on page 84. This record may be kept on separate sheets or on cards, which may be filed alphabetically or numerically for ready reference. The information recorded on this form is taken from the payroll register.

Marvin Carlton's earnings for the last half of the year up to December 18 are shown on this form. The entry for the pay period ended December 18 is posted from the payroll register illustrated on pages 80 and 81. Assuming that Carlton had accumulated $5,500 in wages for the first two quarters of the year, it can be seen from his earnings record that his cumulative earnings passed the $9,000 mark during the week ended October 30. (He received a raise at the beginning of the third quarter.) Although his total earnings for that week amounted to $200, only $43.50 of those wages was subject to the combined FICA tax of 5.2 percent, hence only $2.26 was withheld from his wages for that week. For the remainder of the current calendar year, his entire earnings are exempt from FICA tax withholding.

The payroll register is a summary of the earnings of all employees for each pay period, while the earnings record is a summary of the annual earnings of each employee. The earnings record illustrated on page 84 is

EMPLOYEE'S EARNINGS RECORD

#	1971 PERIOD ENDING	EARNINGS REGULAR	OVERTIME	GROSS	DEDUCTIONS FICA	FEDERAL INC. TAX	CITY TAX	LIFE INSURANCE	PRIVATE HOSP. INS.	CREDIT UNION	OTHER	NET PAY CHECK NO.	AMOUNT
1	7/3	200.00		200.00	10.40	25.10	2.00					12	162.50
2	7/10	200.00		200.00	10.40	25.10	2.00					20	162.50
3	7/17	200.00	10.00	210.00	10.92	26.90	2.10	5.00	2.50	2.00	Savings Bond 5.00	28	155.58
4	7/24	200.00	10.00	210.00	10.92	26.90	2.10					36	170.08
5	7/31	200.00		200.00	10.40	25.10	2.00					44	162.50
6	8/7	200.00		200.00	10.40	25.10	2.00					52	162.50
7	8/14	200.00	7.50	207.50	10.79	25.10	2.08	5.00	2.50	2.00	Savings Bond 5.00	60	155.03
8	8/21	200.00		200.00	10.40	25.10	2.00					68	162.50
9	8/28	200.00		200.00	10.40	25.10	2.00					76	162.50
10	9/4	200.00	5.00	205.00	10.66	25.10	2.05					84	167.19
11	9/11	200.00		200.00	10.40	25.10	2.00					92	162.50
12	9/18	200.00	10.00	210.00	10.92	26.90	2.10	5.00	2.50	2.00	Savings Bond 5.00	100	155.58
13	9/25	200.00		200.00	10.40	25.10	2.00					108	162.50
THIRD QUARTER		2,600.00	42.50	2,642.50	137.41	331.70	26.43	15.00	7.50	6.00	15.00		3,103.46
1	10/2	200.00		200.00	10.40	25.10	2.00					116	162.50
2	10/9	200.00	8.00	208.00	10.82	25.10	2.08					124	170.00
3	10/16	200.00	6.00	206.00	10.71	25.10	2.06	5.00	2.50	2.00	Savings Bond 5.00	132	153.63
4	10/23	200.00		200.00	10.40	25.10	2.00					140	162.50
5	10/30	200.00		200.00	2.26	25.10	2.00					148	170.64
6	11/6	200.00	10.00	210.00		26.90	2.10					156	181.00
7	11/13	200.00	5.00	205.00		25.10	2.05	5.00	2.50	2.00	Savings Bond 5.00	164	163.35
8	11/20	200.00	7.50	207.50		25.10	2.08					172	180.32
9	11/27	200.00		200.00		25.10	2.00					180	172.90
10	12/4	200.00		200.00		25.10	2.00					188	172.90
11	12/11	200.00		200.00		25.10	2.00					196	172.90
12	12/18	200.00	15.00	215.00		26.90	2.15	5.00	2.50	2.00	Savings Bond 5.00	204	171.45
FOURTH QUARTER													
YEARLY TOTAL													

SEX M ✓ F	DEPARTMENT Maintenance	OCCUPATION Supervisor	SOCIAL SECURITY NO. 504-38-8340	NAME – LAST Carlton	FIRST Marvin	MIDDLE Lee	EMPLOYEE NO. 2

Employee's Earnings Record — Manually Prepared

designed so that a record of the earnings of the employee for the first half of the year may be kept on one side and a record of the earnings for the last half of the year may be kept on the other side of the form. Thus, at the end of the year, the form provides a complete record of the earnings of the employee for the year. It also provides a record of the earnings for each calendar quarter needed by the employer in the preparation of his quarterly returns. These returns will be discussed later in this chapter.

Automated Payroll Systems

Automated payroll systems may involve the use of small-capacity bookkeeping machines, large-capacity bookkeeping machines, or electronic data processing equipment. Both bookkeeping machine payroll systems and electronic payroll systems make it possible to prepare a payroll check with deduction stub, an earnings record, and a payroll register simultaneously. This is an application of the *write-it-once principle*, which recognizes that each time the same information is recopied there is another chance for an error.

It is also possible for a person preparing a payroll manually to employ the *write-it-once principle* by using an accounting board on which the payroll register, the checks, check stubs, and the employee earnings records are prepared simultaneously. Manual accounting systems using accounting boards are discussed further in the Appendix, pages A-17 to A-19.

Service Bureaus and Payroll Accounting. The development of automated accounting methods and electronic data processing equipment has led to the establishment of a large number of *service bureaus.* Service bureaus are business organizations engaged in data processing on a contract basis for other businesses of small and medium size. They either are independently operated or are owned and operated by the major business machine manufacturers or by banks. In any case, their employees are trained in accounting and systems work and can set up and operate effective payroll systems for customers.

When payroll accounting is done for a business by a service bureau, the preliminary work that the business needs to do usually is quite limited. One or more cards are punched for each employee with the aid of a keypunch machine for each payroll period, and these cards contain necessary information such as:

(a) Employee name
(b) Employee address
(c) Employee social security number
(d) Regular earnings
(e) Overtime earnings
(f) Federal income tax withheld
(g) FICA (OASDI and HIP) tax withheld
(h) Other deductions

Completed Paycheck — Machine Prepared

These punched cards are picked up by the service bureau at regular intervals, and the payroll records desired by the business customer are prepared.

In a manual payroll system, the payroll register normally is prepared first and serves as a journal. The employee earnings records, checks, and stubs are then prepared from the payroll register information. However, in an automated payroll system all three records are prepared simultaneously. Because of this, the order of their preparation is not of any concern to the accountant.

Employer-Operated Payroll Systems. A payroll check with deduction stub, earnings record, and payroll register entry prepared simultaneously on a bookkeeping machine are illustrated above and on the following pages. Assume that these records were prepared by the Central States Paper & Bag Company for its employee, Marvin L. Carlton, for the same pay period as the manual records previously illustrated on pages 80 to 84, inclusive. Contrast the two types of payroll systems. The primary advantage of the machine system is the saving of time and labor.

In addition to the *write-it-once* features of modern bookkeeping machines, electronic payroll systems can also provide speed and storage as well as needed adding and multiplying ability. Through the use of electronic equipment, adding and multiplying of payrolls can be speeded up, and information such as wage rates and withholding table amounts can be stored inside the equipment. As one would expect, the cost of electronic payroll equipment is noticeably higher than the cost of more conventional bookkeeping machines. The type of electronic data processing system well suited, among other things, to payroll accounting is described and illustrated in the appendix to this textbook.

CENTRAL STATES PAPER & BAG COMPANY
ST. LOUIS, MO.

STATEMENT OF EARNINGS

MISC.	HOSPITAL	BONDS	INSURANCE	CREDIT UNION	PARKING	CHARITY	EMPLOYEE	DATE
	2 50	5 00	5 00	2 00			2	12 18 71
200 00	15 00		26 90		2 15		43 55	171 45
REGULAR	O'TIME	OTHER	W.H. TAX	FICA	CITY	STATE	TOTAL DEDUCTIONS	NET PAY
EARNINGS			TAXES					

NON-NEGOTIABLE

and Deduction Stub

Much of the work usually required to figure employees' gross earnings, deductions, and net pay may be eliminated if the equipment provides sufficient automation, storage capacity, and electronic calculation capability. When conventional electric bookkeeping machines are used, gross earnings are often computed separately on a calculator, and withholding and other tax amounts are either read from tables or worked out manually.

An electronic payroll accounting system completes all of the major payroll records at once, just as do modern electric bookkeeping machines. In addition, an electronic payroll accounting system determines automatically:

(a) The presence of the proper earnings record.
(b) The next available posting line.
(c) Whether overtime earnings are due.
(d) Whether there are other earnings.
(e) Whether the FICA limit has been reached.
(f) What tax deductions should be made.
(g) Whether insurance premiums should be deducted.
(h) Whether there are any other deductions to be made.
(i) Whether there are any delinquent deductions to be made.
(j) Whether there is anything else to be done.

Once this system is properly set up, the operator is relieved of manual figuring and of looking up amounts in tables. The primary job is one of feeding in blank payroll accounting record forms and getting these forms back as completed payroll accounting records. (For a further discussion of automated accounting systems and procedures, see Appendix, page A-1.)

EMPLOYEE'S EARNINGS RECORD

NAME MARVIN LEE CARLTON
ADDRESS 2017 BELLEVUE
CITY ST. LOUIS, MO. 63143

	EARNINGS			DEDUCTIONS								
REGULAR	OVERTIME	GROSS	FICA	FEDERAL INC. TAX	CITY TAX	LIFE INS.	PRIVATE HOSP. INS.	CREDIT UNION	U.S. SAVINGS BONDS	DATE	NET PAY
200.00		200.00	10.40	25.10	2.00					July 3, '71	162.50
200.00		200.00	10.40	25.10	2.00					July 10, '71	162.50
200.00	10.00	210.00	10.92	26.90	2.10	5.00	2.50	2.00	5.00	July 17, '71	155.58
200.00	10.00	210.00	10.92	26.90	2.10					July 24, '71	170.08
200.00		200.00	10.40	25.10	2.00					July 31, '71	162.50
200.00		200.00	10.40	25.10	2.00					Aug. 7, '71	162.50
200.00	7.50	207.50	10.79	25.10	2.08	5.00	2.50	2.00	5.00	Aug. 14, '71	155.03
200.00		200.00	10.40	25.10	2.00					Aug. 21, '71	162.50
200.00		200.00	10.40	25.10	2.00					Aug. 28, '71	162.50
200.00	5.00	205.00	10.66	25.10	2.05					Sept. 4, '71	167.19
200.00		200.00	10.40	25.10	2.00					Sept. 11, '71	162.50
200.00	10.00	210.00	10.92	26.90	2.10	5.00	2.50	2.00	5.00	Sept. 18, '71	155.58
200.00		200.00	10.40	25.10	2.00					Sept. 25, '71	162.50
THIRD QUARTER		2,642.50	137.41	331.70	26.43	15.00	7.50	6.00	15.00		2,103.46
200.00		200.00	10.40	25.10	2.00					Oct. 2, '71	162.50
200.00	8.00	208.00	10.82	25.10	2.08					Oct. 9, '71	170.00
200.00	6.00	206.00	10.71	25.10	2.06	5.00	2.50	2.00	5.00	Oct. 16, '71	153.63
200.00		200.00	10.40	25.10	2.00					Oct. 23, '71	162.50
200.00		200.00	2.26	25.10	2.00					Oct. 30, '71	170.64
200.00	10.00	210.00		26.90	2.10					Nov. 6, '71	181.00
200.00	5.00	205.00		25.10	2.05	5.00	2.50	2.00	5.00	Nov. 13, '71	163.35
200.00	7.50	207.50		25.10	2.08					Nov. 20, '71	180.32
200.00		200.00		25.10	2.00					Nov. 27, '71	172.90
200.00		200.00		25.10	2.00					Dec. 4, '71	172.90
200.00		200.00		25.10	2.00					Dec. 11, '71	172.90
200.00	15.00	215.00		26.90	2.15	5.00	2.50	2.00	5.00	Dec. 18, '71	171.45
FOURTH QUARTER											
YEARLY TOTAL											

Employee's Earnings Record — Machine Prepared

PAYROLL REGISTER

NAME	NO. OF EXEMP.	MARI-TAL STATUS	EARNINGS			DEDUCTIONS							DATE	NET PAY	CK. NO.
			REGULAR	OVER-TIME	GROSS	FICA	FEDERAL INC. TAX	CITY TAX	LIFE INS.	PRIVATE HOSP. INS.	CREDIT UNION	U.S. SAVINGS BONDS			
1. BROWN, HAROLD D.	2	M	120.00		120.00	6.24	13.20	1.20	4.00		2.00		Dec. 18, '71	93.36	203
2. CARLTON, MARVIN L.	3	M	200.00	15.00	215.00		26.90	2.15	5.00	2.50	2.00	5.00	Dec. 18, '71	171.45	204
3. GECKLER, DORENE L.	1	S	95.00		95.00	4.94	12.40	.95		2.00			Dec. 18, '71	74.71	205
4. HEATH, WILLIAM L.	4	M	160.00	15.00	175.00	9.10	17.90	1.75			2.00	5.00	Dec. 18, '71	139.25	206
5. JOHNSON, OSCAR E.	3	M	125.00	15.00	140.00	7.28	14.50	1.40	5.00	2.50	2.00		Dec. 18, '71	107.32	207
6. MYERS, KENT J.	3	M	105.00		105.00	5.46	8.90	1.05	3.00				Dec. 18, '71	86.59	208
7. NICHOLS, JOSEPH E.	2	M	115.00	10.00	125.00	6.50	14.10	1.25			2.00		Dec. 18, '71	101.15	209
8. ROBERTS, JOHN H.	1	S	100.00		100.00	5.20	13.80	1.00	3.00	2.00			Dec. 18, '71	75.00	210
			1,020.00	55.00	1,075.00	44.72	121.70	10.75	20.00	9.00	10.00	10.00		848.83	

Payroll Register — Machine Prepared

<table>
<tr><td colspan="3">Central States Paper & Bag Company, Inc.
5221 Natural Bridge
St. Louis, Missouri 63115
43-0211630</td><td colspan="4">WAGE AND TAX STATEMENT—1971
(For use in States or Cities authorizing combined form)
Employer's State Identification Number
       Copy A—
For Internal Revenue Service</td></tr>
</table>

1

Type or print EMPLOYER'S Federal identification number, name, and address above.

FEDERAL INCOME TAX INFORMATION			SOCIAL SECURITY INFORMATION		STATUS	*
Federal income tax withheld	Wages paid subject to withholding in 1971¹	Other compensation paid in 1971²	F.I.C.A. employee tax withheld³	Total F.I.C.A. wages paid in 1971⁴	1. Single 2. Married	
$1370.40	$10,994		$468.00	$9,000	2	**

EMPLOYEE'S social security number ▶ 504-38-8340

Name of State	State Form No.	State income tax withheld
Missouri		
Name of City	City Form No.	City income tax withheld
St. Louis		

Marvin Lee Carlton
2017 Bellevue
St. Louis, Missouri 63143

*See Circ. E for sick pay reporting. **Gross wages for State if different from Federal.
¹ Includes tips reported by employee. Amount is before payroll deductions or sick pay exclusion.
² Report salary or other employee compensation which was not subject to withholding. See Circular E.
³ One-eighth of this amount was withheld to finance the cost of Hospital Insurance Benefits. The remainder is for old-age, survivors, and disability insurance.
⁴ Includes tips reported by employee.

Type or print EMPLOYEE'S name and address (including ZIP code) above.

FORM **W–2** Department of the Treasury, Internal Revenue Service

16—80571-1

Uncollected Employee Tax on Tips . . . $

EMPLOYER: See instructions on back of copy D.

Completed Withholding Tax Statement (Form W-2)

Withholding Tax Statement

Not later than January 31 of each year the law requires employers to furnish each employee from whom income taxes have been withheld a withholding statement (Form W-2) showing the total amount of wages paid and the amount of such tax withheld during the preceding calendar year. If the employee's wages were subject to FICA taxes as well as income taxes, the employer must report total wages paid and the amounts deducted both for income taxes and for FICA taxes. Information for this purpose should be provided by the employee's earnings record. A completed form W-2 is illustrated above.

The number appearing on the Withholding Tax Statement below the name and address of the employer is an *identification number* assigned to the employer by the Social Security Administration. Every employer of even one person receiving taxable wages must get an identification number within a week of the beginning of such employment. This number must be shown on all reports required of Central States Paper & Bag Company under the Federal Insurance Contributions Act.

Withholding statements must be prepared in quadruplicate (four copies). The first copy goes to the District Director of Internal Revenue with the employer's return of taxes withheld for the fourth quarter of the calendar year. The second and third copies are furnished to the employee, so that he can send one in with his federal income tax return as required and keep one for his files. The fourth copy is kept by the employer for his records. A six-copy form may be used in states or cities which have income tax withholding laws which authorize the use of a combined withholding tax statement form. One of the additional copies goes to the State or City Tax Department, and the other additional copy goes to the employee for filing with his state or city income tax return. In the case of an employee who leaves a job before the end of the year, the employer is expected to furnish the withholding statement within 30 days after the last wage payment is made.

Accounting for Wages and Wage Deductions

In accounting for wages and wage deductions it is desirable to keep separate accounts for (1) wages earned and (2) wage deductions. Various account titles are used in recording wages, such as Wages Expense, Salaries Expense, and Salaries and Commissions Expense. The accounts needed in recording wage deductions depend upon what deductions are involved. A separate account should be kept for recording the liability incurred for each type of deduction, such as FICA taxes, employees' income taxes, and savings bond deductions.

Wages Expense. This is an expense account which should be debited for the total amount of the gross earnings of all employees for each pay period. Sometimes separate

WAGES EXPENSE	
Debit	
to record gross earnings of employees for each pay period.	

wage accounts are kept for the employees of different departments. Thus, separate accounts might be kept for Office Salaries Expense, Sales Salaries Expense, and Factory Wages Expense.

FICA Taxes Payable. This is a liability account which should be credited for (1) the FICA taxes withheld from employees' wages and (2) the FICA taxes imposed on the employer. The account should be debited for amounts paid to apply on

FICA TAXES PAYABLE	
Debit	Credit
to record payment of FICA taxes.	to record FICA taxes (a) withheld from employees' wages and (b) imposed on the employer.

such taxes. When all of the FICA taxes have been paid, the account should be in balance.

Employees' Income Taxes Payable. This is a liability account which should be credited for the total income taxes withheld from employees' wages. The account should be

EMPLOYEES' INCOME TAXES PAYABLE	
Debit	Credit
to record payment of income taxes withheld.	to record income taxes withheld from employees' wages.

debited for amounts paid to apply on such taxes. When all of the income taxes withheld have been paid, the account will be in balance. A city or state earnings tax payable account is used in a similar manner.

Life Insurance Premiums Payable.
This is a liability account which
should be credited with amounts
withheld from employees' wages for
the future payment of life insurance
premiums. The account should be
debited for the subsequent payment

of these premiums to the life insurance company. Accounts for private
hospital insurance premiums payable, credit union contributions payable,
and savings bond deductions payable are similarly used.

Journalizing Payroll Transactions. The payroll register should provide
the information needed in recording wages paid. The payroll register
illustrated on page 89 provided the information needed in drafting the
following general journal entry to record the wages paid on December 18:

```
Dec. 18. Wages Expense.................................  1,075.00
         FICA Taxes Payable............................             44.72
         Employees' Income Taxes Payable...............            121.70
         City Earnings Taxes Payable...................             10.75
         Life Insurance Premiums Payable..............             20.00
         Private Hospital Insurance Premiums Payable...              9.00
         Credit Union Contributions Payable...........             10.00
         Savings Bond Deductions Payable.............             10.00
         Cash.........................................            848.83
            Payroll for week ended December 18.
```

It will be noted that the above journal entry involves one debit and
eight credits. Regardless of the number of debits and credits needed to
record a transaction, the total amount debited must be equal to the total
amount credited.

Report No. 8

Complete Report No. 8 in the workbook and submit your working
papers to the instructor for approval. After completing the report, continue with the following study assignment until the next report is required.

payroll taxes imposed on the employer

The employer is liable to the government for the taxes which he is required by law to withhold from the wages of his employees. These taxes include the federal income taxes and the FICA taxes which must be withheld from wages paid to employees. Such taxes are not an expense of the employer; nevertheless, the employer is required by law to collect the taxes and he is liable for the taxes until payment is made. Certain taxes are also imposed on the employer for various purposes, such as old-age, survivors, and disability insurance benefits; hospital insurance for the aged; and unemployment, relief, and welfare. Most employers are subject to payroll taxes imposed under the Federal Insurance Contributions Act (FICA) and the Federal Unemployment Tax Act (FUTA). An employer may also be subject to the payroll taxes imposed under the unemployment compensation laws of one or more states. These commonly are called "State Unemployment Taxes."

Payroll Tax Expense

All of the payroll taxes imposed on an employer under federal and state social security laws are an expense of the employer. In accounting for such taxes at least one expense account should be maintained. This account may be entitled Payroll Tax Expense. It is an expense account which should be debited for all taxes imposed on the employer under federal and state social security laws. Sometimes separate expense accounts are kept for **(1)** FICA Tax Expense,

Payroll Tax Expense	
Debit to record FICA, FUTA, and State Unemployment Taxes imposed on the employer.	

(2) FUTA Tax Expense, and **(3)** State Unemployment Tax Expense. In small business enterprises it is usually considered satisfactory to keep a single expense account for all federal and state social security taxes imposed on the employer.

Employer's FICA Tax

The taxes imposed under the Federal Insurance Contributions Act apply equally to employers and to employees. As explained on page 80, both the rate and base of the tax may be changed by Congress at any time.

In this discussion it is assumed that the combined rate is 5.2 percent which applies both to the employer and to his employees (a total of 10.4 percent) with respect to taxable wages. Only the first $9,000 of the wages paid to each employee in any calendar year constitutes taxable wages. Any amount of wages paid to an employee during a year in excess of $9,000 is exempt from FICA tax. This is illustrated in Form 941 on page 99. While the employer is liable to the government both for the taxes withheld from his employees' wages and for the taxes imposed on the business, only the latter constitutes an expense of the business.

Employer's FUTA Tax

Under the Federal Unemployment Tax Act, a payroll tax is levied on employers for the purpose of implementing more uniform administration of the various state unemployment compensation laws. Employers who employ one or more individuals in each of 20 different weeks, or who pay wages of $1,500 or more during any calendar quarter in the current or preceding calendar year are subject to this tax. The federal law imposes a specific rate of tax but allows a substantial credit against this levy if the state in which the employer is located has an unemployment compensation law that meets certain requirements. Since all states have such laws, the rate actually paid by most employers is much less than the maximum legal rate. As in the case of the FICA tax, Congress can and does change the rate and base from time to time. For the purpose of this discussion, a rate of 3.2 percent with a credit of 2.7 percent available to most employers is used. The difference, 0.5 percent (3.2 − 2.7) is, then, the effective rate. This is applied to the first $4,200 of compensation paid to each employee during the calendar year. It is important to note this limitation in contrast to the $9,000 limit in the case of the FICA tax. It is also important to note that all of the payroll taxes relate to amounts of wages paid — not to amounts earned. Sometimes wages are earned in one quarter or year, but not paid until the following period.

FUTA Taxes Payable

FUTA TAXES PAYABLE

Debit	Credit
to record payment of FUTA taxes.	to record FUTA taxes imposed on the employer with respect to wages paid.

In recording the federal unemployment tax, it is customary to keep a separate liability account entitled FUTA Taxes Payable. This is a liability account which should be credited for the taxes imposed on employers under the Federal Unemployment Tax Act. The account should be debited for amounts paid to apply on such taxes. When all of the FUTA taxes have been paid, the account should be in balance.

State Unemployment Taxes

All of the states and the District of Columbia have enacted unemployment compensation laws providing for the payment of benefits to qualified unemployed workers. The cost of administering the state unemployment compensation laws is borne by the federal government. Under the federal law an appropriation is made for each year by the Congress from which grants are made to the states to meet the proper administrative costs of their unemployment compensation laws. As a result of this provision, the entire amount paid into the state funds may be used for the payment of benefits to qualified workers. While in general there is considerable uniformity in the provisions of the state laws, there are many variations in coverage, rates of taxes imposed, and benefits payable to qualified workers. Not all employers covered by the Federal Unemployment Tax Act are covered by the unemployment compensation laws of the states in which they have employees.

The number of employees specified under state laws varies from 1 to 4. However, in many of the states an employer who is covered by the federal law and has one or more individuals employed within the state is also covered by the state law. Furthermore, under the laws of most states an employer who is covered by the federal law may elect voluntary coverage in states where he has one or more employees, even though he may have less than the number of employees specified by the law in that particular state. In any event, it is necessary for each employer to be familiar with the unemployment compensation laws of all the states in which he has one or more employees, and if such employees are covered, he must keep such records and pay such taxes for unemployment compensation purposes as are prescribed by those laws.

In most states the unemployment benefit plan is financed entirely by taxes imposed on employers. However, in a few states employees are also required to contribute, and the amount of the tax imposed on the employees must be withheld from their wages.

In most states the maximum tax imposed upon employers is 2.7 percent of the first $4,200 of wages paid to each employee in any calendar year. However, under the laws of most states there is a *merit-rating* system which provides a tax-saving incentive to employers to stabilize employment. Under this system an employer's rate may be considerably less than the maximum rate if he provides steady work for his employees.

There are frequent changes in the state laws with respect to coverage, rates of contributions required, eligibility to receive benefits, and amounts of benefits payable. In the following discussion, it is assumed that the state tax rate is 2.7 percent of the first $4,200 of wages paid each employee each year.

State Unemployment Taxes Payable

In recording the taxes imposed under state unemployment compensation laws, it is customary to keep a separate liability account entitled State Unemployment Taxes Payable.

STATE UNEMPLOYMENT TAXES PAYABLE	
Debit	Credit
to record state unemployment taxes paid.	to record liability for state unemployment taxes required of employers.

This is a liability account which should be credited for the taxes imposed on employers under the state unemployment compensation laws. The account should be debited for the amount paid to apply on such taxes. When all of the state taxes have been paid, the account should be in balance. Some employers who are subject to taxes imposed under the laws of several states keep a separate liability account for the taxes imposed by each state.

Journalizing Employers' Payroll Taxes

The payroll taxes imposed on employers may be recorded periodically, such as monthly or quarterly. It is more common to record such taxes at the time that wages are paid so that the employer's liability for such taxes and related expenses may be recorded in the same period as the wages on which the taxes are based. The payroll register illustrated on page 89 provides the information needed in recording the FICA tax imposed on Central States Paper & Bag Company with respect to wages paid on December 18. The FICA taxable earnings for the pay period involved amounted to $860.00. Assuming that the combined rate of the tax imposed on the employer was 5.2 percent, which is the same as the rate of the tax imposed on the employees, the tax would amount to $44.72. (This amount will not necessarily be the same as that calculated by multiplying the tax rate times total taxable earnings due to the rounding up of amounts in calculating the tax deduction for each employee.)

Assume that by December 18, all of the employees have earned more than $4,200, and their wages will not be subject to federal and state unemployment taxes. If we assume, however, that for the week ending July 10 only $300.00 of the earnings were subject to unemployment taxes, the federal and state taxes will be computed as follows:

State unemployment taxes, 2.7% of $300.00............................ $8.10
FUTA taxes, 0.5% of $300.00... 1.50

Total unemployment taxes.. $9.60

If it is assumed that the employer's portion of the FICA taxes for the week ending July 10 is $45.45, the journal entry shown at the top of the next page would be made to record the payroll taxes imposed on the employer with respect to the wages paid on July 10.

```
July 10.  Payroll Tax Expense...........................    55.05
              FICA Taxes Payable...........................           45.45
              FUTA Taxes Payable...........................            1.50
              State Unemployment Taxes Payable................            8.10
                  Payroll taxes imposed on employer with respect to
                  wages paid July 10.
```

The following journal entry would be made to record the employer's portion of the payroll taxes on the wages paid on December 18:

```
Dec. 18.  Payroll Tax Expense...........................    44.72
              FICA Taxes Payable...........................           44.72
                  Payroll taxes imposed on employer with respect to
                  wages paid December 18.
```

Filing Returns and Paying the Payroll Taxes

The total amount of income taxes withheld and FICA tax contributions made by both employees and employers determines the time the employer is required to remit the taxes to the government. The range of payment dates can vary from deposits which are made weekly to a lump sum payment of the entire quarter's taxes.

When paying the taxes, the employer enters the appropriate deposit amount on Form 501, Federal Tax Deposit—Withheld Income and FICA Taxes, and the related stub. A completed copy of this form is shown below. Form 501, with the check or money order for the amount of tax deposited, is mailed or delivered to an authorized commercial bank depositary or to a Federal Reserve Bank. Form 501 is distributed automatically by mail to employers with the basic information preprinted on the form through the automatic data processing system of the Internal Revenue Service. The serial number from the face of Form 501 should be written on the check or money order remitted to reference it to the related tax deposit form. The stub should be detached and retained as the taxpayer's record of the deposit. The deposit portion will not be returned to the employer, but will be used to credit his tax account as identified by his employer's identification number.

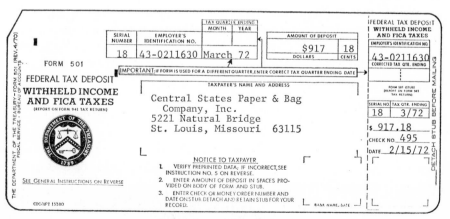

Completed Federal Tax Deposit (Form 501)

The employer must also file the Employer's Quarterly Federal Tax Return, Form 941, on or before the last day of the month following the close of each of the quarters ending March 31, June 30, September 30, and December 31.

To illustrate the accounting procedure in recording the payment of employees' income taxes and FICA taxes withheld, it will be assumed that on February 15, 1972, Central States Paper & Bag Company issued a check in payment of the following taxes imposed with respect to wages paid during the month of January:

Employees' income taxes withheld from wages..............		$478.30
FICA taxes:		
Withheld from employees' wages........................	$219.44	
Imposed on employer.................................	219.44	438.88
Amount of check.....................................		$917.18

A check for this amount accompanied by a Federal Tax Deposit Form 501, was sent to a bank that is qualified as a depositary for federal taxes. (All national banks are qualified.) This transaction may be recorded as indicated by the following general journal entry:

Feb. 15. FICA Taxes Payable..........................	438.88	
Employees' Income Taxes Payable...............	478.30	
Cash......................................		917.18
Remitted $917.18 in payment of taxes.		

Further assume that on March 15, $947.68 was deposited. This covered income tax withholdings of $498.40 during February and the employer's and employees' FICA taxes of $449.28 for February. The proper entry was made to record the payment of $947.68. Also assume that during March, income tax withholdings amounted to $609.00 and FICA taxes (employer's and employees'), $555.36 — a total of $1,164.36. Finally, assume that on April 15, the quarterly return illustrated on page 99 was sent to the nearest office of the District Director of Internal Revenue, accompanied by a check for $1,164.36. The proper entry was made to record the payment of $1,164.36.

The amount on lines 2 and 4 of the quarterly tax return illustration, $1,585.70, is the sum of the employees' income taxes withheld in January ($478.30), February ($498.40), and March ($609.00). The amount on line 5 of this return comes from the total of wages reported on line 21 (the total taxable FICA wages reported on Schedule A) times 10.4 percent (the combined FICA tax rate for employer and employee). The adjusted total FICA taxes on line 9 is added to the adjusted total of income tax withheld, line 4, to give the amount on line 10, which is the total income and FICA taxes due to the federal government.

The amount on line 11 of the quarterly tax return illustration, $3,029.22, is the sum of the taxes remitted to the qualified depositary. Since the

FORM 941
(Rev. Jan. 1971)
Department of the Treasury
Internal Revenue Service

Employer's Quarterly Federal Tax Return

		Dollars	Cents
1. TOTAL WAGES AND TIPS SUBJECT TO WITHHOLDING PLUS OTHER COMPENSATION →		13,880	00
2. AMOUNT OF INCOME TAX WITHHELD FROM WAGES, TIPS, ANNUITIES, etc. (See Instructions)		1,585	70
3. ADJUSTMENT FOR PRECEDING QUARTERS OF CALENDAR YEAR		--	--
4. ADJUSTED TOTAL OF INCOME TAX WITHHELD →		1,585	70
5. TAXABLE FICA WAGES PAID (Item 21) . . $ 13,880.00 multiplied by 10.4% = TAX		1,443	52
6. TAXABLE TIPS REPORTED (Item 22) . . $ multiplied by 5.2% = TAX		--	--
7. TOTAL FICA TAXES (Item 5 plus Item 6) →		1,443	52
8. ADJUSTMENT (See Instructions)		--	--
9. ADJUSTED TOTAL OF FICA TAXES		--	--
10. TOTAL TAXES (Item 4 plus Item 9)		1,443	52
11. TOTAL DEPOSITS FOR QUARTER (INCLUDING FINAL DEPOSIT MADE FOR QUARTER) AND OVERPAYMENT FROM PREVIOUS QUARTER. LIST IN SCHEDULE B. (See instructions on page 4)		3,029	22
		3,029	22

Note: If undeposited taxes due at the end of the quarter are $200 or more, the entire balance must be deposited. This deposit must be entered in Schedule B and included in Item 11.

12a. UNDEPOSITED TAXES DUE (ITEM 10 LESS ITEM 11—THIS SHOULD BE LESS THAN $200), PAY TO INTERNAL REVENUE SERVICE AND ENTER HERE ▶ $

12b. IF ITEM 11 IS MORE THAN 10, ENTER EXCESS HERE ▶ $ AND CHECK IF TO BE: ☐ APPLIED TO NEXT RETURN, or ☐ REFUNDED.

13. If not liable for returns in succeeding quarters write "FINAL" here ▶ and enter date of final payment of taxable wages here ▶

Under penalties of perjury, I declare that I have examined this return, including accompanying schedules and statements, and to the best of my knowledge and belief it is true, correct, and complete.

Date 4/15/72 Signature *Edwin C. Edelmann* Title (Owner, etc.) Treasurer

Employer's name, address, employer identification number, and calendar quarter. (If not correct, please change)

Name (as distinguished from trade name)
Central States Paper & Bag Company, Inc.
Trade name, if any
▶ Central States
Address and ZIP code
5221 Natural Bridge, St. Louis Mo. 63115

Date quarter ended 3/31/72
Employer Identification No. 43-0211630

—— Entries must be made both above and below this line ——

Name (as distinguished from trade name)
Central States Paper & Bag Company, Inc.
Trade name, if any
▶ Central States
Address and ZIP code
5221 Natural Bridge, St. Louis, Mo. 63115

Date quarter ended 3/31/72
Employer Identification No. 43-0211630

| T |
| P |
| D |
| I |
| T |

SCHEDULE A—QUARTERLY REPORT OF WAGES TAXABLE UNDER THE FEDERAL INSURANCE CONTRIBUTIONS ACT (FOR SOCIAL SECURITY)
IF WAGES WERE NOT TAXABLE UNDER THE F.I.C.A. MAKE NO ENTRIES BELOW

14. (First quarter only) Number of employees (except household) employed in the pay period including March 12th. **8**

15. Total pages of this return including this page and any pages of Form 941a. **1**

16. Total number of employees listed. **8**

List for each nonagricultural employee the WAGES taxable under the F.I.C.A. which were paid during the quarter. If you pay an employee more than $9,000 in a calendar year report only the first $9,000 of such wages. In the case of "Tip Income" see instructions on Page 4.

Please be sure to report each employee's name and number exactly as shown on his Social Security card.

17. EMPLOYEE'S SOCIAL SECURITY NUMBER (If number is unknown, see Circular E)	18. NAME OF EMPLOYEE (Please type or print)	19. TAXABLE F.I.C.A. WAGES Paid to Employee in Quarter (Before deductions) Dollars Cents	20. TAXABLE TIPS REPORTED (See page 4) (If amounts in this column are not tips check here ☐) Dollars Cents
258-05-3753	Harold D. Brown	1,600.00	
504-38-8340	Marvin L. Carlton	2,330.00	
810-04-1629	Dorene L. Geckler	1,300.00	
411-02-9708	William L. Heath	2,280.00	
258-08-8221	Oscar E. Johnson	1,870.00	
472-04-2335	Kent J. Myers	1,430.00	
521-08-6503	Joseph E. Nichols	1,650.00	
269-07-1132	John H. Roberts	1,420.00	

If you need more space for listing employees, use Schedule A continuation sheets, Form 941a.
Totals for this page—Wage total in column 19 and tip total in column 20 ▶ **13,880.00**

21. TOTAL WAGES TAXABLE UNDER F.I.C.A. PAID DURING QUARTER.
(Total of column 19 on this page and continuation sheets.) Enter here and in Item 5 above . . $ **13,880.00**

22. TOTAL TIPS REPORTED UNDER F.I.C.A. DURING QUARTER. (If no tips reported, write "None.")
(Total of column 20 on this page and continuation sheets.) Enter here and in Item 6 above . . . ▶ $ **None**

SEE "WHERE TO FILE" ON PAGE 2.

$ 13,880.00

Employer's Quarterly Federal Tax Return and Quarterly Report, Schedule A (Form 941)

quarter's total taxes have been remitted, there is no amount due the Internal Revenue Service (line 12a) nor is Central States Paper & Bag Company entitled to a refund (line 12b).

The amount of the tax imposed on employers under the state unemployment compensation laws must be remitted to the proper state office during the month following the close of the calendar quarter. Each state provides an official form to be used in making a return of the taxes due. Assuming that a check for $374.76 was issued on April 30 in payment of state unemployment compensation taxes on wages paid during the preceding quarter ended March 31, the transaction may be recorded as indicated by the following journal entry:

```
Apr. 30. State Unemployment Taxes Payable...............    374.76
           Cash.......................................              374.76
                Paid state unemployment taxes.
```

The amount of the tax on employers under the Federal Unemployment Tax Act was formerly paid to the District Director of Internal Revenue for the entire year during the month following the close of the calendar year. A recent change in the law requires that for any calendar year after 1969, the FUTA tax must be deposited with an authorized commercial bank depositary or a Federal Reserve Bank with a Federal Tax Deposit Form 508. The deposits are required on a quarterly basis if the amount of tax exceeds $100 for a quarter or period of two or more quarters within the same calendar year.

The amount to be deposited is computed by multiplying the taxable wages (the first $4,200 paid to each employee) by .005. If the product is more than $100, a deposit should be made. If the product is less than $100, no deposit is made, but the amount is carried forward and added to the computation for each succeeding quarter during the year. When the total for two or more quarters exceeds $100, a deposit is required. On or before January 31, an annual return must be filed on Form 940 accompanied by the balance of tax due.

The FUTA tax on the payroll of the Central States Paper & Bag Company, Inc. would not require deposits during the year, since the amount would not exceed $100 until the fourth quarter. If the company for an entire year has eight employees each of whom earn more than $4,200 a year, the federal unemployment taxes for the year will be $168.00 ($4,200 × 8 × .005).

Assuming that a check for $168.00 was issued on January 31 in payment of the taxes imposed under the Federal Unemployment Tax Act with respect to wages paid during the preceding year ended December 31, the transaction may be recorded as indicated by the following journal entry:

Jan. 31. FUTA Taxes Payable............................... 168.00
          Cash..   168.00
          Paid federal unemployment taxes

The check would be accompanied by a Federal Tax Deposit Form 508.
Form 508 is illustrated below.

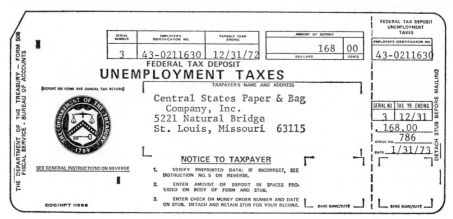

Federal Tax Deposit (Form 508)

Report No. 9

Complete Report No. 9 in the workbook and submit your working
papers to the instructor for approval. After completing the report, you may
continue with the textbook discussion in Chapter 5 until the next report is
required.

chapters 1-4

practical accounting problems

The following problems supplement those in Reports 1 through 9 of the Part 1 Workbook. These problems are numbered to indicate the chapter of the textbook with which they correlate. For example, Problem 1-A and Problem 1-B correlate with Chapter 1. Loose-leaf stationery should be used in solving these problems. The paper required includes plain ruled paper, two-column and four-column journal paper, cash journal paper, and ledger paper.

Problem 1-A

W. S. Dickey is a practicing attorney. As of December 31 he owned the following property that related to his business: Cash, $961; office equipment, $1,500; and an automobile, $2,560. At the same time he owed business creditors $630.

REQUIRED: (1) On the basis of the above information, compute the amounts of the accounting elements and show them in equation form. (2) Assume that during the following year there is an increase in Mr. Dickey's business assets of $1,800 and a decrease in his business liabilities of $75. Indicate the changes in the accounting elements by showing them in equation form after the changes have occurred.

Problem 1-B

H. L. Scholl, a CPA who has been employed by a large national firm of certified public accountants, decides to go into business for himself. His business transactions for the first month of operations were as follows:

(a) Mr. Scholl invested $5,000 cash in the business.

(b) Paid office rent for one month, $100.

(c) Purchased office equipment from the Office Supply Co., $1,840, on account.

(d) Paid telephone bill, $17.

(e) Received $500 for services rendered to James J. Hughes & Co.

(f) Paid $600 to the Office Supply Co. on account.

(g) Received $325 for services rendered to the Barford Garage.

(h) Paid $300 salary to office secretary.

REQUIRED: (1) On a plain sheet of paper rule eight "T" accounts and enter the following titles: Cash, Office Equipment, Accounts Payable, H. L. Scholl, Capital, Professional Fees, Rent Expense, Telephone Expense, and Salary Expense. (2) Record the foregoing transactions directly in the accounts. (3) Foot the accounts and enter the balances where necessary. (4) Prepare a trial balance of the accounts, using a sheet of two-column journal paper.

Problem 2-A

Following is a narrative of the transactions completed by R. H. Blinn, a management consultant, during the first month of his business operations:

Oct. 1. Mr. Blinn invested $3,000 cash in the business.

1. Paid office rent, $125.

2. Purchased office furniture for $975 cash.

3. Paid $16.85 for installation of telephone and for one month's service.

4. Received $225 from The Munger Linen Service for consulting services rendered.

5. Purchased stationery and supplies on account from American Lithofold Co., $189.64.

6. Paid $6 for subscription to a professional management magazine. (Charge Miscellaneous Expense.)

8. Paid $35 to Dr. Leo Shanley, a dentist, for dental service performed for Mrs. Blinn.

(Note: This is equivalent to a withdrawal of $35 by Mr. Blinn for personal use. Charge to his drawing account.)

9. Received $80 from Midwest Pool and Court Co. for professional services rendered.

12. Paid $48.72 for a plane ticket for a business trip.

14. Paid other traveling expenses, $38.70.

19. Paid account of American Lithofold Co. in full, $189.64.

20. Received $265 from Moloney Electric Co. for professional services rendered.

31. Paid $290 monthly salary to secretary.

REQUIRED: Journalize the foregoing transactions, using a sheet of two-column journal paper. Number the pages and use both sides of the sheet, if necessary. Select the account titles from the following chart of accounts:

CHART OF ACCOUNTS

Assets

11 Cash
12 Stationery and Supplies
13 Office Furniture

Liabilities

21 Accounts Payable

Owner's Equity

31 R. H. Blinn, Capital
32 R. H. Blinn, Drawing

Revenue

41 Professional Fees

Expenses

51 Rent Expense
52 Telephone Expense
53 Traveling Expense
54 Salary Expense
55 Miscellaneous Expense

After journalizing the transactions, prove the equality of the debits and credits by footing the amount columns. Enter the footings in pencil immediately under the line on which the last entry appears.

Problem 2-B

L. S. LEES, CERTIFIED PUBLIC ACCOUNTANT
Trial Balance
June 30, 19 - -

Cash	11	$ 942.31	
Office Equipment	12	525.00	
Automobile	13	2,200.00	
Accounts Payable	21		$ 312.36
L. S. Lees, Capital	31		2,512.00
L. S. Lees, Drawing	32	1,800.00	
Professional Fees	41		4,000.00
Rent Expense	51	750.00	
Telephone Expense	52	87.75	
Electric Expense	53	60.00	
Automobile Expense	54	217.90	
Charitable Contributions Expense	55	160.00	
Miscellaneous Expense	56	81.40	
		$6,824.36	$6,824.36

L. S. Lees is a certified public accountant engaged in practice on his own account.

NARRATIVE OF TRANSACTIONS FOR JULY

July   1. (Thursday) Paid one month's rent, $125.
     2. Paid telephone bill, $14.20.
     2. Paid electric bill, $10.25.
     5. Received $325 from Sealtest Foods for services rendered.
     7. Paid a garage bill, $27.60.

July 9. Received $100 from the Mayfair-Lennox Hotels for services rendered.
 12. Paid Scruggs Department Store, $32.40. (Charge to Mr. Lees' drawing account.)
 15. Mr. Lees withdrew $275 for personal use.
 16. Paid Smith-Corona Marchant, Inc., $90 on account.
 19. Received $120 from Tri-City Food Stores for services rendered.
 23. Gave the American Red Cross $15.
 26. Paid the American Institute of Certified Public Accountants $50 for annual membership dues.
 29. Received $52.50 from Goddard Motor Sales Co. for professional services.
 30. Mr. Lees withdrew $25 for personal use.

REQUIRED: (1) Journalize the July transactions, using a sheet of two-column journal paper. Number the pages and use both sides of the sheet, if necessary. Foot the amount columns. (2) Open the necessary accounts, using the standard account form of ledger paper. Allow one page for each account. Record the July 1 balances as shown in the June 30 trial balance and post the journal entries for July. (3) Foot the ledger accounts, enter the balances, and prove the balances by taking a trial balance as of July 31. Use a sheet of two-column journal paper for the trial balance.

Problem 2-C

THE G. C. HETLAGE AGENCY
Trial Balance
January 31, 19 - -

Cash	11	$2,896.41	
Stationery and Supplies	12	562.76	
Office Furniture	13	1,842.00	
Notes Payable	21		$ 900.00
Accounts Payable	22		643.29
G. C. Hetlage, Capital	31		3,516.88
G. C. Hetlage, Drawing	32	630.40	
Professional Fees	41		1,687.20
Rent Expense	51	150.00	
Telephone Expense	52	21.60	
Salary Expense	53	280.00	
Traveling Expense	54	316.52	
Stationery and Supplies Expense	55	18.43	
Miscellaneous Expense	56	29.25	
		$6,747.37	$6,747.37

REQUIRED: (1) Prepare an income statement for The G. C. Hetlage Agency showing the results of operations for the month of January. (2) Prepare a balance sheet in account form showing the financial condition of the agency as of January 31. Use a sheet of two-column journal paper for the income statement. Two sheets of two-column journal paper may be used for the balance sheet. List the assets on one sheet and the liabilities and owner's equity on the other sheet.

Problem 3-A

S. V. Smith is an advertising counselor. The only book of original entry for his business is a four-column journal. He uses the standard account form of general ledger. Following is the trial balance of his business taken as of November 30:

S. V. SMITH, ADVERTISING COUNSELOR
Trial Balance
November 30, 19 - -

Cash	11	$1,673.41	
Office Equipment	13	350.00	
Accounts Payable	21		$ 75.97
S. V. Smith, Capital	31		3,125.00
S. V. Smith, Drawing	32	2,375.00	
Advertising Fees	41		4,240.00
Rent Expense	51	880.00	
Telephone Expense	52	105.20	
Electric Expense	53	67.45	
Salary Expense	54	1,786.50	
Charitable Contributions Expense	55	151.00	
Miscellaneous Expense	56	52.41	
		$7,440.97	$7,440.97

NARRATIVE OF TRANSACTIONS FOR DECEMBER

Dec. 1. (Wednesday) Paid December office rent in advance, $80.
 1. Paid electric bill, $6.52.
 6. Paid telephone bill, $10.75.
 6. Received a check from Moloney Electric Co. for $200 for services rendered.
 6. Received $225 from Drew Foods Co. for services rendered.
 7. Donated $10 to the American Red Cross.
 7. Paid $5.25 for cleaning office.
 8. Received check for $225 from Eden Publishing House for advertising counsel.
 13. Mr. Smith withdrew $200 for personal use.
 15. Paid secretary's salary for the half month, $150.
 16. Purchased office furniture on credit from Lammert Furniture Co., $400.
 17. Paid $3 for having the office windows washed.
 20. Received $150 from Wetterau Grocery Co. for services rendered.
 22. Paid traveling expenses while on business, $22.50.
 24. Donated $20 to the United Fund.
 27. Paid Lammert Furniture Co. $75 on account.
 28. Mr. Smith withdrew $100 for personal use.
 31. Paid secretary's salary for the half month, $150.

REQUIRED: (1) Journalize the December transactions. For the journal use one sheet of four-column journal paper and number the page. (2) Open the necessary ledger accounts. Allow one page for each account and number the accounts. Record the December 1 balances and post the four-column journal entries. Foot and rule the four-column journal and enter the new cash balance. (3) Take a trial balance.

Problem 3-B

Oscar Sutter, a plumber, completed the following transactions with the Delmar Trust and Savings Bank during the month of October:

Oct.	1.	(Friday) Balance in bank per record kept on check stubs..........	$2,500.00	Oct. 12.	Check No. 118....	$ 80.00
				12.	Check No. 119....	45.90
				13.	Check No. 120....	447.75
				14.	Check No. 121....	41.80
				14.	Check No. 122....	247.32
	1.	Deposit........	1,500.00	14.	Deposit..........	381.43
	1.	Check No. 108...	288.20	18.	Check No. 123....	125.00
	4.	Check No. 109...	30.00	18.	Check No. 124....	265.01
	4.	Check No. 110...	475.00	21.	Check No. 125....	97.45
	4.	Check No. 111...	110.00	21.	Deposit..........	971.00
	5.	Check No. 112...	125.00	25.	Check No. 126....	131.42
	6.	Check No. 113...	90.00	25.	Check No. 127....	108.38
	7.	Check No. 114...	155.60	27.	Check No. 128....	277.97
	7.	Check No. 115...	50.00	28.	Check No. 129....	83.00
	7.	Check No. 116...	46.00	29.	Check No. 130....	547.63
	7.	Deposit........	268.45	29.	Deposit..........	825.14
	8.	Check No. 117...	454.32			

REQUIRED: (1) A record of the bank account as it would appear on the check stubs. (2) A reconciliation of the bank statement for October which indicated a balance of $2,930.87 on October 29, with Checks Nos. 116, 126, 129, and 130 outstanding, and a service charge of 45 cents.

Problem 3-C

Alan Taylor, a general contractor, had a balance of $60 in his petty cash fund as of June 1. During June the following petty cash transactions were completed:

June 2. (Wednesday) Paid $1.50 for typewriter repairs. Petty Cash Voucher No. 22.
    4. Paid for telegram, $3.25. Petty Cash Voucher No. 23.
    8. Gave $10 to the United Fund. Petty Cash Voucher No. 24.
    9. Paid garage for washing car, $1.75. Petty Cash Voucher No. 25.
    11. Gave Mr. Taylor's son $3. (Charge Alan Taylor, Drawing.) Petty Cash Voucher No. 26.
    14. Paid for postage stamps, $4. Petty Cash Voucher No. 27.
    18. Paid for newspaper for month, $1.65. Petty Cash Voucher No. 28.

June 22. Paid for window washing, $2.50. Petty Cash Voucher No. 29.
28. Paid $2.00 to the Parent-Teachers Association for dues. (Charge Alan Taylor, Drawing.) Petty Cash Voucher No. 30.
28. Paid for car lubrication, $2.00. Petty Cash Voucher No. 31.
29. Donated $15 to the American Red Cross. Petty Cash Voucher No. 32.
30. Rendered report of petty cash expenditures for month and received the amount needed to replenish the petty cash fund.

REQUIRED: (1) Record the foregoing transactions in a petty cash disbursements record, distributing the expenditures as follows:

Alan Taylor, Drawing
Automobile Expense
Telephone and Telegraph Expense
Charitable Contributions Expense
Miscellaneous Expense

(2) Prove the petty cash disbursements record by footing the amount columns and proving the totals. Enter the totals and rule the amount columns with single and double lines. (3) Prepare a statement of the petty cash disbursements for June. (4) Bring down the balance in the petty cash fund below the ruling in the Description column. Enter the amount received to replenish the fund and record the total.

Problem 4-A

Following is a summary of the hours worked, rates of pay, and other relevant information concerning the employees of The Winston Machine Tool Co., R. J. Winston, Owner, for the week ended Saturday, November 6. Employees are paid at the rate of time and one half for all hours worked in excess of 8 in any day or 40 in any week.

No.	Name	Exemptions Claimed	M	T	W	T	F	S	Regular Hourly Rate	Cumulative Earnings Jan. 1–Oct. 30
1	Blake, Allen H............	3	8	8	8	8	8	6	$3.00	$6,407
2	Harter, Thomas R.........	4	8	9	8	8	8	4	3.30	7,418
3	Markland, Robert E.......	3	8	8	8	8	8	0	3.15	7,280
4	Reardon, John H..........	1	8	8	8	9	8	4	2.90	4,289
5	Stevens, James R..........	2	8	8	8	8	0	4	3.25	5,087
6	Willey, James L...........	1	8	8	8	8	0	0	3.60	5,952

Blake and Reardon each have $3 withheld this payday for group life insurance. Harter and Willey each have $2 withheld this payday for private hospital insurance. Stevens has $5 withheld this payday as a contribution to the United Fund.

REQUIRED: (1) Using plain ruled paper size 8½" by 11", rule a payroll register form similar to that reproduced on pages 80 and 81 and insert the necessary columnar headings. Enter on this form the payroll for the week ended Saturday, November 6. Refer to the Weekly Income Tax Table on page 79 to determine the amounts to be withheld from the wages of each worker for income tax purposes. All of Winston's employees are married. Five and two-tenths percent of the taxable wages of each employee should be withheld for FICA taxes. Checks Nos. 511 through 516 were issued to the employees. Complete the payroll record by footing the amount columns, proving the footings, entering the totals, and ruling. **(2)** Assuming that the wages were paid on November 9, record the payment on a sheet of two-column general journal paper.

Problem 4-B

The Clayton Store employs twelve people. They are paid by checks on the 15th and last day of each month. The entry to record each payroll includes the liabilities for the amounts withheld. The expense and liabilities arising from the employer's payroll taxes are recorded on each payday.

Following is a narrative of the transactions completed during the month of January that relate to payrolls and payroll taxes:

Jan. 15. Payroll for first half of month:

Total salaries..........................		$2,240.00
Less amounts withheld:		
FICA taxes..........................	$116.48	
Employees' income taxes...............	200.20	316.68
Net amount paid......................		$1,923.32

15. Social security taxes imposed on employer:
FICA taxes, 5.2%
State unemployment taxes, 2%
FUTA taxes, 0.5%

28. Paid $710.13 for December's payroll taxes:
FICA taxes, $256.73.
Employees' income taxes withheld, $453.40.

28. Paid State unemployment taxes for quarter ended December 31, $68.80.

28. Paid FUTA taxes for year ended December 31, $572.55.

30. Payroll for last half of month:

Total salaries..........................		$2,360.00
Less amounts withheld:		
FICA taxes..........................	$122.72	
Employees' income taxes...............	196.80	319.52
Net amount paid......................		$2,040.48

30. Social security taxes imposed on employer:
All salaries taxable; rates same as on January 15.

REQUIRED: **(1)** Journalize the foregoing transactions, using two-column general journal paper. **(2)** Foot the debit and credit amount columns as a means of proof.

chapter five

accounting for personal service (attorneys)

In contrast to a manufacturing business which manufactures and sells merchandise, or a mercantile business which buys merchandise for resale, a personal service business is one in which service is rendered to a company or a person. Personal services rendered are of two types:

(a) Professional enterprises
(b) Business enterprises

Professional enterprises include public accountants, attorneys, physicians, dentists, engineers, architects, artists, educators, and other professionals whose income is earned chiefly by performing personal services.

Business enterprises of the personal service type include insurance, brokerage, advertising, real estate, entertainment, storage, transportation, and dry cleaning.

In a personal service firm such as that conducted by attorneys, the most valuable asset the attorney has is his time. The significance of time to a professional firm cannot be overemphasized. Adequate time records must be maintained by each attorney, including the sole practitioner. Many legal firms believe that it is desirable for each attorney to account for a working day by analyzing the activities that cannot be charged to clients. An analysis of nonchargeable time will disclose the amount of time the firm is devoting to community affairs, research, and other desirable activities.

Time records may be kept in various ways; some attorneys maintain a daily diary, and the chargeable time is posted daily to the client's record. In a large law firm, weekly reports of work for each client may be used to reduce paper work. A third method of time reporting is to use a consolidated weekly report of all attorney time. Thus, a secretary posts the billable time to the client's record on a weekly rather than a daily basis.

The Cash Basis of Accounting for a Personal Service Enterprise

Most law firms use the cash basis of accounting which means that income is not recognized until cash is received and expenses are not recorded until paid. Thus, services may be performed in one month, and the revenue may be accounted for the following month, or several months later. The cash basis of accounting violates the *matching principle* which holds that revenues earned and expenses incurred during a period should be matched against each other in order to arrive at as accurate a figure of net income or net loss for the period as possible. In many cases, however, expenses such as rent or telephone bills may be approximately the same each month, so that only a slight distortion is caused by paying and recording an expense in November which actually was incurred in October. The cash basis of accounting is acceptable for federal and state income tax purposes.

It should be noted that accounting cannot be based completely on cash transactions. Property or service accepted in lieu of cash must be recorded as income at the fair market value of the property or service at the time it is received. Also, if income such as interest on a savings account is available for withdrawal by the owner of the account, the income is said to be *constructively received* and must be reported as income even though no cash is withdrawn from the account.

Another exception to the cash basis of accounting is made when depreciation is recorded. Assets which provide benefits for several years, such as automobiles or office equipment, will wear out or *depreciate* with the passage of time. When such assets are purchased, they must be debited to asset accounts. As the asset is used, expense is incurred which should be allocated over the estimated life of the asset. The purpose of depreciation is to charge the expense to the period in which it is actually incurred, in accordance with the matching principle explained above. The portion of cost assigned to each period is called *depreciation expense*.

For example, an automobile, possibly the largest item in the balance sheet of a legal firm, must be charged to the asset account, Automobile.

Depreciation of the automobile is based on the cost, less any residual or scrap value, and the estimated life of the automobile. Since the residual value and the expected useful life are estimates, the amount charged to depreciation expense each period is not entirely accurate, but an allocation of cost over the expected useful life of an asset results in a more equitable profit or loss measurement than charging such assets to expense in the period they are purchased.

When an entry is made at the end of the period debiting Depreciation Expense, the credit is usually to an account called *Accumulated Depreciation* such as Accumulated Depreciation — Automobile. Accumulated depreciation accounts are contra-assets and should be deducted from the related asset accounts in the balance sheet. The difference between the asset account and the accumulated depreciation account is known as the *book value* of the asset. Adjustments for depreciation will be explained further in Chapter 7.

Chart of Accounts

To illustrate the cash basis of accounting for an attorney, a chart of accounts for Harold R. Stewart, Attorney at Law, is reproduced below. Note that all asset accounts have account numbers beginning with 1; liability accounts begin with 2; owner's equity accounts begin with 3; revenue accounts begin with 4; expense accounts begin with 5. New accounts may be added as needed without disturbing the numerical order of the existing accounts.

HAROLD R. STEWART, ATTORNEY AT LAW

CHART OF ACCOUNTS

Assets
- 11 First National Bank
- 12 Petty Cash Fund
- 13 Advances on Behalf of Clients
- 14 Office Equipment
- 014 Accumulated Depreciation — Office Equipment
- 15 Automobile
- 015 Accumulated Depreciation — Automobile

Liabilities
- 21 Accounts Payable
- 22 Employees' Income Taxes Payable
- 23 FICA Taxes Payable
- 24 FUTA Taxes Payable
- 25 State Unemployment Taxes Payable

Owner's Equity
- 31 Harold R. Stewart, Capital
- 031 Harold R. Stewart, Drawing
- 32 Expense and Revenue Summary

Revenue
- 41 Legal Fees Income
- 42 Collection Fees Income

Expenses
- 511 Salary Expense
- 512 Payroll Tax Expense
- 513 Rent Expense
- 514 Telephone and Telegraph Expense
- 515 Office Supplies Expense
- 516 Automobile Expense
- 517 Law Library Expense
- 518 Depreciation Expense
- 519 Charitable Contributions Expense
- 520 Miscellaneous Expense

Note: Words in italics represent headings and not account titles.

Many of the accounts in the preceding list have been explained and their uses illustrated in the previous chapters. Accounts appearing for the first time in this chapter will be discussed before the records of Mr. Stewart are presented.

Advances on Behalf of Clients, Account No. 13. Payment for items such as court filing fees, fees charged by accountants for making audits, or the cost of obtaining depositions are sometimes made for clients. Absorption of these expenses by the attorney would be equivalent to lowering fees for certain clients. To avoid unethical "fee cutting," payments made for clients are charged to the account, Advances on Behalf of Clients, and then billed to the clients on a monthly or quarterly basis. A record of the payments made and remittances received is also made in the client's account on an office docket (an auxiliary record which provides a complete record of each legal case). A minimum amount, usually $.50 to $1.00, can be established below which the firm will absorb the expense to save clerical work.

Expense and Revenue Summary, Account No. 32. The expense and revenue summary account is a clearing account which is used only when the books are closed at the end of the accounting period. Use of this account will be explained further in Chapter 8.

Legal Fees Income, Account No. 41. Legal fees income is a revenue account that is credited for cash received from clients in payment of legal work performed. When the accounts are kept on the cash basis, income is not recorded in the account until cash is received or until a note or other property is accepted in lieu of cash.

Since legal fees are usually not collected until they are billed, billing is very important. The more frequent the billing, the more frequent the collection. If bills are collected frequently, the firm can operate with a smaller cash investment, and in some cases may collect a larger total fee without impairing the client relationship than would be possible if the entire amount were billed at one time. Many clients of a law firm prefer to be billed on a monthly or quarterly basis even though the legal work is not completed, rather than to receive one large bill at the end of the engagement.

Collection Fees Income, Account No. 42. Fees charged for collecting accounts for clients from their customers, clients, or patients are income to the attorney making the collections. The account, Collection Fees Income, is credited for the commissions or fees received for collections made on behalf of clients. When a collection is made in partial or in full settlement of an account, the First National Bank account should be debited for the amount received. If the attorney receives much of his income from making collections for clients, an accounts payable account should be credited for the amount received less the amount of the fee. Collection Fees Income is credited for the amount of the fee. If Harold Stewart undertakes to collect an account amounting to $120 for the City Department Store on a commission basis of 33⅓%, the following entry should be made when cash is received in payment of the account:

April 15. First National Bank..	120	
Accounts Payable..		80
Collection Fees Income..................................		40
Collected an account in the amount of $120 on behalf of the City Department Store and recorded fee of $40.		

When the amount owed to the City Department Store ($80) is paid, an entry should be made as follows:

April 17. Accounts Payable..	80	
First National Bank....................................		80
Payment to City Department Store of collection made for them.		

If many collections are made for clients, it probably would be advisable to maintain a special account at the bank in which all cash, checks, and other cash items received in settlement of collection cases may be deposited. Maintaining this special account would separate funds collected for clients from funds belonging to the firm. Checks drawn payable to clients should be credited to the special account instead of to the regular disbursement account.

Books of Account

Mr. Stewart uses the following books of account:

(a) General books
  (1) Combined cash journal
  (2) General ledger

(b) Auxiliary records
  (1) Petty cash disbursements record
  (2) Lawyers' office docket
  (3) Lawyers' collection docket
  (4) Employee's earnings record

Combined Cash Journal. Mr. Stewart uses only one book of original entry — a combined cash journal. If desired, it is also possible to use separate cash receipts and cash disbursements journals. Mr. Stewart's combined cash journal, reproduced on pages 124–127, contains eight money columns, two on the left of the description column and six on the right. The columnar arrangement is shown at the top of the next page.

The account numbers in the headings are an aid in completing the summary posting at the end of the month. If the combined cash journal used by Mr. Stewart is compared to the four-column journal illustrated in Chapter 3 (page 47) two differences will be noted. The combined cash

(a) First National Bank
    (1) Deposits 11 Dr.
    (2) Checks 11 Cr.
(b) General
    (1) Debits
    (2) Credits
(c) Income
    (1) Legal Fees Income 41 Cr.
    (2) Collection Fees Income 42 Cr.
(d) Wage Deductions
    (1) Employees' Income Taxes Payable 22 Cr.
    (2) FICA Taxes Payable 23 Cr.

journal contains a check number column to the right of the Checks 11 Cr. column, and four special columns to the right of the pair of General columns. Such a journal is sometimes called a special column journal because there are special columns for specific items. As was illustrated by the cash columns in the four-column journal on page 47, special columns for accounts in which frequent entries are made will save time and labor in the bookkeeping process. A narrative of transactions completed by Mr. Stewart during the month of December, 1971 is given on pages 119–123 and 126–127. These transactions are recorded in the combined cash journal on pages 124–127. Note that before any transactions were recorded in this journal, the bank balance at the start of the month, $9,100.27, was entered in the Description column just below the words "Amounts Forwarded."

General Ledger. Mr. Stewart uses the standard form of account. The ledger is reproduced on pages 128–131. In each case, the balance as of December 1 has been entered. The accounts in the general ledger are arranged in the order given in the chart of accounts shown on page 112. All posting to the general ledger accounts is from the combined cash journal. A trial balance is taken at the end of each month to prove the equality of the general ledger account balances. The trial balance as of December 31 appears on page 132.

Auxiliary Records. Auxiliary records are used to record information not recorded in the regular books of account. Mr. Stewart uses a petty cash disbursements record, office docket, and a collection docket as auxiliary records. An employee's earnings record, similar to the one illustrated in Chapter 4 on page 84, is maintained for each employee.

Petty Cash Disbursements Record. Mr. Stewart maintains a petty cash fund in the amount of $50. The petty cash disbursements record is similar to that illustrated on pages 56 and 57.

Lawyers' Office Docket. An *office docket* is a form used to maintain a memorandum record of each legal case with a client. A model filled-in office docket (reproduced on page 117) shows the history of the case of General Manufacturing Corporation, plaintiff, vs. Henry Townsend, defendant. The legal information that may be needed in handling the case is recorded on the upper part of the form, and a memorandum account of the charges and credits to the account of the client is kept on the lower part of the form.

When an attorney keeps his accounts on the cash basis, he does not have a general ledger account for his clients, but the information must be kept on the office docket. The client's account, as recorded on the office docket, should be charged for:

(a) Fees for services rendered.
(b) Disbursements on behalf of the client, such as filing fees and other expenses paid for the client.

The client's account should be credited for:

(a) Payments received for services.
(b) Reimbursements for advances made on behalf of the client.

In the illustration on page 117 the client, General Manufacturing Corporation, is charged for the following:

November 24. Amount of the fee agreed upon at the time the case was taken, $225.
November 29. Amount advanced in payment of suit fee, $5.

The account is credited for the following:

December 1. Amount received as a retainer, $100.
December 23. Amount received in payment of balance due on account, $130.

Lawyers' Collection Docket. Lawyers who collect accounts for clients may use a form known as a *collection docket* to keep a record of the necessary information pertaining to collections. A model filled-in copy of a collection docket is shown on page 118. The docket provides a record of the case of the Madison Department Store, creditor, vs. John L. Harwood, debtor. It also furnishes a record of the amounts collected from the debtor and the amounts paid to the creditor.

Attorneys usually take most collection cases on a percentage basis. Any expenses incurred in making collections should be charged to the expense accounts of the attorney and not to the client. If, however, a client has agreed to pay any expenses incident to a lawsuit, such as court costs, the amounts paid by the attorney should be charged to the client's account just the same as payments made for clients in handling other legal cases.

LAWYER'S OFFICE DOCKET

CLIENT General Manufacturing Corporation   ADDRESS 220 Market St., City   NO. 157

IN RE: General Manufacturing Corporation

vs. Henry Townsend

COURT	Common Pleas, Stone County		
COURT FILE NO.	15743		19 71
CALENDAR NO. 785	ATTORNEY FOR Plaintiff		
OTHER ATTORNEYS			

NATURE OF MATTER Lawsuit

REMARKS

DATE		SERVICES RENDERED	FEES AND DISBURSEMENTS		MONEYS RECEIVED		
					PURPOSE	AMOUNT	
Nov	24	Fee for preparing case	2	25 00			
	29	Suit fee		5 00			
Dec	1				Retainer	100	00
	23				Balance due	130	00
		CARRIED FORWARD					

Lawyer's Office Docket

In the illustration the following transactions were recorded on the collection docket for the Madison Department Store:

LAWYER'S COLLECTION DOCKET		NO. 19
DEBTOR John L. Harwood		DATE CLAIM REC'D. 12-3 1971
ADDRESS 1835 Davidson Road, City		DATE DISPOSED OF 1-31-72
BUSINESS		TOTAL AMOUNT $ 150.00
CREDITOR Madison Department Store		AMOUNT COLLECTED $ 150.
ADDRESS Main and Sims St., City		FEES $ 50.00
REC'D CLAIM FROM		EXPENSE $
ATTORNEY FOR DEBTOR		AMOUNT REMITTED $ 100.
CALLS ON DEBTOR		CHECK NO. 367 & 390

	RECEIVED FROM CREDITOR		
	DATE	FOR	AMOUNT
CORRESPONDENCE	12-21	Com.	30 00
	1-15	Com.	20 00

RECEIVED FROM DEBTOR				PAID TO CREDITOR			
DATE	AMOUNT	DATE	AMOUNT	CHECK NO.	AMOUNT	CHECK NO.	AMOUNT
12-21	90 00			367	60 00		
1-15	60 00			390	40 00		

REMARKS: Statement of account. Collection fee 33 1/3%.
No suit without further instructions.

Lawyer's Collection Docket

December 21. Collected $90 from John L. Harwood, debtor.

December 30. Paid $60 to the Madison Department Store.

January 15. Collected $60 from John L. Harwood, debtor.

January 31. Paid $40 to the Madison Department Store.

The amount of the commission of 33⅓% is deducted from the amounts collected from the debtor and is entered on the collection docket as follows:

December 21. $30.

January 15. $20.

Employee's Earnings Record. The employee's earnings record was discussed in Chapter 4.

Following is a narrative of transactions completed by Harold R. Stewart during the month of December. These transactions are recorded in the combined cash journal on pages 124–127.

HAROLD R. STEWART, ATTORNEY AT LAW

Narrative of Transactions

Wednesday, December 1

Issued Check No. 351 for $250, payable to Henry Stevens, for the December office rent.

Received $100 from General Manufacturing Corporation as a retainer in the lawsuit of General Manufacturing Corporation against Henry Townsend. Case No. 157.

> The amount received as a retainer constitutes income realized on the cash basis. Office docket No. 157 is reproduced on page 117. This docket is an auxiliary record designed to supplement the information recorded in the regular books of account and to facilitate the handling of the case.
>
> The transaction was recorded in the combined cash journal by debiting First National Bank, Account No. 11, and by crediting Legal Fees Income, Account No. 41. Since this entry was recorded in special columns, individual posting is not required, and a check mark was placed in the Posting Reference column.

Thursday, December 2

Issued Check No. 352 for $15.25 to the Columbia Electric Co. for electricity consumed during November. Charge Miscellaneous Expense, Account No. 520.

Received $100 from Mr. Thomas Gardner for services rendered in preparation of a trust agreement.

Friday, December 3

Issued Check No. 353 for $23.18 to the Bell Telephone Co. for November service.

Received a check for $150 from W. C. Macomber in payment of the balance due on Case No. 149.

Received for collection from the Madison Department Store, Main and Sims Street, City, a statement of its account with John L. Harwood, 1825 Davidson Road, City, for $150. This account is over eighteen months past due. Collection fee, 33⅓%; no suit without further instructions. Collection No. 19.

Inasmuch as Mr. Stewart's books are kept on the cash basis, no entry in the regular books of account is required for this transaction. Collection Docket No. 19 is reproduced on page 118. This docket is an auxiliary record of information designed to supplement the information recorded in the regular books of account and to facilitate handling the account.

Monday, December 6

Received a check for $110 from the Adams Manufacturing Company in full payment of Case No. 152.

Issued Check No. 354 for $29.74 to the Johnson Service Station in payment of the December 1 statement for gasoline, oil, and services rendered during November.

Tuesday, December 7

Received a check for $250 from Brown and Scott, certified public accountants, for drafting a partnership agreement.

Wednesday, December 8

Mr. Stewart has been engaged to represent the Martin Howard Advertising Agency, Inc., in the purchase of a building owned by Albert Snowden, at a minimum fee of $625. Case No. 158. Received a check for $150 as a retainer.

Received an invoice of $45.70 from Sanders Stationery Company, 1011 Fifth Avenue, City, for stationery and supplies.

Since Mr. Stewart's books are kept on the cash basis, invoices for expenses are not recorded until they are paid. When expense invoices are received, they are filed in an invoice file until they are paid. When payment is made, the proper entry is made in the combined cash journal.

Thursday, December 9

Received a check for $327.18 from Robert J. Wayne in payment of the amount due on Collection No. 17.

The collection docket shows that Mr. Stewart had agreed to handle this collection on a 33⅓% commission basis. The transaction was entered in the combined cash journal by debiting First National Bank, Account No. 11, for $327.18, by crediting Accounts Payable, Account No. 21, for the amount due to the James Rogers Co., $218.12, and by crediting Collection Fees Income, Account No. 42, for the commission earned, $109.06. A memorandum entry was also made in the collection docket for the amount received from the debtor.

Friday, December 10

Issued Check No. 355, for $558.17 to the Modern Law Book Company for law books.

Proved the footings of the combined cash journal. Deposits of cash receipts have been made in the First National Bank on the day of receipt. Compared the cash balance in the combined cash journal with the balance in the checkbook ($9,411.11). Completed the individual postings from the General Debits and Credits columns of the combined cash journal to the ledger accounts. As each item was posted, the account number was entered in the Posting Reference column of the combined cash journal and the page number of the combined cash journal was entered in the Posting Reference column of the account.

Monday, December 13

Issued Check No. 356 for $25 to the City Christmas Bureau Fund.

> The check is recorded in the combined cash journal by debiting Charitable Contributions Expense, Account No. 519, and crediting First National Bank, Account No. 11.

Received $75 from the Jackson and Harrison Plumbing Co. for preparing and filing a mechanic's lien on the property of C. R. Andrews.

Tuesday, December 14

Issued Check No. 357 for $50 to the State Bar Association for annual dues.

> The amount of this check was charged to Miscellaneous Expense, Account No. 520, since a separate expense account is not maintained for dues.

Received $50 from Mrs. Naomi Bennett for preparing a lease on office space in a building owned by Mrs. Bennett.

Issued Check No. 358 for $273.20 to the First National Bank in payment of the following payroll taxes based on wages paid during the month of November:

Employees' income taxes withheld from wages		$174.40
FICA taxes		
Withheld from employees' wages	$49.40	
Imposed on employer	49.40	98.80
Amount of check		$273.20

A Federal Tax Deposit, Form 501, was filled out and sent with the check. Mr. Stewart does not pay the balances in the FUTA Taxes Payable and State Unemployment Taxes Payable Accounts until January because these taxes are payable on a quarterly rather than monthly basis.

Mr. Stewart telephoned the First National Bank and learned that the check for $327.18 received from Robert J. Wayne had cleared. Issued Check No. 359 to the James Rogers Co. in the net amount of $218.12, which represents the full amount of Collection No. 17, $327.18, less a 33⅓% collection fee, $109.06.

> This transaction was recorded in the combined cash journal by debiting Accounts Payable, Account No. 21, and by crediting the bank for the amount of the check. The collection fee had been recorded at the time the remittance was received from the debtor. A memorandum entry, however, was made in the collection docket to record the amount paid to the creditor. Since the claim was settled in full, the following information was entered in the upper right hand corner of the collection docket: (a) the date the case was disposed of, (b) the total amount collected, (c) the total amount of the attorney's fees, (d) the amount sent to the client, and (e) the check number.

Wednesday, December 15

Mr. Stewart withdrew $547.40 for personal use. Check No. 360.

> The check was recorded in the combined cash journal by debiting Harold R. Stewart, Drawing, Account No. 031, and by crediting the First National Bank.

Issued the following checks in payment of salaries for the first half of the month:

No. 361 for $172.80 to Joseph Larsen, part-time law clerk, in payment of his salary in the amount of $225, less $11.70 withheld for FICA taxes, and $40.50 withheld for income taxes.

No. 362 for $190.30 to Elizabeth Staley, the office secretary, in payment of her salary in the amount of $250 less $13.00 withheld for FICA taxes, and $46.70 withheld for income taxes.

Received a check for $375 from R. E. Olds Company, 225 Lake Avenue, City, in full payment of Case No. 151. This remittance is in payment of the balance due for legal fees, $275, and $100 for payment of an audit fee paid by Mr. Stewart on November 10 and charged to Advances on Behalf of Clients.

> The check was recorded in the combined cash journal by debiting First National Bank, Account No. 11, for $375, and crediting Advances on Behalf of Clients, Account No. 13, for $100, and Legal Fees Income, Account No. 41, for $275.

Thursday, December 16

Issued Check No. 363 for $45.70 to the Sanders Stationery Company in payment of the invoice received on December 8. Office Supplies Expense is debited.

Friday, December 17

Received $25 from Mrs. Ruth Hamilton for drawing a will.

Proved the footings of the combined cash journal. Compared the balance in the combined cash journal with the balance in the checkbook ($8,413.59). Completed the individual postings from the General Debits and Credits columns of the combined cash journal to the ledger accounts.

Monday, December 20

Received $100 as a retainer from Melvin Robertson, 1401 Broadway, City, in the case of Williams vs. Robertson. Minimum fee, $500 and costs. Case No. 159.

Issued Check No. 364 for $620.18 to the City Typewriter Co. in payment for a new electric typewriter.

> This transaction was recorded in the combined cash journal by debiting Office Equipment, Account No. 14, and crediting First National Bank, Account No. 11.

Tuesday, December 21

Received a check for $90 from John L. Harwood to apply on his account with the Madison Department Store, Collection No. 19.

Received a check for $475 from the Martin Howard Advertising Agency, Inc., in payment of the balance due for legal work done in connection with the purchase of a building. Case No. 158.

Wednesday, December 22

Mr. Charles Hunt, 2705 Seneca Avenue, City, has engaged Mr. Stewart to handle the incorporation of an insurance agency. Minimum fee, $350. A check for $100 was received as a retainer. Case No. 160.

Received an invoice for $34.70 from the Legal Supply Co., 70 Church Street, New York City, for legal forms.

> Legal forms used by an attorney are an expense, and invoices for expenses are recorded only when paid in cash.

Thursday, December 23

Received a check for $130 from the General Manufacturing Corporation in payment of the balance due on account. Case No. 157.

> The check was recorded in the combined cash journal by debiting First National Bank, Account No. 11, for $130, and crediting Advances on Behalf of Clients, Account No. 13, for $5, and Legal Fees Income, Account No. 41, for $125.

Friday, December 24

Mr. Stewart directed that Check No. 365 for $49.75 be issued to the Gilbert Department Store in payment of his personal account.

> Since this transaction is a disbursement in payment of a personal account of Mr. Stewart, it was recorded in the combined cash journal by debiting Harold R. Stewart, Drawing, Account No. 031, and by crediting the First National Bank, Account No. 11.

Proved the footings of the combined cash journal. Compared the cash balance in the combined cash journal with the balance in the checkbook ($8,638.66). Completed the individual postings from the General Debits and Credits columns of the combined cash journal to the ledger accounts.

FIRST NATIONAL BANK		CK. NO.	DATE		DESCRIPTION	POST. REF.
DEPOSITS 11 DR.	CHECKS 11 CR.		MO.	DAY		
					AMOUNTS FORWARDED *Balance $9,100.27*	
	250 00	351	Dec.	1	Rent Expense	513
100 00				1	General Mfg. Corp. Case #157	✓
	15 25	352		2	Miscellaneous Expense	520
100 00				2	Thos. Gardner, Trust Agreement	✓
	23 18	353		3	Telephone & Telegraph Expense	514
150 00				3	W. C. Macomber Case #149	✓
110 00				6	Adams Mfg. Co. Case #152	✓
	29 74	354		6	Automobile Expense	516
250 00				7	Brown & Scott, Partnership Agreement	✓
150 00				8	M. Howard Advg. Agency, Inc. Case #158	✓
327 18				9	Accts. Payable - Jas. Rogers Co. Coll.#17	21
	558 17	355		10	Law Library Expense	517
	25 00	356		13	Charitable Contributions Expense *$9,411.11*	519
75 00				13	Jackson & Harrison Mfg. Co. Mech. Lien	✓
	50 00	357		14	Miscellaneous Expense	520
50 00				14	Mrs. Naomi Bennett, Lease	✓
	273 20	358		14	Employees' Income Taxes Payable	22
					F I C A Taxes Payable	23
	218 12	359		14	Accts. Payable - Jas. Rogers Co. Coll.#17	21
	547 40	360		15	Harold R. Stewart, Drawing	031
	172 80	361		15	Salary Expense	511
	190 30	362		15	Salary Expense	511
375 00				15	R. E. Olds Co. Case #151	✓
					Advances on Behalf of Clients	13
	45 70	363		16	Office Supplies Expense	515
25 00				17	Ruth Hamilton, Will	✓
100 00				20	Melvin Robertson Case #159 *$5,413.59*	✓
	620 18	364		20	Office Equipment	14
90 00				21	Accts. Payable - Madison Dept. Store Coll.#19	21
475 00				21	M. Howard Advg. Agency, Inc. Case #158	✓
100 00				22	Charles Hunt Case #160	✓
130 00				23	General Mfg. Corp. Case #157	✓
					Advances on Behalf of Clients	13
	49 75	365		24	Harold R. Stewart, Drawing	031
75 00				27	Thomas Baldwin Case #161 *$5,638.66*	✓
	125 00	366		28	Advances on Behalf of Clients Case #156	13
25 00				29	Marvin Edwards Case #155	✓
	60 00	367		30	Accts. Payable - Madison Dept. Store Coll.#19	21
	600 00	368		31	Harold R. Stewart, Drawing	031
	172 80	369		31	Salary Expense	511
2932 18	4026 59			31	Carried Forward	

Harold R. Stewart, Attorney at Law — Combined Cash Journal (Left Page)

| GENERAL | | INCOME | | WAGE DEDUCTIONS | |
DEBITS	CREDITS	LEGAL FEES 41 CR.	COLL. FEES 42 CR.	EMPLOYEES INC. TAXES PAY. 22 CR.	FICA TAXES PAY. 23 CR.
25000					
		10000			
.1525					
		10000			
2318					
		15000			
		11000			
2974					
		25000			
		15000			
	21812		10906		
55817					
2500					
		7500			
5000					
		5000			
17440					
9880					
21812					
54740					
22500				4050	1170
25000				4670	1300
		27500			
	10000				
4570					
		2500			
		10000			
62018					
	6000		3000		
		47500			
		10000			
		12500			
	500				
4975					
		7500			
12500					
		25000			
6000					
60000					
22500				4050	1170
419069	38312	241000	13906	12778	3640

Harold R. Stewart, Attorney at Law — Combined Cash Journal (Right Page)

Chapter 5 / Accounting for Personal Service (Attorneys)   125

| FIRST NATIONAL BANK | | CK. NO. | DATE | | DESCRIPTION | POST. REF. |
DEPOSITS 11 DR.	CHECKS 11 CR.		MO.	DAY		
2 9 3 2 1 8	4 0 2 6 5 9				AMOUNTS FORWARDED	
	1 9 0 3 0	370	Dec.	31	Salary Expense	511
	3 7 5 2	371		31	Advances on Behalf of Clients	13
					Harold R. Stewart, Drawing	031
					Office Supplies Expense	515
					Automobile Expense	516
					Charitable Contribution Expense	519
					Miscellaneous Expense	520
				31	Payroll Tax Expense $7778.04	512
					F I C A Taxes Payable	✓
2 9 3 2 1 8	4 2 5 4 4 1					
2 9 3 2 1 8	4 2 5 4 4 1					
(11)	(11)					

Harold R. Stewart, Attorney at Law — Combined Cash Journal — Concluded (Left Page)

Monday, December 27

Mr. Stewart has been engaged by Thomas Baldwin to administer the estate of Nicholas Baldwin, deceased. Minimum fee is $300. A check for $75 was received as a retainer. Case No. 161.

Tuesday, December 28

Issued Check No. 366 for $125 to M. J. Horn, CPA, in payment of his statement covering auditing service rendered to our client, F. E. Lyons. Case No. 156.

Wednesday, December 29

Received a check in the amount of $250 from Marvin Edwards in settlement of his account. Case No. 155.

Thursday, December 30

Issued Check No. 367 for $60 to the Madison Department Store to remit a partial collection from John L. Harwood in the amount of $90 less a 33⅓% collection fee. Collection No. 19.

Friday, December 31

Mr. Stewart withdrew $600 for personal use. Check No. 368.

Issued the following checks in payment of salaries for the second half of the month:

No. 369 for $172.80 to Joseph Larsen, part-time law clerk, in payment of his salary in the amount of $225 less $11.70 withheld for FICA taxes and $40.50 withheld for income taxes.

No. 370 for $190.30 to Elizabeth Staley, the office secretary, in payment of her salary in the amount of $250 less $13.00 withheld for FICA taxes and $46.70 withheld for income taxes.

| GENERAL | | INCOME | | WAGE DEDUCTIONS | |
DEBITS	CREDITS	LEGAL FEES 41 CR.	COLL. FEES 42 CR.	EMPLOYEES INC. TAXES PAY. 22 CR.	FICA TAXES PAY. 23 CR.
4 1 9 0 6 9	3 8 3 1 2	2 4 1 0 0 0	1 3 9 0 6	1 2 7 7 0	3 6 4 0
2 5 0 0 0				4 6 7 0	1 3 0 0
1 0 0 0					
8 0 0					
5 9 5					
3 7 2					
3 0 0					
6 8 5					
4 9 4 0					
					4 9 4 0
4 5 2 7 6 1	3 8 3 1 2	2 4 1 0 0 0	1 3 9 0 6	1 7 4 4 0	9 8 8 0
(✓)	(✓)	(41)	(42)	(22)	(23)

Harold R. Stewart, Attorney at Law — Combined Cash Journal — Concluded (Right Page)

Issued Check No. 371 for $37.52 to replenish the petty cash fund.

The following statement provided the information needed in recording this transaction in the combined cash journal:

STATEMENT OF PETTY CASH DISBURSEMENTS FOR DECEMBER

Advances on Behalf of Clients	$10.00
Harold R. Stewart, Drawing	8.00
Office Supplies Expense	5.95
Automobile Expense	3.72
Charitable Contributions Expense	3.00
Miscellaneous Expense	6.85
Total Disbursements	$37.52

Made an entry in the combined cash journal for the employer's portion of the FICA tax for the month of December by debiting Payroll Tax Expense and by crediting FICA Taxes Payable for $49.40. Both of Mr. Stewarts' employees' wages have exceeded $4,200 and there is therefore no expense in the month of December for Federal or State Unemployment Taxes.

Proved the footings, entered the totals, and ruled the combined cash journal. Compared the bank balance in the combined cash journal to the balance in the checkbook ($7,778.04). Completed the individual posting from the General Debits and Credits columns of the combined cash journal to the ledger accounts. Since this was the end of the month, the summary posting was completed, and the account numbers were written immediately below the totals of the columns in the combined cash journal. A trial balance of the general ledger accounts which have balances on December 31 appears on page 132.

ACCOUNT First National Bank — ACCOUNT NO. 11

DATE	ITEMS	POST. REF.	✓	DEBITS	DATE	ITEMS	POST. REF.	✓	CREDITS
1971 Dec 1	Balance	✓		9 1 0 0 27	1971 Dec 31			CJ34	4 2 5 4 41
31	7,778.04	CJ34		2 9 3 2 18					
				1 2 0 3 2 45					

ACCOUNT Petty Cash Fund — ACCOUNT NO. 12

DATE	ITEMS	POST. REF.	✓	DEBITS	DATE	ITEMS	POST. REF.	✓	CREDITS
1971 Dec 1	Balance	✓		5 0 00					

ACCOUNT Advances on Behalf of Clients — ACCOUNT NO. 13

DATE	ITEMS	POST. REF.	✓	DEBITS	DATE	ITEMS	POST. REF.	✓	CREDITS
1971 Dec 1	Balance	✓		1 8 5 00	1971 Dec 15			CJ33	1 0 0 00
28		CJ33		1 2 5 00	23			CJ33	5 00
31	215.00	CJ34		1 0 00					1 0 5 00
				3 2 0 00					

ACCOUNT Office Equipment — ACCOUNT NO. 14

DATE	ITEMS	POST. REF.	✓	DEBITS	DATE	ITEMS	POST. REF.	✓	CREDITS
1971 Dec 1	Balance	✓		2 3 2 1 87					
20		CJ33		6 2 0 18					
				2 9 4 2 05					

ACCOUNT Accumulated Depreciation - Office Equipment — ACCOUNT NO. 014

DATE	ITEMS	POST. REF.	✓	DEBITS	DATE	ITEMS	POST. REF.	✓	CREDITS
					1971 Dec 1	Balance		✓	3 9 4 71

ACCOUNT Automobile — ACCOUNT NO. 15

DATE	ITEMS	POST. REF.	✓	DEBITS	DATE	ITEMS	POST. REF.	✓	CREDITS
1971 Dec 1	Balance	✓		3 6 5 0 23					

ACCOUNT Accumulated Depreciation - Automobile — ACCOUNT NO. 015

DATE	ITEMS	POST. REF.	✓	DEBITS	DATE	ITEMS	POST. REF.	✓	CREDITS
					1971 Dec 1	Balance		✓	1 3 6 8 83

Harold R. Stewart, Attorney at Law — General Ledger

ACCOUNT Accounts Payable   ACCOUNT NO. 21

DATE	ITEMS	POST. REF.	✓	DEBITS	DATE	ITEMS	POST. REF.	✓	CREDITS
1971 Dec. 14		CJ33		2 1 8 1 2	1971 Dec. 9		CJ33		2 1 8 1 2
30		CJ33		6 0 0 0	21		CJ33		6 0 0 0
				2 7 8 1 2					2 7 8 1 2

ACCOUNT Employees' Income Taxes Payable   ACCOUNT NO. 22

DATE	ITEMS	POST. REF.	✓	DEBITS	DATE	ITEMS	POST. REF.	✓	CREDITS
1971 Dec. 14		CJ33		1 7 4 40	1971 Dec. 1	Balance	✓		1 7 4 40
				174.40	31		CJ34		1 7 4 40
									3 4 8 80

ACCOUNT FICA Taxes Payable   ACCOUNT NO. 23

DATE	ITEMS	POST. REF.	✓	DEBITS	DATE	ITEMS	POST. REF.	✓	CREDITS
1971 Dec. 14		CJ33		9 8 80	1971 Dec. 1	Balance	✓		9 8 80
				98.80	Dec. 31		CJ34		9 8 80
									1 9 7 60

ACCOUNT FUTA Taxes Payable   ACCOUNT NO. 24

DATE	ITEMS	POST. REF.	✓	DEBITS	DATE	ITEMS	POST. REF.	✓	CREDITS
					1971 Dec. 1	Balance	✓		75

ACCOUNT State Unemployment Taxes Payable   ACCOUNT NO. 25

DATE	ITEMS	POST. REF.	✓	DEBITS	DATE	ITEMS	POST. REF.	✓	CREDITS
					1971 Dec. 1	Balance	✓		4 05

ACCOUNT Harold R. Stewart, Capital   ACCOUNT NO. 31

DATE	ITEMS	POST. REF.	✓	DEBITS	DATE	ITEMS	POST. REF.	✓	CREDITS
					1971 Dec. 1	Balance	✓		1 2 1 1 1 43

ACCOUNT Harold R. Stewart, Drawing   ACCOUNT NO. 031

DATE	ITEMS	POST. REF.	✓	DEBITS	DATE	ITEMS	POST. REF.	✓	CREDITS
1971 Dec. 1	Balance	✓		1 3 4 5 0 25					
15		CJ33		5 4 7 40					
24		CJ33		4 9 75					
31		CJ33		6 0 0 00					
31		CJ34		8 00					
				1 4 6 5 5 40					

ACCOUNT Expense and Revenue Summary   ACCOUNT NO. 32

DATE	ITEMS	POST. REF.	✓	DEBITS	DATE	ITEMS	POST. REF.	✓	CREDITS

Harold R. Stewart, Attorney at Law — General Ledger (Continued)

ACCOUNT Legal Fees Income   ACCOUNT NO. 41

DATE	ITEMS	POST. REF.	✓	DEBITS	DATE	ITEMS	POST. REF.	✓	CREDITS
					1971 Dec 1	Balance	✓		2891800
					31		CJ34		241000
									3132800

ACCOUNT Collection Fees Income   ACCOUNT NO. 42

DATE	ITEMS	POST. REF.	✓	DEBITS	DATE	ITEMS	POST. REF.	✓	CREDITS
					1971 Dec 1	Balance	✓		142135
					31		CJ34		13906
									156041

ACCOUNT Salary Expense   ACCOUNT NO. 511

DATE	ITEMS	POST. REF.	✓	DEBITS	DATE	ITEMS	POST. REF.	✓	CREDITS
1971 Dec 1	Balance	✓		1045000					
15		CJ33		22500					
15		CJ33		25000					
31		CJ33		22500					
31		CJ34		25000					
				1140000					

ACCOUNT Payroll Tax Expense   ACCOUNT NO. 512

DATE	ITEMS	POST. REF.	✓	DEBITS	DATE	ITEMS	POST. REF.	✓	CREDITS
1971 Dec 1	Balance	✓		81220					
31		CJ34		4940					
				86160					

ACCOUNT Rent Expense   ACCOUNT NO. 513

DATE	ITEMS	POST. REF.	✓	DEBITS	DATE	ITEMS	POST. REF.	✓	CREDITS
1971 Dec 1	Balance	✓		275000					
1		CJ33		25000					
				300000					

ACCOUNT Telephone and Telegraph Expense   ACCOUNT NO. 514

DATE	ITEMS	POST. REF.	✓	DEBITS	DATE	ITEMS	POST. REF.	✓	CREDITS
1971 Dec 1	Balance	✓		24520					
3		CJ33		2318					
				26838					

Harold R. Stewart, Attorney at Law — General Ledger (Continued)

ACCOUNT Office Supplies Expense — ACCOUNT NO. 515

DATE	ITEMS	POST. REF.	✓	DEBITS	DATE	ITEMS	POST. REF.	✓	CREDITS
1971 Dec. 1	Balance	✓		3 3 2 4 0					
16		cg33		4 5 7 0					
31		cg34		5 9 5					
				3 8 4 0 5					

ACCOUNT Automobile Expense — ACCOUNT NO. 516

DATE	ITEMS	POST. REF.	✓	DEBITS	DATE	ITEMS	POST. REF.	✓	CREDITS
1971 Dec. 1	Balance			5 8 7 5 0					
6		cg33		2 9 7 4					
31		cg34		3 7 2					
				6 2 0 9 6					

ACCOUNT Law Library Expense — ACCOUNT NO. 517

DATE	ITEMS	POST. REF.	✓	DEBITS	DATE	ITEMS	POST. REF.	✓	CREDITS
1971 Dec. 10		cg33		5 5 8 1 7					

ACCOUNT Depreciation Expense — ACCOUNT NO. 518

DATE	ITEMS	POST. REF.	✓	DEBITS	DATE	ITEMS	POST. REF.	✓	CREDITS

ACCOUNT Charitable Contributions Expense — ACCOUNT NO. 519

DATE	ITEMS	POST. REF.	✓	DEBITS	DATE	ITEMS	POST. REF.	✓	CREDITS
1971 Dec. 1	Balance	✓		2 8 8 0 0					
13		cg33		2 5 0 0					
31		cg34		3 0 0					
				3 1 6 0 0					

ACCOUNT Miscellaneous Expense — ACCOUNT NO. 520

DATE	ITEMS	POST. REF.	✓	DEBITS	DATE	ITEMS	POST. REF.	✓	CREDITS
1971 Dec. 1	Balance	✓		2 6 9 4 0					
2		cg33		1 5 2 5					
14		cg33		5 0 0 0					
31		cg34		6 8 5					
				3 4 1 5 0					

Harold R. Stewart, Attorney at Law — General Ledger (Concluded)

Trial Balance

December 31, 19—

First National Bank	11	$ 7,778.04	
Petty Cash Fund	12	50.00	
Advances on Behalf of Clients	13	215.00	
Office Equipment	14	2,942.05	
Accumulated Depreciation — Office Equipment.	014		$ 394.71
Automobile	15	3,650.23	
Accumulated Depreciation — Automobile	015		1,368.83
Employees' Income Taxes Payable	22		174.40
FICA Taxes Payable	23		98.80
FUTA Taxes Payable	24		.75
State Unemployment Taxes Payable	25		4.05
Harold R. Stewart, Capital	31		12,111.43
Harold R. Stewart, Drawing	031	14,655.40	
Legal Fees Income	41		31,328.00
Collection Fees Income	42		1,560.41
Salary Expense	511	11,400.00	
Payroll Tax Expense	512	861.60	
Rent Expense	513	3,000.00	
Telephone and Telegraph Expense	514	268.38	
Office Supplies Expense	515	384.05	
Automobile Expense	516	620.96	
Law Library Expense	517	558.17	
Charitable Contributions Expense	519	316.00	
Miscellaneous Expense	520	341.50	
		$47,041.38	$47,041.38

Report No. 10

Complete Report No. 10 in the workbook and submit your working papers to the instructor for approval. After completing the report, you may continue with the textbook discussion in Chapter 6 until the next report is required.

chapter six

accounting for personal service (physicians and surgeons)

Accounting for physicians and surgeons has much in common with accounting for attorneys. Indeed, there are many similarities in accounting for any type of personal service whether professional or business, but each type of service also has its own peculiarities. Some of the items peculiar to accounting for physicians and surgeons will be explained in this chapter.

As with attorneys, the most valuable asset the physician has is his time. A daily service record should be kept showing as a minimum the name of the patient, the kind of service, and the charge to the patient's account or the amount of cash received.

The Cash Basis of Accounting for Physicians and Surgeons

Most physicians and surgeons use the cash basis of accounting. Usually income is not recognized until cash is received and expenses are not recorded until they are paid. The revenue for services performed in one month may be accounted for in a later month, and expenses incurred in one month may be paid in the following month, or sometimes several months later.

Chart of Accounts

As a means of explaining some of the peculiarities of accounting for persons in the medical profession, a system of accounts for Roger Mason and Charles Edwards, physicians and surgeons, is presented. The chart of accounts is reproduced below. All asset accounts have numbers beginning with 1; liability accounts begin with 2; owner's equity accounts begin with 3; revenue accounts begin with 4; and expense accounts begin with 6. If new accounts are needed, they may be added without disturbing the numerical order of the existing accounts.

MASON AND EDWARDS, PHYSICIANS AND SURGEONS
CHART OF ACCOUNTS

Assets
- 111 Clermont Bank
- 112 Petty Cash Fund
- 171 Office Equipment
- 0171 Accumulated Depreciation —
  Office Equipment
- 172 Medical Equipment
- 0172 Accumulated Depreciation —
  Medical Equipment
- 173 X-Ray Equipment
- 0173 Accumulated Depreciation —
  X-Ray Equipment
- 174 Automobiles
- 0174 Accumulated Depreciation —
  Automobiles

Liabilities
- 211 FICA Taxes Payable
- 221 Employees' Income Taxes
  Payable
- 231 FUTA Taxes Payable
- 241 State Unemployment Taxes
  Payable

Owner's Equity
- 311 Roger Mason, Capital
- 0311 Roger Mason, Drawing
- 321 Charles Edwards, Capital
- 0321 Charles Edwards, Drawing
- 331 Expense and Revenue Summary

Revenue
- 411 Professional Fees

Expenses
- 611 Automobile Expense
- 612 Charitable Contributions
  Expense
- 613 Depreciation Expense
- 617 Dues and Subscriptions Expense
- 618 Electricity, Gas & Water
  Expense
- 619 Insurance Expense
- 620 Laundry Expense
- 621 Legal Expense
- 622 Medical Library Expense
- 623 Medical Supplies Expense
- 624 Office Supplies Expense
- 625 Payroll Tax Expense
- 626 Postage Expense
- 627 Rent Expense
- 628 Repairs and Maintenance
  Expense
- 629 Salary Expense
- 630 Surgical Instruments Expense
- 631 Surgical Supplies Expense
- 632 Telephone and Telegraph
  Expense
- 633 Miscellaneous Expense

Note: Items in italics represent headings and not account titles.

Some of the accounts which appear for the first time are discussed in the following paragraphs.

Professional Fees, Account No. 411. Drs. Mason and Edwards use only one general ledger account in which to record their professional fees. In the daily service record there are columns headed Office Calls and Surgery. The totals of these columns at the end of the month will show the amounts entered for office calls and for surgery. If it is desired, separate accounts could be kept for as many types of service as are rendered. For example, office calls might be assigned the number 411, surgery the number 412, and laboratory work the number 413.

Medical Supplies Expense, Account No. 623; Office Supplies Expense, Account No. 624; Surgical Supplies Expense, Account No. 631; Surgical Instruments Expense, Account No. 630. Supplies and instruments are charged to expense when paid for.

Books of Account

Drs. Mason and Edwards use the following books of account:

(a) General books
  (1) Combined cash journal
  (2) General ledger
(b) Auxiliary records
  (1) Petty cash disbursements record
  (2) Daily service record
  (3) Patients' ledger
  (4) Employees' earnings record
  (5) Checkbook

Combined Cash Journal. Drs. Mason and Edwards use one book of original entry, a combined cash journal. The combined cash journal, reproduced on pages 144 to 147, contains two money columns to the left of the description column and six to the right of the description column. The column headings are as follows:

(a) Clermont Bank 111 Dr.
(b) Clermont Bank 111 Cr.
(c) General
  (1) Debits
  (2) Credits
(d) Professional Fees 411 Cr.
(e) Salary Expense 629 Dr.
(f) Employees' Income Taxes Payable 221 Cr.
(g) FICA Taxes Payable 211 Cr.

General Ledger. Drs. Mason and Edwards use a two column account form for the general ledger accounts. The ledger is reproduced on pages 149 to 155. In each case the balance as of October 1 has been entered. The accounts in the general ledger are arranged in the order given in the chart of accounts on page 134. Posting to the general ledger is from the combined cash journal. A trial balance is taken at the end of each month to prove the equality of the general ledger balances. The trial balance as of October 31 appears on page 156.

Auxiliary Records. Drs. Mason and Edwards use a petty cash disbursements record, a daily service record, patients' ledger, employees' earnings records, and a checkbook as auxiliary records. The employees' earnings record kept for each employee is similar to the one illustrated on page 84.

Petty Cash Disbursements Record. A petty cash fund of $75 is maintained. The petty cash disbursements record is similar to that illustrated on pages 56 and 57.

Daily Service Record. A portion of the daily service record is illustrated on page 157. Note that the daily service record is not set up as a double entry record. There is nothing to offset the Payments Column under Patients' Accounts. The amounts in the Charges Column are posted to the Charges column in the appropriate patients' ledger accounts and the amounts in the Payments column are posted to the Payments column in the patients' ledger accounts. The total cash received from patients will be shown in the columns headed "Patients Accounts — Payments" and "Cash Services." The total cash received should be recorded in the combined cash journal in the Clermont Bank Deposits Dr. column and the Professional Fees Cr. column.

Patients' Ledger. The patients' accounts are kept in a file rather than in a bound book to permit using a copying machine to reproduce the accounts as monthly statements. Information in the Charges column in the daily service record is posted to the individual patients' accounts. Credits to the patients' accounts are also posted from the Payments column of the daily service record. A model patient's account for Mr. Henry Marshall is reproduced on page 137.

Following is a narrative of transactions completed by Drs. Mason and Edwards during the month of October. These transactions are recorded in the combined cash journal on pages 144 to 147.

MASON AND EDWARDS, PHYSICIANS AND SURGEONS

NARRATIVE OF TRANSACTIONS

Friday, October 1

Issued Check No. 529 for $1,000.00 payable to the White Realty Corporation for rent of the office for the month of October.

> The transaction was recorded in the combined cash journal by debiting Rent Expense, Account No. 627, in the General Dr. column and crediting Clermont Bank, Account No. 111.

Roger Mason, M.D.   Charles Edwards, M.D.

MASON & EDWARDS
214 East Fourth Street
716-654-3159

Henry Marshall
835 Valley Lane
City

OC—OFFICE CALL   NC—NIGHT CALL   S—SURGICAL   MISC.—MISCELLANEOUS
HC—HOME CALL   M—MEDICAL   P—PRESCRIPTION

DATE	DESCRIPTION	CHARGES		PAYMENTS		BALANCE	
10/1	Balance					350	00
10/2				350	00	-0-	

PAY LAST AMOUNT IN THIS COLUMN ➤

Illustration of patient's account

Saturday, October 2

Issued Check No. 530 for $75.18 payable to Sherman's Garage for the garage bill for September.

This transaction was recorded in the combined cash journal by debiting Automobile Expense, Account No. 611, and crediting Clermont Bank, Account No. 111.

Issued Check No. 531 for $35.18 to the Columbia Electric Co. for electricity consumed during September.

This transaction was recorded in the combined cash journal by debiting Electricity, Gas and Water Expense, Account No. 618, and by crediting Clermont Bank, Account No. 111.

Issued Check No. 532 for $26.32 to the Bell Telephone Co. for September service.

Monday, October 4

Issued Check No. 533 for $6.79 to the Union Natural Gas Corporation for gas consumed during September.

Issued Check No. 534 for $32.50 to the Acme Laundry for laundry service for the month of September.

Issued Check No. 535 for $80.15 to Physicians' Supply Corporation for medical supplies purchased in September.

Tuesday, October 5

Issued Check No. 536 for $25.30 to the Medical Equipment Co. for an equipment repair.

This transaction was recorded in the combined cash journal by debiting Repairs and Maintenance Expense, Account No. 628, and by crediting Clermont Bank, Account No. 111.

Wednesday, October 6

Issued Check No. 537 for $416 to the Evans Insurance Agency for a one year physicians' liability insurance policy.

This transaction was recorded in the combined cash journal by debiting Insurance Expense, Account No. 619, and by crediting Clermont Bank.

Thursday, October 7

Issued Check No. 538 for $96 to the Peerless Cleaning Co. for services rendered during September.

This transaction was recorded in the combined cash journal by debiting Repairs and Maintenance Expense, Account No. 628, and by crediting Clermont Bank.

Friday, October 8

Issued Check No. 539 for $87.35 to the Quality Instrument Co. for surgical instruments purchased in September.

This transaction was recorded in the combined cash journal by debiting Surgical Instruments Expense, Account No. 630, and by crediting Clermont Bank.

Saturday, October 9

Dr. Edwards has given the account of Ross Stevens in the amount of $375, and the account of Arthur Williams in the amount of $1,200 to Harold R. Stewart, an attorney, for collection. If Mr. Stewart collects all or part of these accounts, his fee will be 33⅓ percent. No entry is needed at this time.

Footed the amount columns in the daily service record and obtained the following totals:

Kind of Service:

Office calls...	$ 153.00
Surgery..	4,300.00
Total..	$ 4,453.00

Patients' accounts — Charges................................	$ 4,360.00
Cash services..	93.00
	$ 4,453.00

Posted all entries in the Patients' Accounts Charges and Payments columns to the appropriate individual accounts in the patients' ledger.

The total cash received from patients for the week was found to be:

Payments...	$ 4,195.00
Cash services..	93.00
Total..	$ 4,288.00

Recorded the total cash received ($4,288.00) in the combined cash journal by entering the words "Total receipts" in the Description column and the amount in both the Clermont Bank Deposits Dr. column and the Professional Fees Cr. column.

Footed the amount columns of the combined cash journal and checked the cash balance in the checkbook ($22,524.56) by starting with the checkbook balance on October 1 ($20,117.33) and adding the total of the Clermont Bank Dr. column and subtracting the total of the Clermont Bank Cr. column. Completed the individual postings from the General Dr. and Cr. columns of the combined cash journal. As each item was posted, the account number was entered in the Posting Reference column of the combined cash journal. The page number of the combined cash journal was entered in the Posting Reference column of the accounts to which items from the combined cash journal were posted.

Monday, October 11

Issued Check No. 540 for $10 to the American Medical Association for a subscription to a professional journal.

Tuesday, October 12

Issued Checks No. 541 for $45 to the Johnson Supply Company for surgical supplies.

Wednesday, October 13

Issued Check No. 542 for $20.15 to the Stone County Water Authority for September service.

Thursday, October 14

Issued Check No. 543 for $75.49 to the Scientific Publishing Co. for medical books.

> This transaction was recorded by debiting Medical Library Expense, Account No. 622, and crediting Clermont Bank.

Friday, October 15

Dr. Mason withdrew $500 for personal use. Check No. 544.

Dr. Edwards withdrew $550 for personal use. Check No. 545.

Issued the following checks in payment of salaries for the first half of the month:

No. 546 for $241.80 to Margaret Holmes, R.N., in payment of salary in the amount of $300 less $15.60 withheld for FICA taxes and $42.60 withheld for federal income taxes.

No. 547 for $162.80 to Ruth Browning, secretary, in the amount of $200 less $10.40 withheld for FICA taxes and $26.80 withheld for federal income taxes.

No. 548 for $200.30 to Helen Channing, secretary-bookkeeper, in the amount of $250 less $13 withheld for FICA taxes and $36.70 withheld for federal income taxes.

No. 549 for $225.40 to Alice Weber, X-Ray and laboratory technician, in the amount of $275 less $14.30 withheld for FICA taxes and $35.30 withheld for federal income taxes.

> Drs. Mason and Edwards are subject to the taxes imposed under the federal unemployment tax act and to the state unemployment taxes. These taxes are collected entirely from the employer on the first $4,200 of each employee's earnings during the year. No deductions are made from the salaries of the employees for unemployment taxes.

Saturday, October 16

Issued Check No. 550 for $79.80 to the Madison Department Store in payment of Dr. Edwards' personal account.

<blockquote>Since this transaction is a personal expense, it is recorded in the combined cash journal by debiting Charles Edwards, Drawing, Account No. 0321, and by crediting Clermont Bank.</blockquote>

Footed the amount columns in the daily service record and obtained the following totals:

Kind of Service:

Office calls	$ 135.00
Surgery	2,930.00
Total	$3,065.00

Patients' accounts — Charges	$2,996.00
Cash services	69.00
Total	$3,065.00

Posted all entries in the Patients' Accounts Charges and Payments columns to the appropriate individual accounts in the patients' ledger.

The total cash received from patients for the week was found to be:

Payments	$ 950.00
Cash services	69.00
Total	$1,019.00

Recorded the total cash received ($1,019.00) in the combined cash journal by entering the words "Total receipts" in the Description column and the amount in both the Clermont Bank Deposits Dr. column and the Professional Fees Cr. column.

Footed the amount columns of the combined cash journal and checked the cash balance in the checkbook ($21,432.82) by adding the total of the Clermont Bank Dr. column to the checkbook balance on October 1 ($20,117.33) and subtracting the total of the Clermont Bank Cr. column. Completed the individual postings from the General Dr. and Cr. columns of the combined cash journal.

Monday, October 18

Issued Check No. 551 for $68.90 to the Emerson Office Equipment Co. in payment for a new filing cabinet.

Tuesday, October 19

Issued Check No. 552 for $25.90 to the Sanders Stationery Company for stationery and supplies.

Issued Check No. 553 for $145.17 to Physicians' Supply Co. for medical supplies.

Wednesday, October 20

Issued Check No. 554 for $100 to the United Fund in payment of the part of the pledge due in October.

> This transaction was recorded in the combined cash journal by debiting Charitable Contributions Expense, Account No. 612, and by crediting Clermont Bank.

Thursday, October 21

Issued Check No. 555 for $268.80 to the Evans Insurance Agency in payment of the renewal premium on an insurance policy on Dr. Roger Mason's car.

> Since the car is used exclusively for business purposes, the cost of the policy is charged to Insurance Expense, Account No. 619.

Friday, October 22

Issued Check No. 556 for $12 to the Clermont Bank in payment of the annual rental of a safe deposit box for use of the partnership.

> This transaction was recorded by debiting Miscellaneous Expense, Account No. 633, and by crediting Clermont Bank.

Saturday, October 23

Issued Check No. 557 for $20.75 to the Emerson Office Equipment Co. for typewriter repairs.

Footed the amount columns in the daily service record and obtained the following totals:

Kind of Service:

Office calls	$ 164.00
Surgery	2,535.00
Total	$2,699.00
Patients' accounts — Charges	$2,674.00
Cash services	25.00
Total	$2,699.00

Posted all entries in the Patients' Accounts Charges and Payments columns to the appropriate individual accounts in the patients' ledger.

The total cash received from patients for the week was found to be:

Payments	$3,810.00
Cash services	25.00
Total	$3,835.00

Recorded the total cash received ($3,835.00) in the combined cash journal.

Footed the amount columns of the combined cash journal and checked the cash balance in the checkbook ($24,626.30). Completed the individual postings from the General Dr. and Cr. columns of the combined cash journal.

Monday, October 25

Issued Check No. 558 for $500 to the American Cancer Society.

Tuesday, October 26

Issued Check No. 559 for $1,890.15 to Baker Medical Equipment Co. for medical equipment.

Received $250 from Harold Stewart representing collection of the account of Ross Stevens in the amount of $375. Mr. Stewart deducted his fee of $125 and remitted the balance, $250.

> This transaction was recorded in the combined cash journal by debiting Clermont Bank for $250 and Legal Expense, Account No. 621, for $125, and by crediting Professional Fees, Account No. 411, for $375. In order to avoid a duplication of the $375 credit to Professional Fees, this payment was not entered in the daily service record. An entry was therefore made in Ross Stevens' account in the patients' ledger crediting the account for $375.

Wednesday, October 27

Issued Check No. 560 for $60.28 to the Quality Equipment Co. for repairs to the X-Ray equipment.

Thursday, October 28

Issued Check No. 561 for $25.50 to the Physicians' Publishing Co. for medical books.

Friday, October 29

Received $200 from Harold Stewart to apply on the account of Arthur Williams. Mr. Stewart collected $300 from Mr. Williams and remitted $200 after deducting the fee of $100.

> This transaction was recorded in the combined cash journal by debiting Clermont Bank for $200 and Legal Expense, Account No. 621, for $100, and by crediting Professional Fees, Account No. 411, for $300. An entry was also made in Arthur Williams' account in the patients' ledger crediting the account for $300.

Issued Check No. 562 for $200 in payment of the annual dues for Drs. Mason and Edwards to the Stone County Medical Society.

Saturday, October 30

Dr. Mason withdrew $600 for personal use. Check No. 563.

Dr. Edwards withdrew $550 for personal use. Check No. 564.

Issued the following checks in payment of salaries for the second half of the month:

No. 565 for $241.80 to Margaret Holmes, R.N., in payment of salary in the amount of $300 less $15.60 withheld for FICA taxes and $42.60 withheld for federal income taxes.

DEPOSITS 111 DR.	CHECKS 111 CR.	CK. NO.	DATE MO. DAY	DESCRIPTION	POST. REF.
				AMOUNTS FORWARDED *Balance 20,117.33*	
	1000 00	529	Oct. 1	Rent Expense	627
	75 18	530	2	Automobile Expense	611
	35 18	531	2	Electricity, Gas, and Water Expense	618
	26 32	532	2	Telephone and Telegraph Expense	632
	6 79	533	4	Electricity, Gas, and Water Expense	618
	32 50	534	4	Laundry Expense	620
	80 15	535	4	Medical Supplies Expense	623
	25 30	536	5	Repairs and Maintenance Expense	628
	416 00	537	6	Insurance Expense	619
	96 00	538	7	Repairs and Maintenance Expense	628
	87 35	539	8	Surgical Instruments Expense	630
4288 00			9	Total receipts	✓
	10 00	540	11	Dues and Subscriptions Expense *22,524.56*	617
	45 00	541	12	Surgical Supplies Expense	631
	20 15	542	13	Electricity, Gas, and Water Expense	618
	75 49	543	14	Medical Library Expense	622
	500 00	544	15	Roger Mason, Drawing	0311
	550 00	545	15	Charles Edwards, Drawing	0321
	241 80	546	15	Margaret Holmes	✓
	162 80	547	15	Ruth Browning	✓
	200 30	548	15	Helen Channing	✓
	225 40	549	15	Alice Weber	✓
	79 80	550	16	Charles Edwards, Drawing	0321
1019 00			16	Total receipts	✓
	68 90	551	18	Office Equipment *21,432.82*	171
	25 90	552	19	Office Supplies Expense	624
	145 17	553	19	Medical Supplies Expense	623
	100 00	554	20	Charitable Contributions Expense	612
	26 88 0	555	21	Insurance Expense	619
	12 00	556	22	Miscellaneous Expense	633
	20 75	557	23	Repairs and Maintenance Expense	628
3835 00			23	Total receipts	✓
	500 00	558	25	Charitable Contributions Expense *24,626.30*	612
	1890 15	559	26	Medical Equipment	172
250 00			26	Legal Expense — Ross Stevens	621
	60 28	560	27	Repairs and Maintenance Expense	628
	25 50	561	28	Medical Library Expense	622
200 00			29	Legal Expense — Arthur Williams	621
	200 00	562	29	Dues and Subscriptions Expense	617
9592 00	7308 96		29	Carried Forward	
9592 00	7308 96				

Mason & Edwards — Combined Cash Journal (Left Page)

GENERAL DEBITS	GENERAL CREDITS	PROFESSIONAL FEES 411 CR.	SALARY EXPENSE 629 DR.	EMPLOYEES INC. TAXES PAY. 221 CR.	FICA TAXES PAY. 211 CR.
100000					
7518					
3518					
2632					
679					
3250					
8015					
2530					
41600					
9600					
8735					
		428800			
1000					
4500					
2015					
7549					
50000					
55000					
			30000	4260	1560
			20000	2680	1040
			25000	3670	1300
			27500	3530	1430
7980					
		101900			
6890					
2590					
14517					
10000					
26880					
1200					
2075					
		383500			
50000					
189015					
12500		37500			
6028					
2550					
10000		30000			
20000					
670366		981700	102500	14140	5330
670366		981700	102500	14140	5330

Mason & Edwards — Combined Cash Journal (Right Page)

Chapter 6 / Accounting for Personal Service (Physicians)   145

CLERMONT BANK		CK. NO.	DATE		DESCRIPTION	POST. REF.
DEPOSITS 111 DR.	CHECKS 111 CR.		MO.	DAY		
9 59 2 00	7 30 8 96		Oct.	29	AMOUNTS FORWARDED	
	6 00 00	563		30	Roger Mason, Drawing	0311
	5 50 00	564		30	Charles Edwards, Drawing	0321
	2 41 80	565		30	Margaret Holmes	✓
	1 62 80	566		30	Ruth Browning	✓
	2 00 30	567		30	Helen Channing	✓
	2 25 40	568		30	Alice Weber	✓
	4 96 00	569		30	Employees' Income Taxes Payable	221
				30	FICA Taxes Payable	211
	1 05 30	570		30	State Unemployment Taxes Payable	241
	19 50	571		30	FUTA Taxes Payable	231
2 53 9 00				30	Total receipts	✓
				30	Payroll Tax Expense	625
					State Unemployment Taxes Payable	241
					FUTA Taxes Payable	231
	68 75	572		30	Roger Mason, Drawing	0311
					Charles Edwards, Drawing	0321
					Automobile Expense	611
					Miscellaneous Expense	633
					Office Supplies Expense	624
					Postage Expense $22,269.52	626
12 13 1 00	9 97 8 87					
(111)	(111)					

Mason & Edwards — Combined Cash Journal (Left Page)

No. 566 for $162.80 to Ruth Browning, secretary, in the amount of $200 less $10.40 withheld for FICA taxes and $26.80 withheld for federal income taxes.

No. 567 for $200.30 to Helen Channing, secretary-bookkeeper, in the amount of $250 less $13 withheld for FICA taxes and $36.70 withheld for federal income taxes.

No. 568 for $225.40 to Alice Weber, X-Ray and laboratory technician, in the amount of $275 less $14.30 withheld for FICA taxes and $35.30 withheld for federal income taxes.

Issued Check No. 569 for $496.00 to the Clermont Bank in payment of the following payroll taxes based on wages paid during the month of September.

Employees' federal income taxes withheld from wages.........		$282.80
FICA taxes		
Withheld from employees' wages........................	$106.60	
Imposed on employer.................................	106.60	213.20
Amount of check......................................		$496.00

GENERAL DEBITS	GENERAL CREDITS	PROFESSIONAL FEES 411 CR.	SALARY EXPENSE 629 DR.	EMPLOYEES INC. TAXES PAY. 221 CR.	FICA TAXES PAY. 211 CR.
670366		981700	102500	14140	5330
60000					
55000					
			30000	4260	1560
			20000	2680	1040
			25000	3670	1300
			27500	3530	1430
28280					
21320					
10530					
1950					
		253900			
11940					10660
	1080				
	200				
1250					
1690					
725					
930					
480					
1800					
866261	1280	1235600	205000	28280	21320
(✓)	(✓)	(411)	(629)	(221)	(211)

Mason & Edwards — Combined Cash Journal (Right Page)

Form 501 accompanied the September deposit to the Clermont Bank. Form 501 had also been sent to the Clermont Bank in August and September in payment of employees' income taxes and FICA taxes payable for the months of July and August. Since September was the third month of the third quarter, Form 941 was filed with the Internal Revenue Service.

Issued Check No. 570 for $105.30 to the State Unemployment Bureau for state unemployment taxes for the third quarter.

Issued Check No. 571 in the amount of $19.50 to the Clermont Bank for FUTA taxes for the third quarter.

Footed the amount columns in the daily service record and obtained the following totals:

Kind of Service:

Office calls	$ 119.00
Surgery	2,685.00
Total	$2,804.00
Patients' accounts — Charges	$2,765.00
Cash services	39.00
Total	$2,804.00

Posted all entries in the Patients' Accounts Charges and Payments columns to the appropriate individual accounts in the patients' ledger.

The total cash received from patients for the week was found to be:

Payments..	$2,500.00
Cash services...	39.00
Total...	$2,539.00

Recorded the total cash received ($2,539.00) in the combined cash journal.

Made an entry in the combined cash journal for the payroll taxes imposed on Drs. Mason and Edwards for the month of October by debiting Payroll Tax Expense, Account No. 625, for $119.40 and by crediting FICA Taxes Payable, Account No. 211 for $106.60 ($2,050 times 5.2%), FUTA Taxes Payable, Account No. 231, for $2.00 ($400 times .5%), and State Unemployment Taxes Payable, Account No. 241, for $10.80 ($400 times 2.7%).

By the end of September the wages of all of the employees except Ruth Browning had exceeded $4,200. Drs. Mason and Edwards must still pay unemployment taxes on her wages which were $400 in October.

Issued Check No. 572 for $68.75 to replenish the petty cash fund.

The following statement provided the information needed in recording this transaction in the combined cash journal:

STATEMENT OF PETTY CASH DISBURSEMENTS FOR OCTOBER

Roger Mason, Drawing...	$12.50
Charles Edwards, Drawing..	16.90
Automobile Expense..	7.25
Miscellaneous Expense...	9.30
Office Supplies Expense..	4.80
Postage Expense...	18.00
Total disbursements...	$68.75

Footed the amounts columns of the combined cash journal and checked the cash balance in the checkbook ($22,269.52).

Completed the individual posting from the general columns of the combined cash journal. Since this was the end of the month, the summary posting was completed and the account numbers were written immediately below the totals of the columns in the combined cash journal. A trial balance of the general ledger accounts which have balances on October 31 appears on page 156.

ACCOUNT *Clermont Bank* — ACCOUNT NO. *111*

DATE	ITEMS	POST. REF.	✓	DEBITS	DATE	ITEMS	POST. REF.	✓	CREDITS
1971 Oct. 1	Balance	✓		2 0 1 1 7 3 3	1971 Oct. 31		CJ 43		9 9 7 8 8 1
31	22,264.52	CJ 43		1 2 1 3 1 0 0					

ACCOUNT *Petty Cash Fund* — ACCOUNT NO. *112*

DATE	ITEMS	POST. REF.	✓	DEBITS	DATE	ITEMS	POST. REF.	✓	CREDITS
1971 Oct. 1	Balance	✓		7 5 0 0					

ACCOUNT *Office Equipment* — ACCOUNT NO. *171*

DATE	ITEMS	POST. REF.	✓	DEBITS	DATE	ITEMS	POST. REF.	✓	CREDITS
1971 Oct. 1	Balance	✓		5 7 7 3 4 0					
18		CJ 42		6 8 9 0					

ACCOUNT *Accumulated Depreciation – Office Equipment* — ACCOUNT NO. *0171*

DATE	ITEMS	POST. REF.	✓	DEBITS	DATE	ITEMS	POST. REF.	✓	CREDITS
					1971 Oct. 1	Balance	✓		1 7 3 5 1 0

ACCOUNT *Medical Equipment* — ACCOUNT NO. *172*

DATE	ITEMS	POST. REF.	✓	DEBITS	DATE	ITEMS	POST. REF.	✓	CREDITS
1971 Oct. 1	Balance	✓		1 5 6 1 5 7 3					
26		CJ 42		1 8 9 0 1 5					

ACCOUNT *Accumulated Depreciation – Medical Equipment* — ACCOUNT NO. *0172*

DATE	ITEMS	POST. REF.	✓	DEBITS	DATE	ITEMS	POST. REF.	✓	CREDITS
					1971 Oct. 1	Balance	✓		2 1 8 4 7 2

ACCOUNT *X-Ray Equipment* — ACCOUNT NO. *173*

DATE	ITEMS	POST. REF.	✓	DEBITS	DATE	ITEMS	POST. REF.	✓	CREDITS
1971 Oct. 1	Balance	✓		2 0 8 7 5 4 9					

Mason & Edwards — General Ledger

ACCOUNT Accumulated Depreciation — X-Ray Equipment   ACCOUNT NO. 0173

DATE	ITEMS	POST. REF.	√	DEBITS	DATE	ITEMS	POST. REF.	√	CREDITS
					1971 Oct. 1	Balance	√		3 4 9 2 38

ACCOUNT Automobiles   ACCOUNT NO. 174

DATE	ITEMS	POST. REF.	√	DEBITS	DATE	ITEMS	POST. REF.	√	CREDITS
1971 Oct. 1	Balance	√		8 4 7 5 09					

ACCOUNT Accumulated Depreciation — Automobiles   ACCOUNT NO. 0174

DATE	ITEMS	POST. REF.	√	DEBITS	DATE	ITEMS	POST. REF.	√	CREDITS
					1971 Oct. 1	Balance	√		2 0 1 8 77

ACCOUNT FICA Taxes Payable   ACCOUNT NO. 211

DATE	ITEMS	POST. REF.	√	DEBITS	DATE	ITEMS	POST. REF.	√	CREDITS
1971 Oct. 30		Cg 43		2 1 3 20	1971 Oct. 1	Balance	√		2 1 3 20
					30		cg 43	213.20	2 1 3 20
									4 2 6 4 0

ACCOUNT Employees' Income Taxes Payable   ACCOUNT NO. 221

DATE	ITEMS	POST. REF.	√	DEBITS	DATE	ITEMS	POST. REF.	√	CREDITS
1971 Oct. 30		cg 43		2 8 2 80	1971 Oct. 1	Balance	√		2 8 2 80
					30		cg 43	282.80	2 8 2 80
									5 6 5 6 0

ACCOUNT FUTA Taxes Payable   ACCOUNT NO. 231

DATE	ITEMS	POST. REF.	√	DEBITS	DATE	ITEMS	POST. REF.	√	CREDITS
1971 Oct. 30		Cg 43		1 9 50	1971 Oct. 1	Balance	√		1 9 50
					30		cg 43	2.00	2 00
									2 1 5 0

ACCOUNT State Unemployment Taxes Payable   ACCOUNT NO. 241

DATE	ITEMS	POST. REF.	√	DEBITS	DATE	ITEMS	POST. REF.	√	CREDITS
1971 Oct. 30		cg 43		1 0 5 30	1971 Oct. 1	Balance	√		1 0 5 30
					30		cg 43	10.80	1 0 8 0
									1 1 6 1 0

Mason & Edwards — General Ledger (Continued)

ACCOUNT *Roger Mason, Capital*   ACCOUNT NO. *311*

DATE	ITEMS	POST. REF.	✓	DEBITS	DATE	ITEMS	POST. REF.	✓	CREDITS
					1971 Oct. 1	Balance	✓		1 46 06 45

ACCOUNT *Roger Mason, Drawing*   ACCOUNT NO. *0311*

DATE	ITEMS	POST. REF.	✓	DEBITS	DATE	ITEMS	POST. REF.	✓	CREDITS
1971 Oct. 1	Balance	✓		9 31 5 26					
15		cj 42		5 00 00					
30		cj 43		6 00 00					
30		cj 43		1 2 50					
				10 42 77 6					

ACCOUNT *Charles Edwards, Capital*   ACCOUNT NO. *321*

DATE	ITEMS	POST. REF.	✓	DEBITS	DATE	ITEMS	POST. REF.	✓	CREDITS
					1971 Oct. 1	Balance	✓		1 20 63 00

ACCOUNT *Charles Edwards, Drawing*   ACCOUNT NO. *0321*

DATE	ITEMS	POST. REF.	✓	DEBITS	DATE	ITEMS	POST. REF.	✓	CREDITS
1971 Oct. 1	Balance	✓		1 00 47 85					
15		cj 42		5 50 00					
16		cj 42		79 80					
30		cj 43		5 50 00					
30		cj 43		1 6 90					
				11 24 45 5					

ACCOUNT *Expense and Revenue Summary*   ACCOUNT NO. *331*

DATE	ITEMS	POST. REF.	✓	DEBITS	DATE	ITEMS	POST. REF.	✓	CREDITS

ACCOUNT *Professional Fees*   ACCOUNT NO. *411*

DATE	ITEMS	POST. REF.	✓	DEBITS	DATE	ITEMS	POST. REF.	✓	CREDITS
					1971 Oct. 1	Balance	✓		9 25 60 75
					30		cj 43		1 23 56 00
									10 49 16 75

Mason & Edwards — General Ledger (Continued)

ACCOUNT Automobile Expense   ACCOUNT NO. 611

DATE	ITEMS	POST. REF.	✓	DEBITS	DATE	ITEMS	POST. REF.	✓	CREDITS
1971 Oct. 1	Balance	✓		1 4 8 7 9 8					
2		cg42		7 5 1 8					
30		cg43		7 2 5					
				1 5 7 0 4 1					

ACCOUNT Charitable Contributions Expense   ACCOUNT NO. 612

DATE	ITEMS	POST. REF.	✓	DEBITS	DATE	ITEMS	POST. REF.	✓	CREDITS
1971 Oct. 1	Balance	✓		5 1 2 0 0					
20		cg42		1 0 0 0 0					
25		cg42		5 0 0 0 0					
				1 1 1 2 0 0					

ACCOUNT Depreciation Expense   ACCOUNT NO. 613

DATE	ITEMS	POST. REF.	✓	DEBITS	DATE	ITEMS	POST. REF.	✓	CREDITS

ACCOUNT Dues and Subscriptions Expense   ACCOUNT NO. 617

DATE	ITEMS	POST. REF.	✓	DEBITS	DATE	ITEMS	POST. REF.	✓	CREDITS
1971 Oct. 1	Balance	✓		4 7 0 0 0					
11		cg42		1 0 0 0					
29		cg42		2 0 0 0 0					
				6 8 0 0 0					

ACCOUNT Electricity, Gas and Water Expense   ACCOUNT NO. 618

DATE	ITEMS	POST. REF.	✓	DEBITS	DATE	ITEMS	POST. REF.	✓	CREDITS
1971 Oct. 1	Balance	✓		9 9 2 3 5					
2		cg42		3 5 1 8					
4		cg42		6 7 9					
13		cg42		2 0 1 5					
				1 0 5 4 4 7					

ACCOUNT Insurance Expense   ACCOUNT NO. 619

DATE	ITEMS	POST. REF.	✓	DEBITS	DATE	ITEMS	POST. REF.	✓	CREDITS
1971 Oct. 1	Balance	✓		5 9 0 1 8					
6		cg42		4 1 6 0 0					
21		cg42		2 6 8 8 0					
				1 2 7 4 9 8					

Mason & Edwards — General Ledger (Continued)

ACCOUNT Laundry Expense   ACCOUNT NO. 620

DATE	ITEMS	POST. REF.	✓	DEBITS	DATE	ITEMS	POST. REF.	✓	CREDITS
1971 Oct. 1	Balance	✓		3 2 0 15					
4		Cg 42		3 2 50					
				3 5 2 65					

ACCOUNT Legal Expense   ACCOUNT NO. 621

DATE	ITEMS	POST. REF.	✓	DEBITS	DATE	ITEMS	POST. REF.	✓	CREDITS
1971 Oct. 1	Balance	✓		3 5 0 79					
26		Cg 42		1 2 5 00					
29		Cg 42		1 0 0 00					
				5 7 5 79					

ACCOUNT Medical Library Expense   ACCOUNT NO. 622

DATE	ITEMS	POST. REF.	✓	DEBITS	DATE	ITEMS	POST. REF.	✓	CREDITS
1971 Oct. 1	Balance	✓		4 2 5 00					
14		Cg 42		7 5 49					
28		Cg 42		2 5 50					
				5 2 5 99					

ACCOUNT Medical Supplies Expense   ACCOUNT NO. 623

DATE	ITEMS	POST. REF.	✓	DEBITS	DATE	ITEMS	POST. REF.	✓	CREDITS
1971 Oct. 1	Balance	✓		5 3 7 92					
4		Cg 42		8 0 15					
19		Cg 42		1 4 5 17					
				7 6 3 24					

ACCOUNT Office Supplies Expense   ACCOUNT NO. 624

DATE	ITEMS	POST. REF.	✓	DEBITS	DATE	ITEMS	POST. REF.	✓	CREDITS
1971 Oct. 1	Balance	✓		4 5 9 20					
19		Cg 42		2 5 90					
30		Cg 43		4 80					
				4 8 9 90					

ACCOUNT Payroll Tax Expense   ACCOUNT NO. 625

DATE	ITEMS	POST. REF.	✓	DEBITS	DATE	ITEMS	POST. REF.	✓	CREDITS
1971 Oct. 1	Balance	✓		1 3 4 3 40					
30		Cg 43		1 1 9 40					
				1 4 6 2 80					

Mason & Edwards — General Ledger (Continued)

ACCOUNT *Postage Expense*   ACCOUNT NO. 626

DATE	ITEMS	POST. REF.	✓	DEBITS	DATE	ITEMS	POST. REF.	✓	CREDITS
1971 Oct. 1	Balance	✓		3 1 0 2 8					
30		Cg43		1 8 0 0					
				3 2 8 2 8					

ACCOUNT *Rent Expense*   ACCOUNT NO. 627

DATE	ITEMS	POST. REF.	✓	DEBITS	DATE	ITEMS	POST. REF.	✓	CREDITS
1971 Oct. 1	Balance	✓		9 0 0 0 0 0					
1		Cg42		1 0 0 0 0 0					
				1 0 0 0 0 0 0					

ACCOUNT *Repairs and Maintenance Expense*   ACCOUNT NO. 628

DATE	ITEMS	POST. REF.	✓	DEBITS	DATE	ITEMS	POST. REF.	✓	CREDITS
1971 Oct. 1	Balance	✓		1 6 2 9 5 0					
5		cg42		2 5 3 0					
7		cg42		9 6 0 0					
23		cg42		2 0 7 5					
27		cg42		6 0 2 8					
				1 8 3 1 8 3					

ACCOUNT *Salary Expense*   ACCOUNT NO. 629

DATE	ITEMS	POST. REF.	✓	DEBITS	DATE	ITEMS	POST. REF.	✓	CREDITS
1971 Oct. 1	Balance	✓		1 8 4 5 0 0 0					
30		cg43		2 0 5 0 0 0					
				2 0 5 0 0 0 0					

ACCOUNT *Surgical Instruments Expense*   ACCOUNT NO. 630

DATE	ITEMS	POST. REF.	✓	DEBITS	DATE	ITEMS	POST. REF.	✓	CREDITS
1971 Oct. 1	Balance	✓		8 7 5 3 0					
8		cg42		8 7 3 5					
				9 6 2 6 5					

ACCOUNT *Surgical Supplies Expense*   ACCOUNT NO. 631

DATE	ITEMS	POST. REF.	✓	DEBITS	DATE	ITEMS	POST. REF.	✓	CREDITS
1971 Oct. 1	Balance	✓		4 1 7 2 0					
12		cg42		4 5 0 0					
				4 6 2 2 0					

Mason & Edwards — General Ledger (Continued)

ACCOUNT *Telephone and Telegraph Expense*   ACCOUNT NO. 632

DATE		ITEMS	POST. REF.	√	DEBITS		DATE	ITEMS	POST. REF.	√	CREDITS
1971 Oct.	1	Balance	√		3 2 0 3 9						
	2		eg42		2 6 3 2						
					3 4 6 7 1						

ACCOUNT *Miscellaneous Expense*   ACCOUNT NO. 633

DATE		ITEMS	POST. REF.	√	DEBITS		DATE	ITEMS	POST. REF.	√	CREDITS
1971 Oct.	1	Balance	√		4 9 5 1 8						
	22		eg42		1 2 0 0						
	30		eg43		9 3 0						
					5 1 6 4 8						

Mason & Edwards — General Ledger (Concluded)

Report No. 11

Complete Report No. 11 in the workbook and submit your working papers to the instructor for approval. After completing the report you will then be given instructions as to the work to be done next.

MASON AND EDWARDS, PHYSICIANS AND SURGEONS

Trial Balance

October 31, 1971

Clermont Bank	111	$ 22,269.52	
Petty Cash Fund	112	75.00	
Office Equipment	171	5,842.30	
Accumulated Depreciation — Office Equipment	0171		$ 1,735.10
Medical Equipment	172	17,505.88	
Accumulated Depreciation — Medical Equipment	0172		2,184.72
X-Ray Equipment	173	20,875.49	
Accumulated Depreciation — X-Ray Equipment	0173		3,492.38
Automobiles	174	8,475.09	
Accumulated Depreciation — Automobiles	0174		2,018.77
FICA Taxes Payable	211		213.20
Employees' Income Taxes Payable	221		282.80
FUTA Taxes Payable	231		2.00
State Unemployment Taxes Payable	241		10.80
Roger Mason, Capital	311		14,606.45
Roger Mason, Drawing	0311	10,427.76	
Charles Edwards, Capital	321		12,063.00
Charles Edwards, Drawing	0321	11,244.55	
Professional Fees	411		104,916.75
Automobile Expense	611	1,570.41	
Charitable Contributions Expense	612	1,112.00	
Dues and Subscriptions Expense	617	680.00	
Electricity, Gas and Water Expense	618	1,054.47	
Insurance Expense	619	1,274.98	
Laundry Expense	620	352.65	
Legal Expense	621	575.79	
Medical Library Expense	622	525.99	
Medical Supplies Expense	623	763.24	
Office Supplies Expense	624	489.90	
Payroll Tax Expense	625	1,462.80	
Postage Expense	626	328.28	
Rent Expense	627	10,000.00	
Repairs and Maintenance Expense	628	1,831.83	
Salary Expense	629	20,500.00	
Surgical Instruments Expense	630	962.65	
Surgical Supplies Expense	631	462.20	
Telephone and Telegraph Expense	632	346.71	
Miscellaneous Expense	633	516.48	
		$141,525.97	$141,525.97

| Day | Name of Patient | KIND OF SERVICE | | PATIENTS' ACCOUNTS | | Cash Services |
		Office Calls	Surgery	Charges	Payments	
	Amounts Forwarded					
1	Dorothy Colton		400 00	400 00		
1	Frank Hunter	15 00				15 00
1	Helen Miller — S. Joseph	12 00				12 00
1	Harry Williams		550 00	550 00		
1	Jean Smith	15 00		15 00		
2	Donald Henderson				100 00	
2	Henry Marshall				350 00	
2	Frank Jones — D. Helen		350 00	350 00		
2	David Brown	15 00		15 00		
2	Louise Nelson	15 00		15 00		
4	Stanley Richter	15 00				15 00
4	Thomas Foster		350 00	350 00		
4	Mrs. William Hall				25 00	
4	Gary Peters				550 00	
4	David Carroll		500 00	500 00		
5	Elmer Hart — D. Kathie	12 00				12 00
5	Elizabeth Hoffman				850 00	
5	John Kenyon		600 00	600 00		
5	Timothy Abbott	15 00		15 00		
6	Wilbur Page				735 00	
6	Paul Myers		350 00	350 00		
6	Emily Hamilton	15 00				15 00
6	John Bancroft	12 00				12 00
7	Grace Lindsey				900 00	
8	John Raeburn — S. Jim	12 00				12 00
8	Robert Mullins				250 00	
8	Harriet Wells				435 00	
8	Margaret Thomas		400 00	400 00		
9	Marilyn Abrams				100 00	
9	Helen Kent	15 00		15 00		
9	Robert Feldman	12 00		12 00		
11	Otto Haskins	15 00				15 00
27	Margaret Thomas				400 00	
27	Edward Conley	12 00				12 00
28	George Stanton				175 00	
28	Jean Smith				15 00	
29	Arthur Williams				300 00	
30	Allen Jackson		400 00	400 00		
		571 00	12450 00	12795 00	11455 00	226 00

Daily Service Record for Month of October

chapter seven

the periodic summary

One of the major reasons for keeping accounting records is to accumulate information that will make it possible to prepare periodic summaries of both (1) the revenue and expenses of the business during a specified period and (2) the assets, liabilities, and owner's equity of the business at a specified date. A trial balance of the general ledger accounts will provide most of the information that is required for these summaries (the income statement and the balance sheet). However, the trial balance does not supply the data in a form that is easily interpreted, nor does it reflect changes in the accounting elements that have not been represented by ordinary business transactions. Therefore, at the end of a fiscal period it is necessary, first, to determine the kind and amounts of changes that the accounts do not reflect and to adjust the accounts accordingly and, second, to recast the information into the form of an income statement and a balance sheet. These two steps are often referred to as "the periodic summary."

end-of-period work sheet

An end-of-period *work sheet* is a device that assists the accountant in three ways. It facilitates **(1)** the preparing of the financial statements, **(2)** the making of needed adjustments in the accounts, and **(3)** the closing of the temporary owner's equity accounts. When a number of adjustments are to be made at the end of a period, a work sheet is especially helpful in determining the balance of the accounts after adjustment.

Work sheets are not financial statements; they are devices used to assist the accountant in performing certain of his tasks. Ordinarily it is only the accountant who uses (or even sees) a work sheet.

A Work Sheet for an Attorney

Although an end-of-period work sheet can be in any of several forms, a common and widely used arrangement involves ten amount columns. The amount columns are used in pairs. The first pair of amount columns is for the trial balance. The data to be recorded consist of the name, number, and debit or credit balance of each account. Debit balances should be entered in the left-hand column and credit balances in the right-hand column. The second pair of amount columns is used to record needed end-of-period adjustments. The third pair of amount columns is used to show the account balances as adjusted. This pair of amount columns is headed "Adjusted Trial Balance" because its purpose is to show that the debit and credit account balances as adjusted are equal in amount. The fourth pair of amount columns is for the adjusted balances of the expense and revenue accounts. This pair of columns is headed "Income Statement" since the amounts shown will be reported in that statement. The fifth, and last, pair of amount columns is headed "Balance Sheet" and shows the adjusted account balances that will be reported in that statement.

To illustrate the preparation and use of the end-of-period work sheet, the example of the accounts of Harold R. Stewart, Attorney at Law, will be continued. The journal and ledger for Mr. Stewart for the month of December were reproduced in Chapter 5. In this chapter the income statement for the year and the balance sheet at the end of the year will be reproduced, showing the use of a work sheet as a device for summarizing the data to be presented in those statements.

The Work Sheet for Harold R. Stewart, Attorney at Law

The end-of-year work sheet for Mr. Stewart is reproduced on page 161. Following is a description and discussion of the steps that were followed in the preparation of this work sheet. Each step should be studied carefully with frequent reference to the work sheet itself.

Trial Balance Columns. The trial balance of the general ledger accounts as of December 31 was entered in the first pair of amount columns. This trial balance is the same as the one shown on page 132 except that all of the account titles were included in the work sheet list even though certain of the accounts had no balance at this point.

The Trial Balance Debits and Credits columns were totaled. The totals should be equal. If not, the cause of any discrepancy must be found and corrected before the preparation of the work sheet can proceed.

Adjustments Columns. The second pair of amount columns on the work sheet were used to record certain entries necessary to reflect the depreciation that had occurred during the year.

Two entries involving two debits and two credits were made in the Adjustments columns to reflect these changes. When the account was debited, the amount was entered on the same horizontal line as the name of the Account in the Adjustments Debits column. Amounts credited were entered, of course, in the Credits column. Each entry made on the work sheet was identified by a small letter in parentheses to facilitate cross-reference. The following is an explanation of each of the entries:

Entry (a): This entry recorded the depreciation expense for the year on office equipment by debiting Depreciation Expense, Account No. 518, for $232.19 and by crediting Accumulated Depreciation — Office Equipment, Account No. 014, for $232.19. Office Equipment, Account No. 14, shows that an electric typewriter was purchased on December 20 at a cost of $620.18. Mr. Stewart follows the practice of not taking depreciation on assets that have been owned for less than a month, so the charge to Depreciation Expense is based on the balance of $2,321.87 in Account No. 14 on December 1. The depreciation rate used for furniture and equipment is 10 percent and 10 percent of $2,321.87 is $232.19.

Entry (b): This entry recorded the depreciation expense on the automobile by debiting Depreciation Expense, Account No. 518, for $912.56 and crediting Accumulated Depreciation — Automobile, Account No. 015, for $912.56.

The automobile has been owned for the entire year. The depreciation rate is 25 percent, and the figure of $912.56 is 25 percent of the cost of the car of $3,650.23.

Harold R. Stewart, Attorney at Law

Work Sheet

For the Year Ended December 31, 1971

Account	Acct. No.	Trial Balance Debits	Trial Balance Credits	Adjustments Debits	Adjustments Credits	Adj. Trial Balance Debits	Adj. Trial Balance Credits	Income Statement Debits	Income Statement Credits	Balance Sheet Debits	Balance Sheet Credits
First National Bank	11	777804				777804				777804	
Petty Cash Fund	12	5000				5000				5000	
Advances on Behalf of Clients	13	21500				21500				21500	
Office Equipment	14	294205				294205				294205	
Accumulated Depr.—Office Equip.	014		39471		(a) 23219		62690				62690
Automobile	15	365023				365023				365023	
Accumulated Depr.—Automobile	015		136863		(b) 91256		228139				228139
Accounts Payable	21		17440				17440				17440
Employees Income Tax Payable	22		9880				9880				9880
FICA Taxes Payable	23		75				75				75
FUTA Taxes Payable	24		405				405				405
State Unemployment Taxes Payable	25										
Harold Q. Stewart, Capital	31		1211143				1211143				1211143
Harold R. Stewart, Drawing	031	1465540				1465540				1465540	
Expense and Revenue Summary	32										
Legal Fees Income	41		3132800				3132800		3132800		
Collection Fees Income	42		156041				156041		156041		
Salary Expense	571	1140000				1140000		1140000			
Payroll Tax Expense	572	86160				86160		86160			
Rent Expense	573	300000				300000		300000			
Telephone and Telegraph Expense	574	26838				26838		26838			
Office Supplies Expense	515	38405				38405		38405			
Automobile Expense	516	62096				62096		62096			
Law Library Expense	517	55817				55817		55817			
Depreciation Expense	518			(a) 23219 (b) 91256		23219 91256		23219 91256			
Charitable Contributions Expense	519	31600				31600		31600			
Miscellaneous Expense	520	34150				34150		34150			
		4704138	4704138	114475	114475	4818613	4818613	1889641	3288841	2929072	1529772
Net Income								1399300			1399300
								3288841	3288841	2929072	2929072

Harold R. Stewart, Attorney at Law — Ten-Column Work Sheet

After making the required entries in the Adjustments columns of the work sheet, the columns were totaled to prove the equality of the debit and credit entries.

Adjusted Trial Balance Columns. The third pair of amount columns of the work sheet was used for the *adjusted trial balance*. To determine the balance of each account after making the required adjustments, it was necessary to take into consideration the amounts recorded in the first two pairs of amount columns. When an account balance was not affected by entries in the Adjustments columns, the amount in the Trial Balance columns was extended directly to the Adjusted Trial Balance columns.

When an account balance was affected by an entry in the Adjustments columns, the balance recorded in the Trial Balance columns was increased or decreased, as the case might be, by the amount of the adjusting entry. For example, Accumulated Depreciation — Office Equipment was listed in the Trial Balance Credits column as $394.71. Since there was an entry of $232.19 in the Adjustments Credits column, the amount extended to the Adjusted Trial Balance Credits column was the total of $394.71 and $232.19, or $626.90.

A rule which can always be followed in combining figures in the Trial Balance columns and the Adjustments columns is that if there are debits in both columns or credits in both columns, the two amounts are added and the total is carried to the Adjusted Trial Balance columns. If there is a debit in one column and a credit in the other, the smaller amount is subtracted from the larger and the difference will be a debit or a credit depending on whether the debit or the credit is the larger amount. If the debit is the larger amount, the amount carried to the Adjusted Trial Balance columns will be placed in the Debits column. If the credit is the larger amount, the difference will be placed in the Adjusted Trial Balance Credits column. The Adjusted Trial Balance columns were totaled to prove the equality of the debits and credits.

Income Statement Columns. The fourth pair of amount columns in the work sheet was used to show the amounts that will be reported in the income statement. The amounts for legal fees income and collection fees income were extended to the Income Statement Credits column. The amounts of the expenses were extended to the Income Statement Debits column.

The Income Statement columns were totaled. The difference between the totals of these columns is the amount of the increase or the decrease in owner's equity due to net income or net loss during the accounting period. If the total of the credits exceeds the total of the debits, the difference represents the increase in owner's equity due to net income; if the total of the debits exceeds the total of the credits, the difference represents the decrease in owner's equity due to net loss.

Reference to the Income Statement columns of Mr. Stewart's work sheet will show that the total of the credits amounted to $32,888.41 and the total of the debits amounted to $18,895.41. The difference, amounting to $13,993.00, was the amount of the net income for the year.

Balance Sheet Columns. The fifth pair of amount columns of the work sheet was used to show the amounts that will be reported in the balance sheet. The Balance Sheet columns were totaled. The difference between the totals of these columns also is the amount of the net income or the net loss for the accounting period. If the total of the debits exceeds the total of the credits, the difference represents a net income for the accounting period; if the total of the credits exceeds the total of the debits, the difference represents a net loss for the period. This difference should be the same as the difference between the totals of the Income Statement columns.

Reference to the Balance Sheet columns of the work sheet will show that the total of the debits amounted to $29,290.72 and the total of the credits amounted to $15,297.72. The difference of $13,993.00 represented the amount of the net income for the year.

Completing the Work Sheet. The difference between the totals of the Income Statement columns and the totals of the Balance Sheet columns should be recorded on the next horizontal line below the totals. If the difference represents net income, it should be so designated and recorded in the Income Statement Debits and in the Balance Sheet Credits columns. If, instead, a net loss has been the result, the amount should be so designated and entered in the Income Statement Credits and in the Balance Sheet Debits columns. Finally, the totals of the Income Statement and Balance Sheet columns, after the net income (or net loss) has been recorded, are entered, and a double line is ruled immediately below the totals.

Proving the Work Sheet. The fact that the difference between the Income Statement columns and the difference between the Balance Sheet columns is the same amount is not a coincidence. This occurs because an excess of revenue over expenses results in net income. Likewise, an excess of expenses over revenue results in a net loss. It is also true, but not quite so obvious, that if there is a net income, it will result in an increase in assets in the Balance Sheet columns in the form of additional cash, accounts receivable, or other assets. Sometimes cash received is used to pay liabilities, so that the assets at the end of the period may not have increased in total, but the liabilities have decreased. The increase in owner's equity, however, which results from profitable operations has not yet been recorded in the permanent owner's equity account at the time the work sheet is prepared. The balance of the owner's capital account is the amount of his equity at the beginning of the period, because the day by day changes are recorded in the temporary owner's equity accounts — the revenue and expense accounts.

When the amount of the net income is added to the Income Statement Debits column, the total of expenses and net income is equal to the revenue items in the Income Statement Credits column; and when the amount of net income is added to the Balance Sheet Credits column, the total assets equal the total liabilities and owner's equity which is the accounting equation presented on page 5. After the temporary accounts are closed at the end of the period and the net amount of income for the period has been transferred to the owner's capital account, that account includes the net income for the period.

Report No. 12

Complete Report No. 12 in the workbook and submit your working papers to the instructor for approval. After completing the report, continue with the following study assignment until the next report is required.

the financial statements

The financial statements usually consist of (1) an income statement and (2) a balance sheet.

The Income Statement

An income statement is a formal statement of the results of the operation of an enterprise during an accounting period. Other titles sometimes used for this statement include *profit and loss statement, income and expense statement, revenue and expense statement, operating statement,* and *report of earnings.* Whatever the title, the purpose of the statement or report is to show the types and amounts of revenue and expenses that the business had during the period involved, and the resulting net income or net loss for this accounting period.

Importance of the Income Statement. The income statement is now generally considered to be the most important financial statement of a business. A business cannot exist indefinitely unless it has profit or net income. The income statement is essentially a "report card" of the enterprise. The statement provides a basis for judging the overall effectiveness of the management. Decisions as to whether to continue a business, to expand it, or to contract it are often based upon the results as reported in the income statement. Actual and potential creditors are interested in income statements because one of the best reasons for extending credit or for making a loan is that the business is profitable.

Various government agencies are interested in income statements of businesses for a variety of reasons. Regulatory bodies are concerned with the earnings of the enterprises they regulate, because a part of the regulation usually relates to the prices, rates, or fares that may be charged. If the enterprise is either exceptionally profitable or unprofitable, some change in the allowed prices or rates may be needed. Income tax authorities, both federal and local, have an interest in business income statements. Net income determination for tax purposes differs somewhat from the calculation of net income for other purposes, but, for a variety of reasons, the tax authorities are interested in both sets of calculations.

Form of the Income Statement. The form of the income statement depends in part upon the type of enterprise. For a professional practice, the professional revenue is listed first, the professional expenses are listed next, and the total of the professional expenses is subtracted from the professional revenue to determine the net professional income. The amounts of any income from other sources such as dividend income from investments are added to, and the amounts of any other expenses such as interest on a loan from the bank are subtracted from, the net professional income to arrive at the final amount of net income (or net loss).

It is essential that the income statement be properly headed. The name of the business (or of the individual if the enterprise is a professional practice or if the owner operates a business in his own name) should be shown first. The name of the statement is placed on the second line, and the period of time that the statement covers appears on the third line. An income statement always covers a period of time and if the period is a year, it may be stated, for example, "For the Year Ended December 31, 19—."

The income statement presented to the owner (or owners) of an enterprise and to potential creditors or other interested parties is usually typewritten. The income statement for Mr. Stewart for the year ended December 31, 1971, is shown on page 166. The information needed to prepare the statement was obtained from the work sheet shown on page 161.

HAROLD R. STEWART, ATTORNEY AT LAW
Income Statement
For the Year Ended December 31, 1971

Professional revenue:

Legal fees income..........................		$31,328.00
Collection fees income......................		1,560.41
Total professional revenue....................		$32,888.41

Professional expenses:

Salary expense...........................	$11,400.00	
Payroll tax expense.........................	861.60	
Rent expense.............................	3,000.00	
Telephone and telegraph expense.............	268.38	
Office supplies expense......................	384.05	
Automobile expense........................	620.96	
Law library expense........................	558.17	
Depreciation expense.......................	1,144.75	
Charitable contributions expense..............	316.00	
Miscellaneous expense......................	341.50	
Total professional expenses.................		18,895.41
Net income................................		$13,993.00

The Balance Sheet

A formal statement of the assets, liabilities, and owner's equity in an enterprise at a specified date is known as a *balance sheet.* The title of the statement had its origin in the equality of the elements, that is, in the balance between the sum of the assets and the sum of the liabilities and owner's equity. Sometimes the balance sheet is called a *statement of assets and liabilities,* a *statement of condition,* or a *statement of financial position.*

Importance of the Balance Sheet. The balance sheet of a business is of considerable interest to various parties for several reasons. The owner or owners of a business are interested in the kinds and amounts of assets and liabilities, and the amount of the owner's equity or capital element.

Creditors of the business are interested in the financial condition of the enterprise, particularly as it pertains to the claims they have and the prospects for prompt payment. Potential creditors or possible lenders are concerned about the financial position of the business. Their decision as to whether to extend credit or to make loans to the business may depend, in large part, upon the condition of the enterprise as revealed by a balance sheet.

Persons considering buying an ownership interest in a business are greatly interested in the character and amount of the assets and liabilities, though this interest is probably secondary to their concern about the future earnings possibilities.

Finally, various regulatory bodies are interested in the financial condition of the businesses that are under their jurisdiction. Examples of regulated businesses include banks, insurance companies, public utilities, railroads, and airlines.

Form of the Balance Sheet. Traditionally, balance sheets have been presented either in *account form* or in *report form*. When the account form is followed, the assets are listed on the left side of the page (or on the left of two facing pages) and the liabilities and owner's equity on the right. This form is similar to the debit-side and credit-side arrangement of the standard ledger account. The balance sheet of Harold R. Stewart, Attorney at Law, as of December 31, 1971, in account form is reproduced on pages 168 and 169. The data for the preparation of the statement were secured from the work sheet.

When the report form of the balance sheet is followed, the assets, liabilities, and owner's equity elements are listed underneath each other. This arrangement is usually preferable when the statement is typed on letter-size paper ($8\frac{1}{2}'' \times 11''$).

Whichever form is used, it is essential that the statement have the proper heading. This means that three things must be shown: **(1)** the name of the business must be given (or name of the individual if the business or professional practice is carried on in the name of an individual), followed by **(2)** the name of the statement — usually just "Balance Sheet," and finally **(3)** the date — month, day, and year. Sometimes the expression "As of Close of Business December 31, 1971" (or whatever date is involved) is included. It must be remembered that a balance sheet relates to a particular moment of time. This is in contrast to the Income Statement which always refers to a certain period of time.

Classification of Data in the Balance Sheet. The purpose of the balance sheet and of all other financial statements and reports is to convey as much information as possible. This aim is furthered by some classification of the data being reported. It has become almost universal practice to classify both assets and liabilities in the balance sheet as either "current," or "non-current" or "long-lived."

Current Assets. *Current assets* include cash and all other assets that may be reasonably expected to be realized in cash or sold or consumed during the normal operating cycle of the business. In a professional practice the current assets may include cash and receivables, such as advances on behalf of clients.

Assets

Current assets:

Cash in bank.....................	$ 7,778.04	
Petty cash fund.................	50.00	
Advances on behalf of clients......	215.00	
Total current assets.............		$ 8,043.04

Long-lived assets:

Office equipment................	$ 2,942.05		
Less: Accumulated depreciation — office equipment..........	626.90	$ 2,315.15	
Automobile.....................	$ 3,650.23		
Less: Accumulated depreciation — automobile...............	2,281.39	1,368.84	
Total long-lived assets.........			3,683.99
Total assets......................			$11,727.03

Long-Lived Assets. Property that is used in the operation of a professional practice may include such assets as land, buildings, office equipment, professional equipment, professional libraries, and automobiles. Such assets are called *long-lived assets* because they have a useful life that is comparatively long. Of these assets only land, however, is really permanent.

Reference to the balance sheet of Harold R. Stewart will show that his long-lived assets consist of office equipment and an automobile. In both cases the amount of the accumulated depreciation is shown as a deduction from the cost of the asset. The difference represents the book value of the equipment. The book value is the amount that will be recorded as depreciation expense in future periods.

Current Liabilities. *Current liabilities* include those obligations that will be due in a short time and paid with monies provided by the current assets. As of December 31, Mr. Stewart's current liabilities consisted of employees' income taxes payable, FICA taxes payable, FUTA taxes payable, and state unemployment taxes payable.

Long-Term Liabilities. *Long-term liabilities* (sometimes called *fixed liabilities*) include those obligations that will not be due for a relatively long time. The most common of the long-term liabilities is mortgages payable.

ATTORNEY AT LAW
Sheet
31, 1971

Liabilities

Current liabilities:

Employees' income taxes payable...	$ 174.40	
FICA taxes payable..............	98.80	
FUTA taxes payable.............	.75	
State unemployment taxes payable.	4.05	
Total current liabilities.........		$ 278.00

Owner's equity

Harold R. Stewart, capital

Capital, January 1..............		$12,111.43	
Net income...................	$13,993.00		
Less: withdrawals.............	14,655.40	(662.40)	
Capital, December 31...........			11,449.03
Total liabilities and owner's equity....			$11,727.03

A *mortgage payable* is a debt or an obligation that is secured by a *mortgage*, which provides for the conveyance of certain property upon failure to pay the debt at maturity. When the debt is paid, the mortgage becomes void. It will be seen, therefore, that a mortgage payable differs little from an account payable or a note payable except that the creditor holds the mortgage as security for the payment of the debt. Usually debts secured by mortgages run for a longer period of time than ordinary notes payable or accounts payable. A mortgage payable should be classified as a long-term liability if the maturity date extends beyond the normal operating cycle of the business (usually a year). Mr. Stewart has no long-term liabilities.

Owner's Equity. As previously explained, accounts relating to the owner's equity element may be either permanent or temporary owner's equity accounts. The permanent owner's equity accounts used in recording the operations of a particular enterprise depend upon the type of organization, that is, whether the enterprise is organized as a sole proprietorship, as a partnership, or as a corporation.

In the case of a sole proprietorship, one or more accounts representing the owner's interest or equity in the assets may be kept. Reference to the chart of accounts shown on page 112 will show that the following accounts are classified as owner's equity accounts:

Account No. 31, Harold R. Stewart, Capital
Account No. 031, Harold R. Stewart, Drawing
Account No. 32, Expense and Revenue Summary

Account No. 31 reflects the amount of Mr. Stewart's equity. It may be increased by additional investments or by the practice of not withdrawing cash or other assets in an amount as large as the net income of the enterprise; it may be decreased by withdrawals in excess of the amount of the net income or by sustaining a net loss during one or more accounting periods. Usually there will be no changes in the balance of this account during the accounting period, in which case the balance represents the owner's investment in the business as of the beginning of the accounting period and until the books are closed at the end of the accounting period.

Account No. 031 is Mr. Stewart's drawing account. This account is charged for any withdrawals of cash or other property for personal use. It is a temporary account in which is kept a record of the owner's personal drawings during the accounting period. Ordinarily such drawings are made in anticipation of earnings rather than as withdrawals of capital. The balance of the account, as shown by the trial balance at the close of an accounting period, represents the total amount of the owner's drawings during the period.

Reference to the work sheet shown on page 161 will reveal that the balance of Mr. Stewart's drawing account is listed in the Balance Sheet Debits column. This is because there is no provision on a work sheet for making deductions from owner's equity except by listing them in the Debits column. Since the balance of the owner's capital account is listed in the Balance Sheet Credits column, the listing of the balance of the owner's drawing account in the Debits column is equivalent to deducting the amount from the balance of the owner's capital account.

Account No. 32 is used only at the close of the accounting period for the purpose of summarizing the temporary owner's equity accounts. Sometimes this account is referred to as a *clearing account*. No entries should appear in the account before the books are closed at the end of the accounting period.

The owner's equity section of Mr. Stewart's balance sheet is arranged to show the major changes that took place during the year in the owner's equity element of the law practice. Mr. Stewart's interest in the practice amounted to $12,111.43 at the beginning of the year. His interest was increased $13,993.00 as the result of profitable operations, and decreased $14,655.40 as the result of withdrawals during the year. Thus, the owner's equity decreased by $662.40 because withdrawals were greater than the income for the period. Mr. Stewart's anticipation of income was greater than the amount actually earned. The owner's equity element on December 31 amounted to $11,449.03.

Report No. 13

Complete Report No. 13 in the workbook and submit your working papers to the instructor for approval. After completing the report, you may continue with the textbook discussion in Chapter 8 until the next report is required.

chapter eight

adjusting and closing accounts at end of accounting period

As explained in the preceding chapter, the adjustment of certain accounts at the end of the accounting period is required because of changes that have occurred during the period that are not reflected in the accounts. Since the purpose of the temporary owner's equity accounts is to assemble information relating to a specified period of time, at the end of the period the balances of these accounts must be removed to allow the accounts to be ready to perform their function in the following period. Accounts of this type must be "closed."

adjusting entries

In preparing the work sheet for Harold R. Stewart, Attorney at Law, (reproduced on page 161), adjustments were made to accomplish the following purposes:

(a) To record the estimated amount of depreciation of office equipment for the year.

(b) To record the estimated amount of depreciation of the automobile for the year.

Note that each of the adjusting entries affects both the balance sheet and the income statement. If an adjusting entry increases an expense, as when depreciation expense is recorded in entries (a) and (b) then the balance sheet accounts, Accumulated Depreciation — Office Equipment and Accumulated Depreciation — Automobile, are also increased. It should also be noted that adjusting entries for accumulated depreciation do not affect cash because the long-lived asset has already been paid for. Depreciation, as explained in Chapter 5, is simply a way of allocating the original cost of the asset to the periods in which it is used up.

The effect of these adjustments was reflected in the financial statements reproduced on pages 166, 168, and 169. To bring the ledger into agreement with the financial statements, the adjustments should be recorded in the proper accounts. It is customary, therefore, at the end of each accounting period to journalize the adjustments and to post them to the accounts.

Journalizing the Adjusting Entries

Adjusting entries may be recorded in either a general journal or a combined cash journal. If the entries are made in a combined cash journal, the only amount columns used are the General Debits and Credits columns. A portion of a page of a combined cash journal showing Mr. Stewart's adjusting entries is reproduced on page 174. Note that when the adjusting entries are recorded in the combined cash journal, they are entered in exactly the same manner as they would be entered in a general journal. Since the heading "Adjusting Entries" explains the nature of the entries, a separate explanation of each adjusting entry is unnecessary. The information needed in journalizing the adjustments was obtained from the Adjustments columns of the work sheet reproduced on page 161. The account numbers were not entered in the Posting Reference column at the time of journalizing; they were entered as the posting was completed.

Posting the Adjusting Entries

The adjusting entries should be posted individually to the proper general ledger accounts. The accounts of Mr. Stewart that were affected by the adjusting entries are reproduced in type below. The entries in the accounts for December transactions that were posted prior to posting the adjusting entries are the same as appeared in the accounts reproduced in script on pages 128–131. The number of the combined cash journal page on which the adjusting entries were recorded was entered in the Posting Reference column of the general ledger accounts affected, and the account numbers were entered in the Posting Reference column of the combined cash journal as the posting was completed. This provided a cross-reference in both books.

COMBINED CASH JOURNAL FOR MONTH OF *December* 1971   PAGE 35

DATE MO. DAY	DESCRIPTION	POST. REF.	GENERAL DEBITS	GENERAL CREDITS
	AMOUNTS FORWARDED			
Dec. 31	*Adjusting Entries*			
	Depreciation Expense	518	2 3 2 1 9	
	Accum. Deprec.-Office Equip.	014		2 3 2 1 9
	Depreciation Expense	518	9 1 2 5 6	
	Accum. Deprec.-Automobile	015	1 1 4 4 7 5	1 1 4 4 7 5

Harold R. Stewart — Adjusting Entries

ACCUMULATED DEPRECIATION — OFFICE EQUIPMENT   Account No. 014

1971			
Dec. 1	Balance	√	394.71
31		CJ35	232.19
			626.90

ACCUMULATED DEPRECIATION — AUTOMOBILE   Account No. 015

1971			
Dec. 1	Balance	√	1,368.83
31		CJ35	912.59
			2,281.39

DEPRECIATION EXPENSE   Account No. 518

1971			
Dec. 31	CJ35	232.19	
31	CJ35	912.56	
		1 144.75	

Report No. 14

Complete Report No. 14 in the workbook and submit your working papers to the instructor for approval. Continue with the following study assignment until Report No. 15 is required.

closing procedure

After the adjusting entries have been posted, all of the temporary owner's equity accounts should be closed. This means that the accountant must remove ("close out") **(1)** the balance of every account that enters into the calculation of the net income (or net loss) for the accounting period and **(2)** the balance of the owner's drawing account. The purpose of the closing procedure is to transfer the balances of the temporary owner's equity accounts to the permanent owner's equity account. This could be accomplished simply by debiting or crediting each account involved, with an offsetting credit or debit to the permanent owner's equity account. However, it is considered better practice to transfer the balances of all accounts that enter into the net income or net loss determination to a summarizing account called Expense and Revenue Summary (sometimes called *Income Summary, Profit and Loss Summary*, or just *Profit and Loss*). Then, the resulting balance of the expense and revenue summary account (which will be the amount of the net income or net loss for the period) is transferred to the permanent owner's equity account.

The final step in the closing procedure is to transfer the balance of the owner's drawing account to the permanent owner's equity account. After this is done, only the asset accounts, the liability accounts, and the permanent owner's equity account have balances. If there has been no error, the sum of the balances of the asset accounts (less balances of any contra accounts) will be equal to the sum of the balances of the liability accounts plus the balance of the permanent owner's equity account. The accounts will agree exactly with what is shown by the balance sheet as of the close of the period. Reference to the balance sheet of Harold R. Stewart reproduced on pages 168 and 169 will show that the assets, liabilities, and owner's equity as of December 31 may be expressed in equation form as follows:

$$\text{ASSETS} = \text{LIABILITIES} + \text{OWNER'S EQUITY}$$
$$\$11,727.03 \qquad \$278.00 \qquad \$11,449.03$$

Journalizing the Closing Entries

Closing entries, like adjusting entries, may be recorded in either a general journal or a combined cash journal. If the entries are made in a combined cash journal, only the General Debits and Credits columns are used. A portion of a page of a combined cash journal showing the closing entries for Mr. Stewart is reproduced on page 177. Since the heading "Closing Entries" explains the nature of the entries, a separate explanation of each closing entry is not necessary. The information required in preparing the closing entries was obtained from the work sheet illustrated on page 161.

The first closing entry was made to close the revenue accounts, Legal Fees Income and Collection Fees Income. Since these accounts have credit balances, each account must be debited for the amount of its balance in order to close it. The debits to these two accounts are offset by a credit of $32,888.41 to Expense and Revenue Summary.

The second closing entry was made to close the expense accounts. Since these accounts have debit balances, each account must be credited for the amount of its balance in order to close it. The credits to these accounts are offset by a debit of $18,895.41 to Expense and Revenue Summary.

The posting of the first two closing entries causes the expense and revenue summary account to have a credit balance of $13,993.00, the net income for the year. The account has now served its purpose and must be closed. The third closing entry closes the expense and revenue summary account by debiting that account and crediting Harold R. Stewart, Capital, for $13,993.00.

The final closing entry was made to close the Harold R. Stewart drawing account. Since this account has a debit balance, it must be credited to close it. The offsetting entry is a debit of $14,655.40 to Harold R. Stewart, Capital.

The account numbers shown in the Posting Reference Column were not entered at the time the closing entries were made — they were entered as the posting was completed.

Posting the Closing Entries and Completing the Accounts

Closing entries should be posted in the usual manner. Proper cross-references are provided by using the Posting Reference columns of the

| DATE | | DESCRIPTION | POST REF. | GENERAL | | | |
MO.	DAY			DEBITS		CREDITS	
		AMOUNTS FORWARDED					
Dec	31	Closing Entries					
		Legal Fees Income	41	3 1 3 2 8 0 0			
		Collection Fees Income	42	1 5 6 0 4 1			
		Expense and Revenue Summary	32			3 2 8 8 8 4 1	
		Expense and Revenue Summary	32	1 8 8 9 5 4 1			
		Salary Expense	511			1 1 4 0 0 0 0	
		Payroll Tax Expense	512			8 6 1 6 0	
		Rent Expense	513			3 0 0 0 0 0	
		Telephone and Telegraph Exp.	514			2 6 8 3 8	
		Office Supplies Expense	515			3 8 4 0 5	
		Automobile Expense	516			6 2 0 9 6	
		Law Library Expense	517			5 5 8 1 7	
		Depreciation Expense	518			1 1 4 4 7 5	
		Charitable Contributions Exp.	519			3 1 6 0 0	
		Miscellaneous Expense	520			3 4 1 5 0	
		Expense and Revenue Summary	32	1 3 9 9 3 0 0			
		Harold R. Stewart, Capital	31			1 3 9 9 3 0 0	
		Harold R. Stewart, Capital	31	1 4 6 5 5 4 0			
		Harold R. Stewart, Drawing	031	1 4 6 5 5 4 0		1 4 6 5 5 4 0	
				8 0 4 3 2 2 2		8 0 4 3 2 2 2	

Harold R. Stewart — Closing Entries

combined cash journal and the ledger accounts. After all the closing entries have been posted, the accounts affected appear as shown on pages 178 to 180. The income statement accounts are now in balance.

After the income statement accounts have been closed, the accounts still open are the balance sheet accounts, that is, the asset, liability, and the permanent owner's equity accounts. If a new general ledger is to be opened in which to record the transactions of the new year, it is not necessary to rule the balance sheet accounts in the old ledger. In the new ledger the balances of the open accounts which have debit balances should be entered in the Debit Balance columns. The open accounts which have credit balances should be entered in the Credit Balance columns. The date will be January 1, even though the new ledger may be opened a few days after January 1.

ACCOUNT Harold R. Stewart, Capital   ACCOUNT NO. 31

DATE	ITEMS	POST. REF.	✓	DEBITS	DATE	ITEMS	POST. REF.	✓	CREDITS
1971 Dec. 31		CJ36		1 46 55 40	1971 Dec. 1	Balance	✓		1 21 11 43
					31		cJ36		1 39 93 00

ACCOUNT Harold R. Stewart, Drawing   ACCOUNT NO. 031

DATE	ITEMS	POST. REF.	✓	DEBITS	DATE	ITEMS	POST. REF.	✓	CREDITS
1971 Dec. 1	Balance	✓		1 34 50 25	1971 Dec. 31		cJ36		1 46 55 40
15		cJ33		5 47 40					
24		cJ33		49 75					
31		cJ33		6 00 00					
31		cJ34		8 00					
				1 46 55 40					
				1 46 55 40					1 46 55 40

ACCOUNT Expense and Revenue Summary   ACCOUNT NO. 32

DATE	ITEMS	POST. REF.	✓	DEBITS	DATE	ITEMS	POST. REF.	✓	CREDITS
1971 Dec. 31		cJ36		1 88 95 41	1971 Dec. 31		cJ36		3 28 88 41
31		cJ36		1 39 93 00					
				5 28 88 41					
				3 28 88 41					3 28 88 41

ACCOUNT Legal Fees Income   ACCOUNT NO. 41

DATE	ITEMS	POST. REF.	✓	DEBITS	DATE	ITEMS	POST. REF.	✓	CREDITS
1971 Dec. 31		cJ36		3 13 28 00	1971 Dec. 1	Balance	✓		2 89 18 00
					31		cJ34		24 10 00
									3 13 28 00
				3 13 28 00					3 13 28 00

ACCOUNT Collection Fees Income   ACCOUNT NO. 42

DATE	ITEMS	POST. REF.	✓	DEBITS	DATE	ITEMS	POST. REF.	✓	CREDITS
1971 Dec. 31		cJ36		1 56 0 41	1971 Dec. 1	Balance	✓		1 42 1 35
					31		cJ34		13 90 6
									1 56 0 41
				1 56 0 41					1 56 0 41

Harold R. Stewart — Partial General Ledger

ACCOUNT Salary Expense — ACCOUNT NO. 511

DATE	ITEMS	POST. REF.	✓	DEBITS	DATE	ITEMS	POST. REF.	✓	CREDITS
1971 Dec. 1	Balance	✓		1045000	1971 Dec. 31		cj 36		1140000
15		cj 33		22500					
15		cj 33		25000					
31		cj 33		22500					
31		cj 34		25000					
				1140000					1140000

ACCOUNT Payroll Tax Expense — ACCOUNT NO. 512

DATE	ITEMS	POST. REF.	✓	DEBITS	DATE	ITEMS	POST. REF.	✓	CREDITS
1971 Dec. 1	Balance	✓		81220	1971 Dec. 31		cj 36		86160
31		cj 34		4940					
				86160					86160

ACCOUNT Rent Expense — ACCOUNT NO. 513

DATE	ITEMS	POST. REF.	✓	DEBITS	DATE	ITEMS	POST. REF.	✓	CREDITS
1971 Dec. 1	Balance	✓		275000	1971 Dec. 31		cj 36		300000
1		cj 33		25000					
				300000					300000

ACCOUNT Telephone and Telegraph Expense — ACCOUNT NO. 514

DATE	ITEMS	POST. REF.	✓	DEBITS	DATE	ITEMS	POST. REF.	✓	CREDITS
1971 Dec. 1	Balance	✓		24520	1971 Dec. 31		cj 36		26838
3		cj 33		2318					
				26838					26838

ACCOUNT Office Supplies Expense — ACCOUNT NO. 515

DATE	ITEMS	POST. REF.	✓	DEBITS	DATE	ITEMS	POST. REF.	✓	CREDITS
1971 Dec. 1	Balance	✓		33240	1971 Dec. 31		cj 36		38405
16		cj 33		4570					
31		cj 34		595					
				38405					38405

Harold R. Stewart — Partial General Ledger (Continued)

ACCOUNT *Automobile Expense* ACCOUNT NO. 516

DATE	ITEMS	POST. REF.	✓	DEBITS	DATE	ITEMS	POST. REF.	✓	CREDITS
1971 Dec 1	Balance	✓		587 50	1971 Dec 31		CJ36		620 96
6		CJ33		29 74					
31		CJ34		3 72					
				620 96					
				620 96					620 96

ACCOUNT *Law Library Expense* ACCOUNT NO. 517

DATE	ITEMS	POST. REF.	✓	DEBITS	DATE	ITEMS	POST. REF.	✓	CREDITS
1971 Dec 10		CJ33		558 17	1971 Dec 31		CJ36		558 17

ACCOUNT *Depreciation Expense* ACCOUNT NO. 518

DATE	ITEMS	POST. REF.	✓	DEBITS	DATE	ITEMS	POST. REF.	✓	CREDITS
1971 Dec 31		CJ35		232 19	1971 Dec 31		CJ36		1144 75
31		CJ35		912 56					
				1144 75					
				1144 75					1144 75

ACCOUNT *Charitable Contributions Expense* ACCOUNT NO. 519

DATE	ITEMS	POST. REF.	✓	DEBITS	DATE	ITEMS	POST. REF.	✓	CREDITS
1971 Dec 1	Balance	✓		288 00	1971 Dec 31		CJ36		316 00
13		CJ33		25 00					
31		CJ34		3 00					
				316 00					
				316 00					316 00

ACCOUNT *Miscellaneous Expense* ACCOUNT NO. 520

DATE	ITEMS	POST. REF.	✓	DEBITS	DATE	ITEMS	POST. REF.	✓	CREDITS
1971 Dec 1	Balance	✓		269 40	1971 Dec 31		CJ36		341 50
2		CJ33		15 25					
14		CJ33		50 00					
31		CJ34		6 85					
				341 50					
				341 50					341 50

Harold R. Stewart — Partial General Ledger (Concluded)

If the old general ledger is to be used for the new year, the open accounts either may or may not be ruled. If they are not ruled, the December 31 balance automatically becomes the balance on January 1. The open accounts, however, may be ruled with a double line under all the columns except the "Items" columns. The number of the new year should be

ACCOUNT First National Bank   ACCOUNT NO. 11

DATE	ITEMS	POST. REF.	✓	DEBITS	DATE	ITEMS	POST. REF.	✓	CREDITS
1971 Dec 1	Balance	✓		9 100 27	1971 Dec 31		cj34		4 254 41
31		cj34		2 932 18	31	Balance	✓		7 778 04
				1 203 245					1 203 245
				1 203 245					1 203 245
1972 Jan 1	Balance	✓		7 778 04					

ACCOUNT FICA Taxes Payable   ACCOUNT NO. 23

DATE	ITEMS	POST. REF.	✓	DEBITS	DATE	ITEMS	POST. REF.	✓	CREDITS
1971 Dec 14		cj33		98 80	1971 Dec 1	Balance	✓		98 80
31	Balance	✓		98 80	Dec 31		cj34		98 80
				1 97 60					1 97 60
				1 97 60					1 97 60
					1972 Jan 1	Balance	✓		98 80

ACCOUNT Harold R. Stewart, Capital   ACCOUNT NO. 31

DATE	ITEMS	POST. REF.	✓	DEBITS	DATE	ITEMS	POST. REF.	✓	CREDITS
1971 Dec 31		cj36		14 655 40	1971 Dec 1	Balance	✓		12 111 43
31	Balance	✓		11 449 03	31		cj36		13 993 00
				26 104 43					26 104 43
				26 104 43					26 104 43
					1972 Jan 1	Balance	✓		11 449 03

Harold R. Stewart — Balancing and Ruling Open Accounts

entered below the double ruling and the account balance, dated January 1, should be brought down in the Debits or Credits column depending upon whether the account has a debit or credit balance.

To illustrate the procedure in ruling open accounts when the old ledger is to be used for the new year, the following accounts in Mr. Stewart's ledger are reproduced above.

First National Bank, Account No. 11
FICA Taxes Payable, Account No. 23
Harold R. Stewart, Capital, Account No. 31

Account No. 11, First National Bank, has a debit balance of $7,778.04 which was brought down in the Debits column on a line dated January 1. This debit balance must be included when the balance of the account is determined at the end of January. It will not be necessary to rule the ledger at the end of January, since the amount of the balance in the account on January 31 automatically becomes the beginning balance for the month of February, and so on throughout the year. The reason for the change in procedure at the end of the year is that it is necessary to make a formal closing of the income statement accounts at the end of the year and if it is decided to rule the open accounts, it is necessary to carry the balances of the balance sheet accounts into the new year as beginning balances.

Account No. 23, FICA Taxes Payable, has a credit balance of $98.80. This balance was brought down in the Credits column on a line dated January 1.

Account No. 31, Harold R. Stewart, Capital, has a credit balance of $11,449.03 which was brought down in the Credits column. The balance represents Mr. Stewart's equity in his law practice on January 1.

Trial Balance After Closing

A trial balance of the general ledger accounts that remain open after the temporary owner's equity accounts have been closed is usually referred to as a *post-closing trial balance*. The purpose of the post-closing trial balance is to prove that the general ledger is in balance at the beginning of a new accounting period. It is advisable to know that such is the case before any transactions for the new accounting period are recorded.

The post-closing trial balance should contain the same accounts and amounts as appear in the Balance Sheet columns of the work sheet, except that (1) the owner's drawing account is omitted because it has been closed, and (2) the owner's capital account has been adjusted for the amount of the net income (or net loss) and the amount of his drawings.

A post-closing trial balance of Mr. Stewart's general ledger is shown on page 183. Some accountants advocate that the post-closing trial balance should be dated as of the close of the old accounting period, while others advocate that it should be dated as of the beginning of the new accounting period. In this illustration the trial balance is dated December 31, the end of the period.

The Accounting Cycle

The steps involved in handling the effect of all transactions and events completed during an accounting period, beginning with entries in the the books of original entry and ending with the post-closing trial balance, are known as the *accounting cycle*. The following is a list of the steps in the accounting cycle.

(a) Journalizing the transactions.
(b) Posting to the ledger accounts.
(c) Taking a trial balance.
(d) Determining the needed adjustments.

HAROLD R. STEWART, ATTORNEY AT LAW
Post-Closing Trial Balance
December 31, 1971

Account	Acct. No.	Debit Balance	Credit Balance
First National Bank......................	11	$7,778.04	
Petty Cash Fund.........................	12	50.00	
Advances on Behalf of Clients..............	13	215.00	
Office Equipment.........................	14	2,942.05	
Accumulated Depreciation — Office Equipment.	014		$ 626.90
Automobile..............................	15	3,650.23	
Accumulated Depreciation — Automobile......	015		2,281.39
Employees' Income Taxes Payable	22		174.40
FICA Taxes Payable......................	23		98.80
FUTA Taxes Payable......................	24		.75
State Unemployment Taxes Payable.........	25		4.05
Harold R. Stewart, Capital................	31		11,449.03
		$14,635.32	$14,635.32

(e) Completing an end-of-period work sheet.

(f) Preparing an income statement and a balance sheet.

(g) Journalizing and posting the adjusting and closing entries.

(h) Taking a post-closing trial balance.

In visualizing the accounting cycle, it is important to realize that steps (c) through (h) in the foregoing list are performed *as of the last day of the accounting period.* This does not mean that they necessarily are done *on* the last day. The accountant or bookkeeper may not be able to do any of these things until the first few days of the next period. Nevertheless, the work sheet, statements, and entries are prepared or recorded as of the closing date. While the journalizing of transactions in the new period proceeds in regular fashion, it is not usual to post to the general ledger any entries relating to the new period until the steps relating to the period just ended have been completed.

Income and Self-Employment Taxes

An unincorporated business or professional practice is not subject to income taxes. The owner — not the business or practice — is subject to income taxes and he must report the amounts of business or professional revenue and expenses in his personal income tax return regardless of the amount of money or other property he has actually withdrawn from the enterprise during the year. In the case of a sole proprietorship or a partnership, there is no legal distinction between the enterprise and the owner.

In order to bring a large class of self-employed individuals into the federal social security program, the law requires all self-employed persons (except those specifically exempted) to pay a self-employment tax. Currently the rate of tax is 2.3 percent more than the prevailing FICA rate. (With a combined FICA tax rate of 5.2 percent, the self-employment tax rate is 7.5 percent.) The tax is applied to "self-employment income" up to a maximum of $9,000. The rate and base of the tax may be changed by Act of Congress at any time. In general, *self-employment income* means the net income of a professional practice or business conducted by an individual or a partner's distributive share of the net income of a partnership whether or not any cash is distributed. Earnings of less than $400 from self-employment are ignored.

A taxable year for the purpose of the tax on self-employment income is the same as the taxpayer's taxable year for federal income tax purposes. The self-employment tax is reported along with the regular federal income tax. For calendar-year taxpayers, the tax return and full or final payment is due on April 15 following the close of the year. Like the personal income tax, the self-employment tax is treated as a personal expense of the owner. If the taxes are paid with business funds, the amount should be charged to the owner's drawing account.

Report No. 15

Complete Report No. 15 in the workbook and submit your working papers to the instructor for approval. You will then be given instructions as to the work to be done next.

chapters 5-8

practical accounting problems

Problem 5-A

Mr. Charles Owens, Miss Helen Courtney, and Mr. William Harris decide to form a partnership for the practice of law. The firm will be known as Owens, Courtney, and Harris. Miss Jean Leonard has been hired as a secretary and Miss Rita Johnson has been hired as a secretary-bookkeeper. It has been decided that the firm's books will be kept on the cash basis and that the books of account will be a combined cash journal and a general ledger. There are several auxiliary records which are not involved in this problem. The following transactions were completed during the month of July:

July 1. The partners invested the following amounts in the enterprise and opened an account in the Security National Bank:

Charles Owens...................................	$15,000
Helen Courtney..................................	$12,000
William Harris..................................	$ 5,000

Mr. Harris also contributed an automobile valued at $3,200. (In the combined cash journal debit Automobile and credit William Harris, Capital.)

July 1. Paid William Morse for rent for July, $500.
 2. Purchased supplies for cash, $85.10.
 6. Received payment for drawing a will for Louis Kent, $35.00.
 8. Paid the State Bar Association for annual dues for the three partners, $150.
 12. The firm was engaged to represent Acme Products Co. in the lawsuit of Acme Products Co. against George Henderson. Received retainer, $200.
 15. Paid wages of employees for first half of month as follows:
  Rita Johnson, $300 less income taxes payable $43.90 and FICA taxes payable $15.60.
  Jean Leonard, $250 less income taxes payable $34.00 and FICA taxes payable $13.00.
 19. Paid Modern Law Book Co. for law books purchased, $3,227.35.
 21. Drafted a partnership agreement for Kelly and Hanson, stockbrokers. Received $250.
 23. Paid City Oil Co. for repairs on automobile used for professional purposes, $73.20.
 27. Paid Quality Office Furniture Co. for office furniture and equipment purchased, $4,877.92.
 29. Paid Richards Insurance Agency for a three-year insurance policy on the law library and furniture and equipment, $192.35.
 30. Paid wages of employees for second half of month as follows:
  Rita Johnson, $300 less income taxes payable $43.90 and FICA taxes payable $15.60.
  Jean Leonard, $250 less income taxes payable $34.00 and FICA taxes payable $13.00.

REQUIRED: (1) Record each transaction in the combined cash journal using the following accounts:

100 Security National Bank	300 Charles Owens, Capital
110 Supplies	310 Helen Courtney, Capital
130 Law Library	320 William Harris, Capital
140 Office Furniture and	400 Legal Fees
Equipment	500 Automobile Expense
150 Automobile	510 Insurance Expense
200 Employees' Income Taxes	520 Miscellaneous Expense
Payable	530 Rent Expense
210 FICA Taxes Payable	540 Salary Expense

For the combined cash journal, use a sheet of paper like that shown in the illustration on pages 124 and 125. A column for collection fees will not be needed in this problem. Number the page of the journal. (2) Prove the combined cash journal by footing the amount columns; then total and rule the journal. (3) Open the necessary accounts using account forms like those illustrated on pages 128–131. Post the combined cash journal entries for July, foot the accounts, and enter the balances. (4) Take a trial balance as of July 31, using a sheet of two-column journal paper.

Problem 5-B

The law firm of Kennedy and Field has seventeen employees. The employees are paid by checks on the 15th and last business day of each month. The entry to record each payroll includes the liabilities for the amounts withheld. The employer's payroll taxes are recorded on each payday. The social security and withheld income taxes exceed $2,000 a month by the end of the month, and it is therefore necessary for Kennedy and Field to deposit the taxes each month within three banking days of the last day of the month. Thus the taxes for January must be paid within three banking days following January 31.

Following is a narrative of the transactions completed during the month of February of the current year that relate to payrolls and payroll taxes:

Feb. 2. Paid $3,597.57 for January's payroll taxes:

Employees' income taxes withheld.........	$2,059.32	
FICA taxes...........................	1,538.25	

15. Payroll for the first half of month:

Total salaries.........................		$7,383.33
Less amounts withheld:		
Employees' income taxes...............	$1,029.40	
FICA taxes.........................	383.93	1,413.33
Net amount paid......................		$5,970.00

15. Social security taxes imposed on employer:

FICA taxes @ 5.2%
State unemployment taxes @ 2.5%
FUTA taxes @ .5%

26. Payroll for second half of month:

Total salaries.........................		$7,423.33
Less amounts withheld:		
Employees' income taxes...............	$1,037.80	
FICA taxes.........................	386.01	1,423.81
Net amount paid......................		$5,999.52

26. Social security taxes imposed on employer:

All salaries taxable; rates same as on February 15.

REQUIRED: **(1)** Journalize the foregoing transactions, using two-column general journal paper. **(2)** Foot the debit and credit amount columns as a means of proof.

Problem 5-C

Eugene Whittier and John Yates are partners engaged in the practice of law. They employ a secretary and a secretary-bookkeeper. The books, which are kept on the cash basis, consist of a combined cash journal and a general ledger. For the combined cash journal, use a sheet of paper like that shown in the illustration on pages 124 and 125. A column for collection fees will not be needed in this journal. Number the page of the journal using number 29. The trial balance taken as of May 31, 19— follows:

WHITTIER AND YATES — ATTORNEYS AT LAW
Trial Balance
May 31, 19—

Cash	100	$13,815.43	
Petty Cash	101	50.00	
Law Library	120	8,835.41	
Accumulated Depreciation — Law Library	125		$ 3,145.18
Furniture and Equipment	130	5,927.42	
Accumulated Depreciation — Furn. and Equip.	135		1,123.27
Employees' Income Taxes Payable	200		155.80
FICA Taxes Payable	210		114.40
State Unemployment Taxes Payable	220		59.40
FUTA Taxes Payable	230		27.50
Eugene Whittier, Capital	300		11,027.46
Eugene Whittier, Drawing	310	6,000.00	
John Yates, Capital	320		8,929.29
John Yates, Drawing	330	5,000.00	
Legal Fees	400		25,122.00
Insurance Expense	500	254.62	
Payroll Tax Expense	510	462.00	
Rent Expense	520	3,000.00	
Salary Expense	530	5,500.00	
Stationery and Supplies Expense	540	380.22	
Utilities Expense	550	479.20	
		$49,704.30	$49,704.30

NARRATIVE OF TRANSACTIONS FOR JUNE

June 1. Paid rent for June, $600.

2. Paid the following bills:
   Telephone bill, $65.82
   Electric bill, $17.63

3. Received $1,500 from the U.S. Government. Mr. Whittier acted as an expert witness before a government committee.

7. Received $1,275 from Philip Meloni for balance due on Case No. 221.

9. Paid cash for office supplies, $35.10.

10. Received $400 for work in connection with the incorporation of the Thomas Manufacturing Corporation.

14. Paid the Internal Revenue Service as follows for May payroll taxes:

Employees' income taxes withheld	$155.80
FICA taxes	114.40
	$270.20

June 15. Paid wages of employees for first half of month as follows:

$300 less income taxes payable $43.90, and FICA taxes payable $15.60.

$250 less income taxes payable $34.00, and FICA taxes payable $13.00.

17. Received $780 from Ramsay and Shulman for balance due on Case No. 219.

21. Paid for additions to the law library, $227.81.

23. Received $350 for work in connection with planning the estate of A. G. Hermann.

24. Received $50 for drawing a will for Raphael Sanchez.

25. Received $50.35 for overcharge on law books purchased in May. (Law Library, Account No. 120, had been charged for the total amount of the invoice.)

28. Received $700 for work in connection with preparing a pension plan for the Star Manufacturing Co.

30. Paid wages of employees for the second half of the month as follows:

$300 less income taxes payable $43.90, and FICA taxes payable $15.60.

$265 less income taxes payable $35.80, and FICA taxes payable $13.78.

30. Mr. Whittier withdrew $1,200 for personal use.

30. Mr. Yates withdrew $1,000 for personal use.

30. Replenished the petty cash fund. The following disbursements had been made:

Stationery and Supplies Expense	$12.49
Utilities Expense — Collect telegram	2.27
John Yates, Drawing	18.56
Total Disbursements	$33.32

30. Made an entry in the combined cash journal for the employer's portion of the FICA tax and for the state unemployment tax and for the FUTA tax for the month of June by debiting Payroll Tax Expense for $93.67 and crediting FICA Taxes Payable for $57.98, State Unemployment Taxes Payable for $30.11 and FUTA Taxes Payable for $5.58.

REQUIRED: (1) Record each transaction in the combined cash journal. (2) Prove the combined cash journal by footing the amount columns; total and rule the journal. (3) Open the necessary general ledger accounts using account forms like those illustrated on pages 128–131. Record the June 1 balances as shown in the May 31 trial balance and complete the individual posting from the combined cash journal. Determine the balances of the accounts. (4) Take a trial balance as of June 30, using a sheet of two-column journal paper.

Problem 6-A

Dr. Philip Oliveri is engaged in the practice of medicine and surgery. The only book of original entry is a combined cash journal. A general ledger is kept and also several auxiliary records including a daily service record and a patients' ledger. Dr. Oliveri has one employee, a secretary, Alma Weaver, who also keeps the books. The books are kept on the cash basis. The trial balance as of January 31 follows:

DR. PHILIP OLIVERI — PHYSICIAN AND SURGEON
Trial Balance
January 31, 19—

First National Bank	100	$ 3,418.46	
Professional Equipment	120	10,117.85	
Accumulated Depreciation — Prof. Equip.	121		$ 4,629.42
Office Equipment	130	2,721.35	
Accumulated Depreciation — Office Equip.	131		960.48
Automobile	140	3,807.91	
Accumulated Depreciation — Automobile	141		1,051.72
Employees' Income Taxes Payable	200		78.00
FICA Taxes Payable	210		62.40
FUTA Taxes Payable	220		3.00
Philip Oliveri, Capital	300		7,568.95
Philip Oliveri, Drawing	310	810.15	
Professional Fees	400		8,125.00
Automobile Expense	500	145.72	
Laundry Expense	510	35.25	
Miscellaneous Expense	520	19.85	
Payroll Tax Expense	530	34.20	
Professional Supplies Expense	540	126.64	
Rent Expense	550	500.00	
Salary Expense	560	600.00	
Stationery and Office Supplies Expense	570	30.95	
Telephone and Telegraph Expense	580	35.49	
Utilities Expense	590	75.15	
		$22,478.97	$22,478.97

NARRATIVE OF TRANSACTIONS FOR FEBRUARY

Feb. 1. Paid rent for February, $500.

3. Paid oil company bill for January, $59.70.

4. Paid for professional equipment, $3,515.82.

6. The amount columns in the daily service record for the week ended February 6 contained the following totals:

Kind of service

Office calls	$ 80.00
Surgery	1,150.00
Total	$1,230.00

Feb. 6. Patients' accounts — Charges....................... $1,180.00
      Cash services.................................... 50.00
        Total....................................... $1,230.00

The total cash received from patients during the week ended February 6 was:

Payments....................................... $ 800.00
Cash services.................................... 50.00
    Total... $ 850.00

8. Paid laundry bill for January, $32.27.

10. Paid the following bills:
    Gas and electric bill, $65.32.
    Water bill, $12.48.

10. Paid for professional supplies, $61.22.

13. The amount columns in the daily service record contained the following totals:

Kind of service
    Office calls.................................... $ 85.00
    Surgery.. 1,700.00
        Total....................................... $1,785.00

Patients' accounts — Charges.................... $1,765.00
Cash services.................................. 20.00
    Total....................................... $1,785.00

The total cash received from patients during the week ended February 13 was:

Payments....................................... $1,295.00
Cash services.................................... 20.00
    Total... $1,315.00

15. Paid salary to Alma Weaver for first half of month, $300 less income taxes payable, $39.00, and FICA taxes payable, $15.60.

17. Paid for professional supplies, $70.15.

18. Paid telephone bill, $34.67.

19. Paid for automobile repairs, $85.35.

20. The amount columns in the daily service record contained the following totals:

Kind of service
    Office calls.................................... $ 75.00
    Surgery.. 1,485.00
        Total....................................... $1,560.00

Patients' accounts — Charges.................... $1,548.00
Cash services.................................. 12.00
    Total....................................... $1,560.00

Feb. 20. The total cash received from patients during the week ended February 20 was:

Payments...................................... $1,935.00
Cash services.................................. 12.00
　Total....................................... $1,947.00

24. Paid for stationery and supplies, $25.70.

26. Paid the American Medical Association for a subscription to a professional journal, $12. (Charge Miscellaneous Expense.)

27. Dr. Oliveri withdrew $1,000 for personal use.

27. Paid salary to Alma Weaver for second half of the month, $300 less income taxes payable, $39.00, and FICA taxes payable, $15.60.

27. The amount columns in the daily service record contained the following totals:

Kind of service

Office calls................................... $ 110.00
Surgery....................................... 1,520.00
　Total....................................... $1,630.00

Patients' accounts — Charges.................. $1,610.00
Cash services................................. 20.00
　Total....................................... $1,630.00

The total cash received from patients for the week ended February 27 was:

Payments...................................... $3,150.00
Cash services................................. 20.00
　Total....................................... $3,170.00

27. Made an entry in the combined cash journal for the employer's portion of the FICA tax and for the FUTA tax for the month of February by debiting Payroll Tax Expense and by crediting FICA Taxes Payable for $31.20 and FUTA Taxes Payable for $3.00.

REQUIRED: (1) Record the transactions in the combined cash journal using a sheet of paper like that illustrated on pages 144–147. (2) Prove the journal by footing the amount columns; total and rule the journal. (3) Open the necessary general ledger accounts using account forms like those illustrated on pages 149–155. Record the February 1 balances as shown on the January 31 trial balance and complete the posting from the combined cash journal. Determine the balances of the accounts. (4) Take a trial balance using a sheet of two-column journal paper.

Problem 6-B

John C. Lang and Terence A. Lang, physicians and surgeons, operate a clinic known as the Lang Clinic. They employ five other physicians and seven other employees. The books are closed each year as of December

31, but interim statements are prepared monthly. The following information is presented so that certain entries can be made in the month of April:

(a) Apr. 18.	Employees' income taxes withheld from wages paid on April 15......		$1,496.60
	FICA taxes		
	Withheld from employees' wages.....................	$351.00	
	Imposed on employer..........	351.00	702.00
			$2,198.60

The Lang Clinic is required to deposit the income and FICA taxes withheld and the employer's share of the FICA taxes within three banking days of the fifteenth and of the last day of each month, since the cumulative unpaid tax is more than $2,000 on the fifteenth and on the last day of the month.

(b)   29. State unemployment tax due for quarter ending March 31 $858.60.

(c)   30. Payroll tax expense for the month of April:

FICA tax............................	$702.00
State unemployment tax.................	$113.40
FUTA tax............................	$ 16.80

(d)   30. Statement of petty cash disbursements for April:

Terence Lang, Drawing..................	$ 14.85
Automobile Expense.....................	13.50
Miscellaneous Expense...................	40.27
Professional Supplies Expense.............	10.16
Stationery and Office Supplies Expense...	5.77
Total Disbursements...................	$ 84.55

REQUIRED: Prepare entries in general journal form to record the information given above.

Problem 6-C

Dr. Raymond Burton, a physician and surgeon, keeps his books on the cash basis. A trial balance taken as of August 31, 19— does not balance. A check of the records reveals the following information:

(1) The correct total of the First State Bank Dr. column in the combined cash journal is $5,694. This amount was posted in the cash account in the general ledger as $5,649.

(2) The combined cash journal was out of balance by $169 because a payment for professional supplies was charged to the proper account, but was not entered in the First State Bank Cr. column.

(3) The balance in the office equipment account was entered in the trial balance as $260 instead of the correct figure of $2,600.

(4) The miscellaneous expense account in the amount of $114.00 was omitted from the trial balance.

(5) All accounts have normal balances.

DR. RAYMOND BURTON

Trial Balance

August 31, 19—

First State Bank..............................	$12,368.00	
Professional Equipment........................	15,215.00	
Accumulated Depreciation — Professional Equipment.		$ 4,735.00
Office Equipment..............................	260.00	
Accumulated Depreciation — Office Equipment......		792.00
Employees' Income Taxes Payable................		96.00
FICA Taxes Payable...........................		62.00
FUTA Taxes Payable...........................		24.00
Raymond Burton, Capital.......................		9,110.00
Raymond Burton, Drawing......................	12,250.00	
Professional Fees..............................		44,215.00
Payroll Tax Expense...........................		276.00
Professional Supplies Expense....................		1,300.00
Rent Expense.................................	9,600.00	
Salary Expense...............................	4,855.00	
Utilities Expense..............................	580.00	
	$55,128.00	$60,610.00

REQUIRED: Prepare a corrected trial balance.

Problem 7-A

Albert Lewis and Anthony Sardis have formed a partnership for the practice of civil engineering. They employ ten engineers and draftsmen, a secretary, and a secretary-bookkeeper. The partners share profits and losses equally. The Trial Balance columns of the work sheet for the current year ended December 31 are shown on the next page.

Note: Problems 7-B and 8-A are based on the work sheet for Lewis and Sardis. If these problems are to be solved, the work sheet should be retained for reference until they are solved, when the solutions of all three problems may be submitted to the instructor.

REQUIRED: Prepare a ten-column work sheet making the necessary entries in the Adjustments columns to record the following:

Depreciation:
Furniture and equipment, 10% a year, $1,342.80.
Professional equipment, 10% a year, $1,201.36.
Automotive equipment, 25% a year, $5,119.53.

LEWIS AND SARDIS
Work Sheet
For the Year Ended December 31, 19—

Account	Acct. No.	Trial Balance Debits	Trial Balance Credits
Cash................................	100	27,264.38	
Petty Cash...........................	101	50.00	
Furniture and Equipment..................	140	13,427.98	
Accumulated Depreciation — Furn. and Equip..	141		1,845.02
Professional Equipment..................	150	12,013.62	
Accumulated Depreciation — Prof. Equip......	151		943.67
Automotive Equipment...................	160	20,478.13	
Accumulated Depreciation — Auto.Equipment..	161		3,782.15
Employees' Income Taxes Payable...........	220		1,259.20
FICA Taxes Payable.....................	230		828.00
FUTA Taxes Payable....................	240		7.50
State Unemployment Taxes Payable.........	250		40.50
Albert Lewis, Capital...................	300		22,392.67
Albert Lewis, Drawing...................	310	12,415.30	
Anthony Sardis, Capital.................	320		21,849.73
Anthony Sardis, Drawing.................	330	13,079.20	
Expense and Revenue Summary.............	340		
Professional Fees......................	400		162,425.00
Automotive Expense.....................	500	2,462.30	
Depreciation Expense....................	505		
Insurance Expense......................	510	550.35	
Miscellaneous Expense..................	515	372.93	
Payroll Tax Expense....................	520	5,382.00	
Rent Expense.........................	525	12,000.00	
Salary Expense........................	530	92,400.00	
Stationery, Supplies, and Blueprint Expense...	535	2,170.55	
Telephone and Telegraph Expense..........	540	528.70	
Charitable Contributions Expense...........	550	778.00	
		215,373.44	215,373.44

Problem 7-B

Refer to the work sheet for Lewis and Sardis (based on Problem 7-A) and from it prepare the following financial statements:

(1) An income statement for the year ended December 31.

(2) A balance sheet in account form as of December 31.

Problem 8-A

Refer to the work sheet for Lewis and Sardis (based on Problem 7-A) and draft the general journal entries required:

(1) To adjust the general ledger accounts so they will be in agreement with the financial statements.

(2) To close the temporary owner's equity accounts on December 31.

Problem 8-B (Complete cycle problem)

Arthur Hamilton and David Leonardi for several years have been partners engaged in the practice of architecture. They share profits and losses equally. The accounting records consist of a combined cash journal and a general ledger. The column headings in the combined cash journal are as follows:

Provident National Bank Dr.   General Dr.
Provident National Bank Cr.   General Cr.
Professional Fees Cr.
Stationery, Office, and Blueprint Supplies Expense Dr.
Salary Expense Dr.
Employees' Income Taxes Payable Cr.
FICA Taxes Payable Cr.

The accounts in the general ledger are in the two-column form.

The trial balance as of November 30 is on page 197. The trial balance includes all the accounts in the general ledger, some of which do not have balances as of November 30.

The firm employs seven persons, two architects, two draftsmen, two secretaries, and a secretary-bookkeeper.

NARRATIVE OF TRANSACTIONS FOR DECEMBER

Dec. 1. Paid the Grossman Realty Co. $3,000 for rent of the office for the month of December. Check No. 314.

1. Received $3,559 from A. H. Wells Co. for work completed.

2. Paid the Bell Telephone Co. bill, $180.13. Check No. 315.

6. Paid the Valley Gas and Electric Co. for November service, $175.15. Check No. 316.

6. Paid for gasoline and oil used in the company cars during November, $48.35. Check No. 317.

7. Received $2,525 from Superior Products Co. for work completed.

8. Paid the Professional Supply Co. for blueprint supplies, $139.85. Check No. 318.

8. Reimbursed Mr. Leonardi for expenses incurred in attending a professional meeting, $140.28. Check No. 319.

10. Paid the Roberts Insurance Agency $786 for a three-year professional liability insurance policy. Check No. 320.

HAMILTON AND LEONARDI, ARCHITECTS
Trial Balance
November 30, 19—

Provident National Bank	100	$ 39,790.04	
Petty Cash	101	75.00	
Office and Professional Equipment	140	26,314.28	
Accumulated Dep. — Office and Prof. Equip.	141		$ 4,925.72
Automobiles	145	7,865.10	
Accumulated Depreciation — Automobiles	146		4,021.36
Employees' Income Taxes Payable	205		807.60
FICA Taxes Payable	210		144.00
FUTA Taxes Payable	215		
State Unemployment Taxes Payable	220		
Arthur Hamilton, Capital	300		33,912.55
Arthur Hamilton, Drawing	305	22,300.00	
David Leonardi, Capital	310		31,478.85
David Leonardi, Drawing	315	20,150.00	
Expense and Revenue Summary	340		
Professional Fees	400		161,026.59
Automobile Expense	500	1,760.14	
Charitable Contributions Expense	505	4,972.00	
Depreciation Expense	510		
Heat, Light, Power, and Water Expense	515	2,569.70	
Insurance Expense	520	822.37	
Miscellaneous Expense	525	341.70	
Payroll Tax Expense	530	2,910.00	
Rent Expense	535	33,000.00	
Repairs and Maintenance Expense	540	1,830.50	
Salary Expense	545	63,433.37	
Stationery, Office, and Blueprint Sup. Exp.	550	3,420.72	
Telephone and Telegraph Expense	555	1,876.20	
Travel and Entertainment Expense	560	2,885.55	
		$236,316.67	$236,316.67

Dec. 13. Paid the following payroll taxes based on wages paid during the month of November by sending Check No. 321 in the amount of $951.60 to the Provident National Bank.

Employees' income taxes withheld from wages		$807.60
FICA taxes:		
Withheld from employees' wages	$72.00	
Imposed on employer	72.00	144.00
Total		$951.60

A Federal Tax Deposit, Form 501, was filled out and sent with the check.

Dec. 13. Paid the Valley Country Club $30.25 for entertainment of a client. Check No. 322.

14. Paid the Acme Cleaning Co. $145 for office cleaning services rendered during November. Check No. 323.

14. Received $1,700 from Edward Murphy for work completed.

15. Paid salaries for the first half of the month, $2,883.34 less employees' withholding taxes, $403.80, and FICA taxes payable, $36.00. Checks No. 324–330 inclusive were issued for the net amounts payable to the employees.

15. Paid the Square Deal Garage $89.75 for repairs to one of the company cars. Check No. 331.

16. Paid the Harper Stationery Co. $145 for stationery and supplies. Check No. 332.

17. Received $8,300 from Jackson County in payment for work completed.

20. Contributed $25.00 to the Community Christmas Fund. Check No. 333. Charge Charitable Contributions Expense, Account No. 505.

21. Paid the Jackson County Water Authority $55.70 for November service. Check No. 334.

22. Received $7,000 from the Jackson County Airport for work completed.

23. Paid the balance due on the pledge to the United Fund, $500. Check No. 335. Charge Charitable Contributions Expense, Account No. 505.

23. Paid the Fine Line Furniture Co. $1,850 for office furniture. Check No. 336. Charge Office and Professional Equipment, Account No. 140.

28. Paid the Modern Stationery Co. $55.67 for office supplies. Check No. 337.

30. Paid the Provident National Bank $15 for annual rental of a safe deposit box for use of the partnership. Check No. 338. Charge Miscellaneous Expense, Account No. 525.

30. Paid the Sherwood Office Equipment Co. $25.50 for typewriter repairs. Check No. 339.

31. Mr. Hamilton withdrew $1,200 for personal use. Check No. 340.

31. Mr. Leonardi withdrew $1,100 for personal use. Check No. 341.

31. Paid salaries for the second half of the month, $2,883.34 less employees' withholding taxes, $403.80, and FICA taxes payable, $36.00. Checks No. 342–348 inclusive were issued for the net amounts payable to the employees.

31. Issued Check No. 349 to replenish the petty cash fund. A statement of petty cash disbursements for December follows:

Arthur Hamilton, Drawing...................	$10.00
Automobile Expense.........................	12.25
Charitable Contributions Expense.................	5.00
Miscellaneous Expense.......................	7.35
Stationery, Office, and Blueprint Supplies Expense...	3.70
Travel and Entertainment Expense.................	32.86
	$71.16

Dec. 31. Made an entry in the combined cash journal for the employer's portion of the FICA tax for the month of December, $72.00.

REQUIRED: (1) Journalize the December transactions. (2) Open the necessary general ledger accounts and record the December 1 balances, using the November 30 trial balance as the source of the needed information. Complete the individual and summary posting from the combined cash journal. (3) Take a trial balance of the general ledger accounts and enter the figures in the first two columns of a ten-column work sheet. (4) Complete the ten-column work sheet making the required adjustments from the information given below.

Depreciation:
Office and professional equipment, 10% a year, $2,631.43 based on the balance at the beginning of the year. No depreciation is taken this year on the purchase of December 23.
Automobiles, 25% a year, $1,966.28.

(5) Prepare an income statement for the year ending December 31 and a balance sheet in report form as of December 31. (6) Record the adjusting entries in the combined cash journal and post. (7) Record the closing entries in the combined cash journal and post. The page numbers of the combined cash journal begin with No. 12. (8) Take a post-closing trial balance.

appendix

automated accounting systems and procedures

Structure of Accounting Systems

The design of a system of books and records depends in large measure on the nature of the enterprise by which the system is used. The number of transactions to be recorded in a given time period has much to do with the planning and arrangement of the chart of accounts and of the procedures for gathering and processing transaction information. Physical location of factory buildings and warehouses and the transaction volume at each location also influence the design of an accounting system.

The nature of the enterprise, the kinds of transactions to be recorded and summarized, the transaction volume, and the location of physical facilities together comprise the *structure* of an accounting system. All of these factors together make careful systems planning essential.

The Language of Automated Accounting Systems

The original or immediate records of many kinds of business transactions have been presented in this textbook. The receipt has been discussed as the immediate record of a cash received transaction. The check stub has been discussed and illustrated as the immediate record of a cash payment transaction. The immediate record is always the key record in an automated accounting system just as it is in a manual accounting system.

Whether an immediate record is prepared by hand or by machine, the data which it contains must be collected and recorded by people. In automated accounting the immediate record is usually referred to as the *source document*.

Some modern businesses are quite large, and this relative size affects their accounting systems. Modern systems for relatively large businesses include some equipment, called *automated equipment*, that operates without human guidance other than the press of a button. The use of such equipment in an accounting system makes it an *automated accounting system*.

Automated accounting has brought about the development of a new language as well as new procedures. In automated accounting, information such as ledger account titles, dollar amounts, and physical quantities is known as *data*. The use of these data in different ways for different business purposes is known as *data processing*. Accounting involves the processing of data in several different forms. In fact, the original preparation of the source document for a business transaction is a form of data processing. Likewise, the recording of transactions in books of original entry, posting to ledger accounts, taking trial balances, and preparing financial statements are also forms of data processing.

Those who use automated equipment to process accounting records must apply accounting principles to each step. The same principles of debit and credit apply whether the work is done with automated equipment, with conventional accounting machines, or by the manual bookkeeper. Equipment and machines are merely tools of the accountant. Such tools reduce routine manual work, increase the speed of producing records, and permit more accurate financial reporting.

Data processing is usually described in two ways. The processing of business transactions by the use of simple office machines with card punches or tape punches attached is known as *integrated data processing* (IDP). The processing of business transactions by the use of an electronic computer is known as *electronic data processing* (EDP).

The Write-It-Once Principle as a Laborsaving Device

A source document, such as a purchase invoice or a sales ticket, usually is prepared manually by handwriting or typing on the document at the time of the transaction. The first step in automated accounting is the preparation of some form of input media by a machine operator from a source document. The most common forms of input media are punched cards, punched paper tape, magnetic tape, and paper with symbols printed in magnetic ink.

If the operator types the source document on an office machine with a card punching or tape punching attachment, the card or tape is being punched at the same time that the source document is being typed. If the office machine used is not an integrated data processing machine, the card or tape must be punched later as a separate operation.

The process of recording the basic information about a business transaction in a form that makes later hand copying unnecessary has been called the *write-it-once principle*. This first step in automated accounting makes it possible to save labor in completing the later steps of the accounting cycle. Once a punched card or a punched paper tape has been prepared by a machine operator, the recorded information can be used over and over again when and where needed. The only further human effort needed is to feed the cards or tape into automatic machines. These machines then perform automatically the functions of journalizing, posting, taking trial balances, preparing financial statements, and adjusting and closing ledger accounts.

Importance of Locating Errors in the Write-It-Once Operation

If errors in the punching of cards or paper tape are not discovered before the cards or tape are fed into automated machines, such errors will be repeated in each step of the automated accounting cycle. The repetition of errors in this manner may pyramid with disastrous results.

Designers of automated accounting systems have recognized the seriousness of the error problem. Errors in automated systems are normally located in either of two ways:

      (a) Transaction information is verified as soon as it has been recorded.

      (b) Automatic error-locating procedures built into the automated accounting equipment are used later on in the accounting cycle.

Verifying transaction information already punched into cards or tape is a process of running the cards or tape through manually operated machines a second time. A different machine operator reads the information from the source document and goes through the same punching motions as did the original operator. If each punching stroke hits a hole in the card or tape, the card or tape passes right on through the machine. If a punching stroke hits a solid section of card or tape, an error is indicated, and the machine notches the edge of the card or tape next to the error. Notched cards or tapes are set aside and corrected later.

Businesses that find errors very difficult to control may decide not only to verify source document information before cards or tape are processed but also to use automatic error-locating procedures later in the accounting cycle. Automated accounting equipment also may be set up to locate certain errors electronically. When such errors are so located, an error light on the equipment usually goes on, and the equipment stops running.

Basic Phases of Automated Data Processing

The automated processing of any data in the completion of the accounting cycle consists of five basic phases. These five phases are common to all automated equipment, regardless of manufacturer. They are:

(a) Input   (d) Arithmetic
(b) Control   (e) Output
(c) Storage

A diagram of a basic automated data processing machine is shown below:

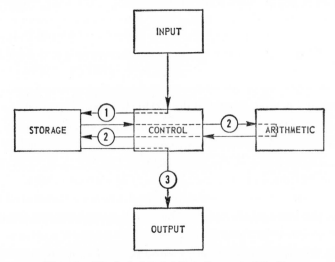

Diagram of Basic Automated Data Processing Machine

Input. In order that automated equipment may complete the accounting process, the immediate record must be rewritten in a form that the equipment can interpret. Information about a business transaction in a form acceptable for use in automated data processing equipment is known as *input*. Any acceptable means for presenting this information to an automated machine is known as an *input device*.

Input devices are fed into automated data processing machines to provide them with information about individual business transactions. The process by which an automated data processing machine receives information is similar in function to the intake of food by the human body.

Control. *Control* is the nerve center, or "action central" of the automated data processing system. It is like the central hall in a home or the lobby of a hotel. People must pass through the lobby of a hotel to get to their rooms. In the same way, transaction information must be routed through control in each step of automated data processing. Transaction information received as input is sent by control to storage, as shown by the flow line labeled "1" in the diagram on page A-4.

Storage. Transaction information stops in *storage* to await further use in automated accounting. Because storage holds information for future use just as does the human mind, it is often referred to as "memory." But unlike the human mind, storage must be told in great detail what to do with each item of transaction information that it holds. A detailed list of steps to be followed in completing the automated accounting cycle is known as a *program*. A person who designs programs is called a *programmer*. The detailed work of arranging transaction information in the most efficient manner for automated processing is called *programming*.

Arithmetic. The primary work of automated accounting is done in the *arithmetic* phase. Transaction information is routed from storage through control to arithmetic. In the arithmetic phase, addition, subtraction, multiplication, or division is performed as needed; and the result is returned by control to storage. This round trip is shown by the flow line labeled "2" in the basic automated machine diagram. Arithmetic also can compare two numbers and tell whether the first number is smaller than, equal to, or larger than the second number. This feature is useful in controlling inventories and expenses.

Output. When ledger account balances, financial statement items, or other data are desired, they are obtained from the automated data processing system in the output phase. Business information in a form acceptable for human use is known as *output*. Any acceptable means for converting coded machine information into English language is known as an *output device*.

Business information requested by management from the data processing system is routed from storage through control to output, as shown by the flow line labeled "3" in the basic automated machine diagram. Output devices are prepared which are used later to print in English the particular business information requested.

The Punched Card as an Input Device

At present, the punched card is the most frequently used input device. One form of punched card is the IBM (International Business Machines Corporation) card, illustrated at the top of page A-6.

Utility companies, oil companies, magazine publishers, and mail order houses use punched cards as statements of account. The federal

Standard IBM Card

government and many large private companies use punched cards for payroll checks and other remittance checks.

The small figures on the IBM card above show that it has 80 columns, numbered from left to right. The large figures on the card show that it has ten rows, numbered 0 to 9 inclusive from top to bottom. In addition, as the above illustration shows, the blank space at the top of the card provides room for two more rows, called the twelve row and the eleven row.

As shown by the punches in the illustration, a single numerical digit may be formed by punching a small hole in a column at one of the ten positions numbered zero through nine. A single letter or symbol may be formed by punching two holes in a column. One of these holes is punched through a position numbered one through nine. The other hole is punched through a position numbered twelve, eleven, or zero, as shown in the illustration above. The three top rows on the card are called the "zone" rows, and a hole punched in one of these rows is called a "zone" punch.

Planning the Use of the Punched Card. The first step in the use of a punched card as an input device is to plan the arrangement of the information on the card. A punched card that is to be used as a statement of account in a company selling merchandise will contain the following information:

(a) Customer's name and address   (e) Current sales to the customer
(b) Customer's account number   (f) Amount received on account
(c) Billing date   (g) Sales returns and allowances
(d) Customer's previous balance   (h) Customer's new balance

In a professional practice, a punched card might contain the following information:

(a) Client's or patient's name and address
(b) Client's or patient's account number

(c) Billing date

(d) Client's or patient's previous balance

(e) Current services rendered to the client or patient

(f) Amount received on account

(g) Adjustments to the account

(h) Client's or patient's new balance

Each item of information requires that several holes be punched into the card. An estimate is made of the longest group of letters or numbers required for each of the eight items to be placed on any statement of account. The punched card (or cards if two are needed) is then subdivided into eight groups of columns of sufficient size.

A group of columns used for a single item of information on a punched card is known as a *field*. There is a field for the customer's name and address, and a field for each of the other seven items of information.

Punching Information Into the Punched Card. After the information for preparing a customer's statement of account has been provided by the automated accounting system, a machine operator enters this information into a machine which in turn punches information holes into the card. One field on the card is used for each of the eight information items.

A machine used to punch information holes into punched cards from source documents is known as a *key punch*. The machine used has a keyboard very similar to a typewriter. An IBM key punch machine is illustrated below:

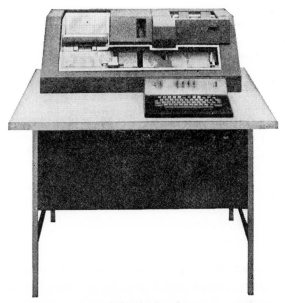

IBM Key Punch

Verifying the Information on the Punched Card. As soon as a batch of cards has been punched, the cards are checked in an attempt to avoid errors. A machine that looks exactly like a key punch and is used to find punching errors is called a *verifier*. As mentioned earlier, another operator reading from the same source document as the key punch operator enters the data into the verifier. The IBM verifier machine "feels" each card electronically to determine whether the correct holes have been punched. Each correct card is notched in a special "verify" position. If the verifier machine "feels" a missing hole or a hole in the wrong position, it notches a special "error" position on the card and the keyboard on the machine locks up.

Printing the Information on a Punched Card. The punched information on each IBM card is printed on a two-part statement card consisting of a statement and a stub. The printing is done by running the punched cards through a special printing machine. An automatic printing machine that lists, totals, and prints information previously punched onto cards is called a *tabulator* or *high-speed printer*. The information may either be printed on the same punched card from which it comes or on a separate sheet of paper.

Completing a Punched Card Statement of Account. After each of the two-part statement cards has been tabulated, the customer's account number and balance due are punched into the stub portion of the card. The statement card is then ready to be mailed to the customer. A completed two-part statement card is illustrated below:

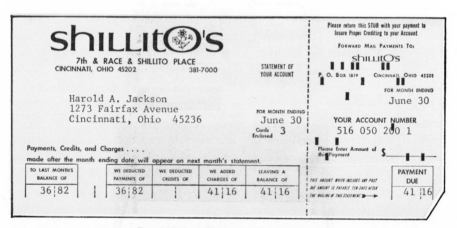

Punched Card Statement of Account

Sorting Customer Remittance Stubs. When the customer receives a statement like the one illustrated above, he detaches the stub and returns it with his remittance. When a remittance arrives, the amount received is keypunched into the stub that comes with the remittance. The stubs are then grouped into piles and run through a machine called a *sorter* which sorts them by customer's account number. A sorter in common use is illustrated below.

The stubs received from customers are placed in the hopper of the sorter. The hopper can be seen to extend from the upper right hand portion of the machine. The sorted stubs drop into the pockets that can be seen across the front of the machine. There is a "reject" pocket for cards that the machine is unable to sort.

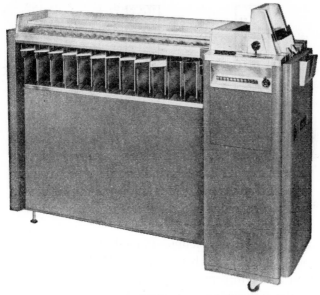

IBM Sorter

Posting Customer Remittance Stubs. The final process in accounting for customer remittances is to run the stubs through the printer or tabulator in account number order. This machine process posts the remittances to individual customers' ledger account cards and determines the new account balances.

The same basic operations are followed in processing punched card checks, except that cash payment transactions are involved rather than cash receipt transactions. The transaction information must still be keypunched, verified, printed, sorted, and posted. These are basic data processing operations in automated accounting.

Punched Paper Tape as an Input Device

Punched paper tape is used as an input device almost as much as the punched card. Punched paper tape was originally used in sending telegrams. A section of five-channel paper tape is shown on page A-10.

It can be seen from the illustration that holes are punched the length of the tape to record and store transaction data. Data can be stored more tightly on paper tape than on punched cards. This is because the holes are smaller and closer together. Reels of paper tape are easier to carry and require less storage space than punched cards.

Punched cards are better for arranging data in different ways, because they can be sorted in different ways. Once data is punched into paper tape, the arrangement of the data on the tape cannot be changed.

A	-		Q	1
B	$		R	4
C	N.P.		S	/
D	Tab		T	5
E	3		U	7
F			V	Punch Off
G	&		W	2
H			X	
I	8		Y	6
J	Error		Z	
K	P.R.		Space	
L			Carriage Return	
M			On 1, On 2	
N	,		Stop Code	
O	9		Letters Shift	
P	0		Figures Shift	

Friden Five-Channel Punched Paper Tape

Punched Paper Tape and IDP

Tape punching attachments often are found on typewriters, adding machines, and bookkeeping machines in modern offices. At the same time that an immediate record is being prepared, the punching attachment records the transaction information on tape for later automated processing.

An automatic writing machine with a tape-punching attachment is called a *flexowriter*. One model of flexowriter is shown below:

Friden Flexowriter

The flexowriter illustrates a practical application of IDP and the write-it-once principle. A tape can be punched along with the manual typing of a permanent record. Or, a permanent record can be automatically typed from a tape previously punched.

Magnetic Tape as an Input Device

Magnetic tape usually is used as an input device in EDP systems. It is prepared for input by depositing small magnetized spots on reels of tape. This tape comes from the factory coated with a magnetic metal substance.

The chief advantage of magnetic tape is the speed with which it can be used as input. Like paper tape, it is easy to carry and compact to store.

Magnetic Ink Symbol Numbers as Input Devices

As discussed in Chapter 3, the American Bankers Association recommends the use of symbol numbers printed in magnetic ink on each bank check. The use of these magnetic ink symbol numbers permits the automated processing of checks.

The use of magnetic ink symbol numbers in the processing of bank checks is called *magnetic ink character recognition.* The common abbreviation for this process is *MICR.* A bank check with magnetic ink symbol numbers printed across the bottom of the check is illustrated below:

No. 76   ST. LOUIS *County National* BANK   80-459 / 810

CLAYTON (ST. LOUIS) MO. *May 10* 19 71

PAY TO THE ORDER OF *Meyer's Hardware Store* $ 25 54

Twenty-five 54/100 ———————————————— DOLLARS

JOHN F. NELSON

John F. Nelson

⑈0810⭑04591⑈ 121 077 3⑆

Bank Check with Magnetic Ink Symbol Numbers

Note that the symbol numbers at the bottom of the check use a style that is different from regular Arabic numerals. This is because these numbers are read by a device that "feels" the surface area of each number and recognizes its shape. Regular Arabic numerals, especially 2, 5, 6, and 9, are too much alike to be easily distinguished one from the other by an electronic reading machine.

Encoding Symbol Numbers on Bank Checks. Magnetic ink symbol numbers are printed on checks using special printing machines. A special machine for printing magnetic ink characters on checks is called an *encoder.*

Encoding may be done by the company that prints the blank checks, or by the bank that supplies the blank checks to its depositors. Most banks have their check suppliers encode the appropriate symbol numbers on the checks.

Clearing Encoded Bank Checks Through the Federal Reserve System. The first series of encoded numerals in the check illustration (0810-0459) is adapted from the ABA number in the upper right-hand corner of the check. Notice that the number 80, which represents the State of Missouri, has been dropped from the encoded symbol number. This is because 0810 locates the bank in the Eighth Federal Reserve District (08) and the Greater St. Louis area (10), and the State of Missouri is understood.

The Federal Reserve system sorts checks encoded with magnetic ink symbol numbers as follows:

Step 1. The bank in which the check is deposited forwards it to the Federal Reserve clearing house in its district.

Step 2. The Federal Reserve clearing house sorts the check along with other checks received from banks in its district on special sorting equipment using the first two encoded symbol numbers (08 in the illustration). This results in twelve batches of checks for the twelve Federal Reserve districts.

Step 3. Each Federal Reserve clearing house forwards the checks drawn on banks in other Federal Reserve districts to the proper districts. In this process, the check illustrated on the previous page is forwarded to the Eighth Federal Reserve District clearing house in St. Louis.

Step 4. The clearing house in St. Louis sorts on the next two encoded symbol numbers (10 in the illustration) for distribution of the checks to regional clearing houses. Since the bank on which the illustrated check is drawn is a Greater St. Louis bank, this check is not forwarded to a regional clearing house.

Step 5. Each district or regional clearing house sorts on the next four symbol numbers (0459 in the illustration) for distribution to individual banks. These four symbol numbers are individual bank numbers.

Step 6. Batches of sorted checks are forwarded to the banks on which they were drawn. The illustrated check is sent to St. Louis County National Bank.

Processing Encoded Bank Checks in Individual Banks. The second series of encoded numerals on the illustrated check (121-077-3) is the account number of the individual depositor at his bank. The depositor's bank sorts its own checks by account number. It uses the same type of MICR sorting equipment as that used in the Federal Reserve clearing houses. This equipment can sort as many as 90,000 checks per hour, which is about 20 times faster than manual sorting.

In smaller banks, checks sorted by depositor's account number are posted by using conventional bank posting machines. Larger banks having encoders of their own print the amount of each check in magnetic ink under the signature line. This is done before the checks are sorted by depositor's account number. Encoding amounts of individual checks makes it possible to sort and post electronically to depositors' ledger accounts in one operation.

The Control Phase in Automated Accounting

The control phase of an electronic system receives commands from input devices and sees that they are carried out. These commands are received electronically. Each command refers to some item of transaction information which is in storage. The control phase searches storage locations one by one in carrying out commands from input devices.

The commands received from input devices are steps in the program to complete the automated accounting cycle. The control phase keeps track of the location of each command as it is carried out. This avoids skipping program steps.

The Storage Phase in Automated Accounting

In manual accounting, the journal, the ledger, and the trial balance are methods of storing transaction information. The journal in which a transaction is first recorded stores complete information about the transaction in one place. After a journal entry has been posted, the ledger accounts to which it has been posted store the transaction information in the accounts affected by the journal entry. After a trial balance has been taken, the trial balance stores the information temporarily awaiting financial statement preparation. The information is stored permanently on the financial statements.

In automated accounting, means of storage must be used which make it possible to complete the accounting cycle automatically. Means of storing journal entries, ledger account balances, and trial balance information must be found. Any means of storing accounting information in between the steps of the automated accounting cycle is known as a *storage device*.

External Storage Devices. Storage devices physically removed from an automated data processing system that can be fed into the system when desired are known as *external storage devices*. Punched cards, punched paper tape, and magnetic tape have already been discussed as input devices. All three of these input devices are able to retain transaction information for long periods of time. For this reason, in conjunction with the fact that they can be physically removed from the system, punched cards, punched paper tape, and magnetic tape are used also as data (external) storage devices.

Externally Stored Journal Entries. External storage devices may be used either for temporary storage or for permanent storage of transaction information. Punched cards are excellent storage devices for journal entries. This is because a separate punched card can be used to record each debit part of a journal entry and a separate punched card can be used to record each credit part of a journal entry. The cards can then be machine sorted by ledger account titles for machine posting.

Journal entries may also be stored on punched paper tape or magnetic tape. However, reels of tape cannot be sorted in the same way that punched cards are sorted. Journal entries on reels of tape must be machine posted in the order in which they were recorded. This is the same order in which journal entries would be posted manually. The only advantage that the posting of tape reels by machine has over manual posting is that machine posting is faster and relatively free of error.

Internal Storage Devices. The storage phase of an electronic system is contained within the machinery. The storage phase receives instructions from control, which have been passed on from input. These instructions are of four types:

(a) Take data from input   (c) Receive data from arithmetic
(b) Send data to arithmetic   (d) Send data to output

As mentioned earlier, each individual computer storage location is known as a storage address. Devices for storing accounting information within a computer are known as *internal storage devices.*

Accounting information may be stored internally on tiny doughnut-shaped metal cores, on cylinder-shaped metal drums, or on large metal disks. Metal cores, metal drums, and metal disks must all be magnetized for use as internal storage devices. Electronic transistors may also be used as internal storage devices.

Internally Stored Ledgers. Internal storage devices are used in automated accounting to keep ledger accounts up-to-date. Each account in the ledger is assigned a storage address. Debits and credits are fed in on punched cards or reels of tape. Control instructs input to transfer a debit or a credit amount into storage.

The incoming debit or credit amount must go to a storage address different from the address assigned to the related ledger account. Since this address is needed only for the current posting operation, it is not permanently assigned. However, the accountant must keep a chart of storage addresses in order to know at all times which addresses are assigned and which are open. This chart corresponds to the chart of accounts in manual accounting.

Automatic Posting. Automatic posting requires the following steps:

Step 1. Control instructs storage to transfer the old balance of the ledger account from its assigned address to the arithmetic unit.

Step 2. Control instructs storage to transfer the related debit or credit amount, which has just come into storage, to arithmetic.

Step 3. Control instructs arithmetic to combine the debit and credit amounts with the old balances of the ledger accounts in accordance with the rules governing debit and credit. A debit amount will be added to a ledger account having a debit balance and a credit will be subtracted. A credit amount will be added to a ledger account having a credit balance and a debit will be subtracted.

Step 4. Control instructs storage to receive the new ledger account balance from arithmetic and to store it in the assigned storage address for the particular ledger account. This is the same address in which the old ledger account balance was stored.

In an automated accounting system, when a new item is stored electronically in the same storage address as a previous item, the new item replaces the old item at that address.

To illustrate the automated posting process, suppose that the cash account is assigned storage address number 10. The beginning cash balance, a debit of $1,200, becomes input by means of a punched card and is sent to address number 10 by the control unit. Suppose also that a debit to the cash account, in the amount of $50, is placed in input by means of another punched card and is sent by control to address number 100 for temporary storage. (There are 2,000 internal storage addresses in the automated data processing system that we are using to illustrate automatic posting.)

The posting process will proceed as follows:

Step 1. Control instructs storage to transfer the beginning cash balance of $1,200 from address number 10 to arithmetic.

Step 2. Control instructs storage to transfer the $50 debit to the cash account from address number 100 to arithmetic.

Step 3. Control instructs arithmetic to add the $50 cash debit to the beginning balance of $1,200.

Step 4. Control instructs storage to receive the new cash balance, $1,250, and to store it back in address number 10, the address permanently assigned to the cash account.

This process is repeated for each succeeding debit and each succeeding credit to the cash account. A similar process is used for all automated posting.

Limitations of Internal Storage. The illustration of automated posting demonstrates that internal storage is used both for permanent storage of ledger account balances and for temporary storage of debits and credits to ledger accounts. A small business having relatively few ledger accounts could get along with a rather small amount of internal storage. However, a large business having a great many ledger accounts would need a rather large amount of internal storage. Internal storage either must be large enough to handle the ledger accounts and the posting operations of the automated accounting system in which it is used, or ledger account balances will have to be stored externally on magnetic tape or punched cards.

The Arithmetic Phase in Automated Accounting

The arithmetic phase of an electronic system receives instructions from control to add, subtract, multiply, divide, or to compare two numbers. Arithmetic works with only two numbers at a time, having received them from different storage locations. To avoid returning subtotals or partial products to storage, however, arithmetic has a temporary electronic storage unit of its own. The electronic storage device in the arithmetic phase of a computer system used to store subtotals and partial products for further processing is known as an *accumulator*.

The Output Phase in Automated Accounting

In many ways, the output phase in automated accounting is just the reverse of the input phase. Punched cards, punched paper tape, and magnetic tape have already been described as input devices and as storage devices. Cards and reels of tape may also be used effectively as output devices.

Upon request, control will instruct storage to punch out cards or tape or to write on magnetic tape any information desired. This information might be journal entries, ledger account balances, trial balances, or financial statements. The cards or tapes must then be converted to English language information.

The Tabulator as an Output Device. The tabulator has already been discussed in connection with the use of the punched card. As indicated, it can list, total, or print journal entries, ledger account balances, trial balances, or financial statements whenever desired. The tabulator prints a line at a time and can handle up to 90 lines a minute.

The Flexowriter as an Output Device. The flexowriter has already been discussed in connection with the use of punched paper tape. As indicated, it can be used to prepare any accounting record or statement automatically from a tape punched by the output unit of an electronic computer or punched by itself.

The High-Speed Printer as an Output Device. High-speed printing machines are now available into which punched cards, paper tape, or magnetic tape may be fed. These machines use electronic grids or type wheels in the printing process instead of the type bars used by the tabulator. High-speed printing machines are capable of printing in excess of 1200 lines of information per minute.

The Use of Automated Accounting by Professional Persons

It is unlikely that lawyers or physicians, even large law firms or a number of physicians practicing in a clinic, will have sufficient accounting work to warrant the acquisition of automated equipment. This does not mean, however, that all work in such law firms or clinics must be done manually. Sometimes it is possible to have all or part of the accounting work done by a public accountant who has some form of automated equipment, or the work may be done by an organization known as a *service bureau*. The public accountant or service bureau will take the basic accounting data and process it. For example, financial statements, payroll reports, and income tax returns may be prepared and returned to the client.

In some localities it is possible for professional persons and persons engaged in business to have much of their accounting work done by the bank which handles their checking account. The bank must be provided with the account numbers used in the chart of accounts. Special checks and deposit tickets are then used which have spaces for the account numbers and amounts. Adjustment forms are used to correct accounts, delete or add accounts, or to handle items not reflected in activity in the checking account. For example, a person may wish to enter interest from savings into his income classification. This may be done with the adjustment form without having to make a deposit. Cash purchases could be entered in the same way.

Based on the coded information, the bank prepares monthly statements of income and expense by category. These statements may show data for the month and year to date as well as a comparison with the previous year. Also the data may be shown both by dollar amount and percentage.

If some of the accounting work is done by an outside organization, the secretary-bookkeeper in the employ of the professional person or persons will keep the basic records. This will usually be the information recorded in the book or books of original entry. In a physician's office, for example, the secretary-bookkeeper will probably keep the daily service record and the records of cash receipts and disbursements. This information together with supplementary data on such things as depreciation rates on the long-lived assets will make it possible for an accountant in public practice or a service bureau, or a bank to complete the accounting records and prepare the financial statements.

Systems Using Accounting Boards

Another method of speeding up accounting work in a professional enterprise is through the use of a manual system which employs some type of accounting board. An *accounting board* is a device with posts on the left side. One or more printed forms with holes on the left side can be positioned on the board. When the forms are fitted over the posts, they are held in place and information written on the top form will also appear in the proper place on the forms below. For example, in recording payrolls, it is possible to create three records with one writing — the check, payroll journal, and the employee's earnings record. The use of a system designed for physicians can create the daily service record, the patient's individual account record, and the patient's receipt with just one writing. In the accounting board illustrated on page A-19, a disbursements journal is given for Hensel, Berry, and Moore, Attorneys at Law. Use of this accounting board enables the secretary-bookkeeper to record the entry in the disbursements journal while writing the check (see left side of journal). It also eliminates the need to fill in a check stub and address an envelope (see lower right corner of journal). Records prepared by using an accounting board system can also be sent to an outside accountant or service bureau for further processing, if desired.

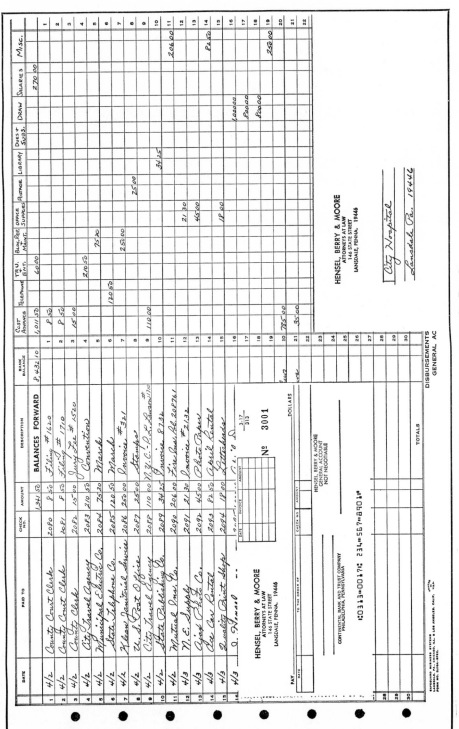

Hensel, Berry & Moore — Accounting Board

glossary

Account — The form of record kept for each asset, liability, owner's equity, revenue, and expense on the books of the enterprise.

Account form of balance sheet — A balance sheet in which the assets are presented on the left and the liabilities and owner's equity accounts are presented on the right.

Accounting — The recording, classification, storage, summarization, reporting, and interpretation of financial information.

Accounting board — A device on which one or more printed forms can be positioned so that several records such as checks, payroll journals, and employees' earnings records are created with one writing.

Accounting cycle — The steps involved in handling all of the transactions and events completed during an accounting period beginning with recording in a journal and ending with a post-closing trial balance.

Accounts payable — Unwritten promises to pay creditors for property such as merchandise, supplies, and equipment purchased on credit, or for services rendered.

Accounts receivable — Unwritten promises by customers to pay for goods purchased on credit or for services rendered.

Accumulated depreciation — The accumulated portions of the cost of a long-lived asset which have been charged to depreciation expense.

Accumulator — The electronic storage device in the arithmetic phase of a computer system used to store subtotals and partial products for further processing.

Adjusted trial balance — A trial balance which contains the balances of the ledger accounts after the required adjustments have been made.

Adjusting entries — Entries made to bring certain accounts up to date at the close of the accounting period.

Arithmetic — The phase of automated accounting in which the primary work is done.

Assets — Properties of value that are owned by an enterprise.

Automated equipment — Equipment that operates without human guidance other than the press of a button.

Balance sheet — A statement which shows the assets, liabilities, and owner's equity of a business or professional practice at a specified date; also referred to as a statement of financial condition, or a statement of financial position.

Bank service charge — A charge made by a bank for the handling of checks and other items.

Bank statement — A statement rendered by a bank to each depositor showing the activity in the account during the period of time covered by the statement.

Book of original entry — The first formal double-entry record of a transaction, also referred to as a journal.

Book value — The difference between the cost of a long-lived asset and the accumulated depreciation of the asset.

Capital — The amount by which the assets of the enterprise exceed its liabilities; also referred to as owner's equity, proprietorship, or net worth.

Cashbook — A book in which only transactions involving cash receipts and disbursements are recorded.

Cash payments journal — A separate record of cash payments or disbursements.

Cash receipts journal — A separate record of cash receipts.

Chart of accounts — A list of the accounts in the ledger usually arranged in the order of assets, liabilities, owner's equity, revenue, and expense.

Check — A written negotiable form signed by the depositor ordering the bank to pay a specified sum of money to a designated person or to his order from funds credited to the depositor's account.

Check register — A journal used by an enterprise when all disbursements are made by check.

Clearing account — An account used only at the close of the accounting period for the purpose of summarizing the revenue and expense accounts.

Combined cash journal — A journal with four or more columns which combines the features of a two-column general journal and a cashbook.

Control — The nerve center, or "action central," of the automated data processing system.

Credit — The right side of an account.

Credit entry — An entry recorded on the right side of an account.

Creditors — Those persons or business establishments who supply products and services which will be paid for later, or who lend money to the enterprise.

Current assets — Cash and all other assets that may be reasonably expected to be realized in cash or sold or consumed during the normal operating cycle of the enterprise.

Current liabilities — Obligations that will be due in a short time and paid with monies provided by the current assets.

Debit — The left side of an account.

Debit entry — An entry recorded on the left side of an account.

Deposit ticket — A form banks provide depositors to use for a detailed listing of items being deposited.

Depreciation expense — The portion of the cost of a long-lived asset charged to expense in each accounting period.

Dishonored check — A check that a bank refuses to pay.

Double-entry bookkeeping — A recording system that involves the making of a record of each of the two or more aspects that are involved in every transaction.

Electronic data processing — The processing of business transactions by the use of an electronic computer.

Encoder — A special machine for printing magnetic ink characters on checks.

Endorsement — The signature or stamp of a depositor on the back of a check.

Equity — Interest in or claim on assets of a business.

Expense — A decrease in the owner's equity in an enterprise caused by a transaction other than a withdrawal by the owner.

Expense and revenue summary — An account to which the balances of the revenue and expense accounts are transferred when closing them at the end of the accounting period, a clearing account; also referred to as income summary, profit and loss summary, or summary account. The balance of the expense and revenue summary account represents the net income or net loss for the period.

External storage device — Storage devices physically removed from an automated data processing system that can be fed into the system when desired.

Field — A group of columns on a punched card used for a single item of information such as a customer's name and address.

Financial statements — Reports prepared to summarize and communicate economic information about the enterprise to interested persons.

Fiscal year — The annual accounting period, which may or may not be a calendar year, adopted by an enterprise.

Flexowriter — An automatic writing machine with a tape-punching attachment.

Footing — The process of totaling the debit and credit amounts in each account before taking a trial balance.

High-speed printer — High-speed printing machine into which punched cards, paper tape, or magnetic tape may be fed and which will print in excess of 1,200 lines of information per minute.

Income statement — A report showing the net income or net loss of an enterprise for a specified period of time and how it was calculated; also referred to as operating statement or profit and loss statement.

Input — Information about a business transaction in a form acceptable for use in automated data processing equipment.

Input device — Any acceptable means for presenting information about a business transaction to an automated machine.

Integrated data processing — The processing of business transactions by the use of office machines with card punches or tape punches attached.

Internal storage device — Devices for storing accounting information within a computer.

Journal — The first formal double-entry record of a transaction, also referred to as a book of original entry.

Journalizing — The act of recording transactions in a journal.

Key punch — A machine used to punch information holes into punched cards from source documents.

Ledger — A group of related accounts for a specific enterprise.

Liabilities — Debts owed by an enterprise to its creditors.

Long-lived assets — Assets such as land, buildings, and equipment which have a useful life that is comparatively long.

Long-term liabilities — Obligations such as mortgages payable that will not be due for a relatively long time.

Magnetic ink character recognition (MICR) — The use of magnetic ink symbol numbers in the processing of bank checks.

Matching principle — A principle which holds that revenues earned and expenses incurred during a period should be matched against each other.

Mortgage payable — A debt or obligation secured by a mortgage which provides for the surrender of certain property if the debt is not paid at maturity.

Net income — The amount by which revenue earned exceeds the expenses necessary to earn the revenue.

Net loss — The amount by which expenses necessary to earn revenue exceed the revenue earned.

Net worth — The amount by which the assets of the enterprise exceed its liabilities; also referred to as owner's equity, capital, or proprietorship.

Notes payable — Formal written promises to pay creditors or lenders specified sums of money at some future time.

Notes receivable — Formal written promises by debtors to pay specified sums of money at some future time.

Operating statement — A report showing the net income or net loss of an enterprise for a specified period of time and how it was calculated; also referred to as an income statement or profit and loss statement.

Output — Business information from a data processing system in a form acceptable for human use.

Output device — Any acceptable means for converting coded machine information into English language.

Outstanding checks — Checks issued during the period covered by the bank statement, but which have not been presented to the bank for payment.

Overdraft — A check or checks issued against a bank in excess of the amount on deposit.

Owner's equity — The amount by which the assets of the enterprise exceed its liabilities; also referred to as capital, proprietorship, or net worth.

Petty cash fund — A small cash fund established for paying small items.

Post-closing trial balance — A trial balance containing only the balance sheet accounts prepared at the end of the accounting period after the revenue and expense accounts have been closed.

Postdated check — A check dated later than the date of issue.

Posting — The process of transferring information entered in the journal to the ledger.

Posting reference — A cross reference between the journal and the ledger.

Profit — The amount by which revenue earned exceeds the expenses necessary to earn the revenue.

Profit and loss statement — A report showing the net income or net loss of an enterprise for a specified period of time and how it was calculated; also referred to as an operating statement or income statement.

Program — A detailed list of steps to be followed in completing the automated accounting cycle.

Proprietorship — The amount by which the assets of the enterprise exceed its liabilities; also referred to as capital, owner's equity, or net worth.

Reconciliation of bank statement — A determination of the reason for differences between the balance on the bank statement and the balance on the depositor's books.

Report form of balance sheet — A balance sheet in which the assets are presented at the top and the liabilities and owner's equity accounts are presented below.

Restrictive endorsement — An endorsement that limits the holder of the check as to the use to be made of the amount collected.

Revenue — An increase in the owner's equity in an enterprise resulting from transactions of any kind except the investment of assets in the enterprise by its owner.

Self-employment income — The net income of a professional practice or business conducted by an individual, or a partner's distributive share of the net income of a partnership.

Service bureau — An organization which will take the basic accounting data and process such items as financial statements, payroll reports, and income tax returns.

Signature card — A card signed by a depositor to give the bank a sample of his signature.

Sorter — A machine that automatically groups all punched cards of a similar kind and arranges them in some order.

Source document — The immediate record prepared either by hand or by machine which is always the key record in an automated accounting system.

Statement of financial condition — A statement which shows the assets, liabilities, and owner's equity of a business or professional practice at a specified date; also referred to as balance sheet.

Statement of financial position — A statement which shows the assets, liabilities, and owner's equity of a business or professional practice at a specified date; also referred to as balance sheet

Storage — Location of information awaiting further use in automated accounting, often referred to as "memory."

Storage device — Any means of storing accounting information in between the steps of the automated accounting cycle.

Summary account — An account to which the balances of the revenue and expense accounts are transferred when closing them at the end of each accounting period; a clearing account, also referred to as expense and revenue summary, income summary, profit and loss summary. The balance of the summary account represents the net income or net loss for the period.

Tabulator — An automatic printing machine that lists, totals, and prints information previously punched onto cards.

Taxes payable — Obligations of an enterprise to pay sums of money based on established rates to various governmental units.

Temporary owner's equity accounts — Revenue and expense accounts.

Time deposits — Interest bearing deposits which are expected to remain in the bank for a period of time.

Transactions — The events or conditions taking place in an enterprise which must be recorded in terms of money or value.

Trial balance — A list of all the accounts showing the title and balance of each account.

Verifier — A machine that looks exactly like a key punch and is used to find punching errors.

Withholding allowances — Additional withholding exemptions granted to employees with large itemized deductions.

Work sheet — A columnar device that assists the accountant in preparing the financial statements, the making of needed adjustments in the accounts, and the closing of the revenue and expense accounts.

Write-it-once principle — The basic idea in systems which prepare several records at once such as a payroll check, an earnings record, and a payroll register.

index

B

Balance sheet, 9,10, 41, 43, 166; account form, 42, 43, 167; classification of data, 167; columns of ten-column work sheet, 163; form of, 167; importance of, 166; report form, 167; Harold R. Stewart, Attorney at Law, 168–169; The Whitman Advertising Agency, 42–43
Balances, credit, 19; debit, 19
Balancing and ruling open accounts, 180; illustrated, 181
Bank, 59, ABA magnetic ink symbol numbers, illustrated, A-11; ABA transit numbers, 60; automatic teller machines, 61; checking account, 59–72; deposits, 63; electronic processing of checks, 66; keeping a ledger account with, 71; processing of encoded checks, A-12; recording transactions, 67; records kept by, 67; savings account, 72; service charges, 71; signature card, 59; time deposits, 72
Bank checks, *see* Checks
Bank statement, 68; illustrated, 69; reconciling the, 68, 71
Bank transactions, recording, 67
Banking procedure, 59–73
Basic phases of automated data processing, A-4
Book of original entry, 22
Book value, 112, 168
Bookkeeper, definition of, 4
Bookkeeping, double-entry, 21, 44
Books of account, 114, 135
Business accounting, nature of, 1; purpose of, 1
Business assets, 5
Business enterprises, 110
Business papers, 22

C

Calendar year, 16
Capital, 4
Cash, 45; accounting for 44–73; definition of, 45; disbursements, 46; items, 45; petty, 53–58; proving, 52, 71; receipts, 45; recording receipts and disbursements, 46; short and over, 53
Cash account, 45; in balance, 45; short and over, 53
Cash basis of accounting, for a personal service enterprise, 111; for physicians and surgeons, 133
Cash disbursements, 46; recording the, 46
Cash disbursements journal, 51
Cash journals, 51; cash disbursements, 51; cash payments, 51; cash receipts, 51; check register, 51; *see* Combined cash journal
Cash payments journal, 51
Cash receipts, 45; recording, 46
Cash receipts journal, 51
Cashbook, 51
Certified Public Accountant (CPA), 2
Charge, 13
Charges, service, 71
Chart of accounts, 24, 25, 112, 134; code of, 25; Mason and Edwards, Physicians and Surgeons, 134; Harold R. Stewart, At-

torney at Law, 112; The Whitman Advertising Agency, 25
Check register, 51
Check stub, 64, 67
Checkbook, 64
Checking account, 59; bank statement, 69; credit advice, 68; debit advice, 63; deposit ticket, 59; deposits by mail, 63; night deposits, 63; opening a, 59; overdraft, 66; recording bank transactions, 67; records kept by bank, 67; service charges, 70; signature card, 59; withdrawing from, 64
Checks, 67; ABA numbers, 60, A-11; checkbook, 64; checkwriter, 65; clearing encoded through Federal Reserve System, A-12; counter, 70; dishonored, 62; electronic processing of, 66, A-12; encoding symbol numbers on, A-11; endorsement of, 61; magnetic ink character recognition (MICR), 66, A-11; magnetic ink symbol numbers, illustrated, A-11; not sufficient funds (NSF), 62; postdated, 63; processing encoded in individual banks, A-12; restrictive endorsement, 61; sorted by Federal Reserve system, A-12; and stubs, illustrated, 67; writing, 65
Checkwriter, 65
Classification of data, in balance sheet, 167
Classifying, in accounting, 3
Clearing account, 170
Closed accounts, ruling the, 177–180
Closing accounts at end of accounting period, 172–184
Closing entries, 175; for Harold R. Stewart, Attorney at Law, 177; journalizing the, 176; posting the, 176
Closing procedure, 175
Code of accounts, 25
Collection docket, lawyer's, 116, 118
Collection fees income, 113
Columns of standard two-column journal, 23
Combined cash journal, 51, 114, 135; adjusting entries, 173; closing entries, 176; Mason and Edwards, Physicians and Surgeons, 144–147; Harold R. Stewart, Attorney at Law, 124–127
Compensation, types of, 75
Compound entry, 58
Contra-assets, 112
Control, in automated data processing, A-4, A-13
Counter checks, 70
Credit advice, 68
Credit balances, 19
Creditors, definition of, 1
Credits, 12, 13
Current assets, 167
Current liabilities, 168
Customer remittance stubs, posting the, A-9; sorting the, A-8
Cycle, accounting, 182; normal operating, 167

D

Daily service record, 136, 157
Data processing, A-2
Debit advice, 62; illustrated, 63
Debit balances, 19
Debits, 12, 13

Decrease in asset offset by decrease in liability, 8, 15; in asset offset by decrease in owner's equity resulting from expense, 8, 18
Deduction stub, machine prepared, 87; manually prepared, 83
Deductions, and earnings, 75–92; from total earnings, 77
Deposit, Federal Tax (Form 501), 97
Deposit ticket, 59, 60
Deposits, 63; by mail, 63; night, 63; time, 72
Depreciation, 111, 173
Depreciation expense, 111, 112
Determination of total earnings, 76
Disbursements, cash, 46; petty cash, 54–58; recording cash, 46, 51
Discounting commercial paper, 68
Dishonored checks, 62
Double-entry bookkeeping, 11
Double-entry mechanism, 11–20
Dual effect of transactions, 11

E

Earnings, and deductions, 75, 92; deductions from total, 77; determination of total, 76; types of compensation, 75
Earnings record, 83; employee's machine prepared, 88; employee's manually prepared, 84
EDP systems, magnetic tape as input device, A-11; magnetic ink symbols as input devices, A-11
Electronic data processing (EDP), A-2; of checks, 66, A-12; of payrolls, 85
Employee, defined, 75
Employees' earnings record, 83; machine prepared, 88; manually prepared, 84
Employees' FICA taxes withheld, 80
Employees' income taxes payable, 91
Employees' income taxes withheld, 77
Employees' payroll register, machine prepared, 89; manually prepared, 80–81
Employer-employee relationships, 75
Employer's FICA tax, 80, 93
Employer's FUTA tax, 94
Employer's identification number, 90
Employer's payroll taxes, filing returns and payment of, 97; journalizing, 96
Employer's Quarterly Federal Tax Return and Quarterly Report, Schedule A (Form 941), 99
Employer's state unemployment taxes, 95, 96
Encoder, A-11
Encoding symbol numbers on bank checks, A-11
End-of-period adjustments, 173
End-of-period work sheet, 159–164; illustrated, 161; see Work sheet
Endorsement, 61; restrictive, 61
Entries, adjusting, 173–174; closing, 176–177; compound, 58; journalizing the adjusting, 173; journalizing the closing, 176; posting the adjusting, 174; posting the closing, 176
Equation, accounting, 5; effect of transactions on, 7
Equity, 4
Equity, owner's, 4, 169–170
Exemptions, withholding, 177

Expense, defined, 16; depreciation, 112; employer's payroll tax, 93; payroll tax expense account, 93; and revenue, 15; use of expense and revenue accounts, 17; wages expense account, 91
Expense and revenue summary, 113, 175
External storage devices, A-13
Externally stored journal entries, A-13

F

Federal Deposit Tax Form (Form 501), 97
Federal Fair Labor Standards Act, 76
Federal income tax withholding table, portion of married persons weekly, 79
Federal Insurance Contributions Act (FICA), 80, 90, 93
Federal Reserve system, clearing encoded bank checks through, A-12; sorting checks, A-12
Federal Unemployment Tax Act (FUTA), 94
Fee, 75; collection, 113; legal, 113; professional, 134
FICA tax, employer's, 80, 93
FICA taxes payable, 91; employees' withheld, 80; employer's, 93
Field, A-7
Filing returns and paying payroll taxes, 97
Financial condition statement, 10
Financial information, users of, 1, 2
Financial position statement, 10
Financial statements, 9, 39–43, 164–170; balance sheet, 10, 41–43, 166; income statement, 9, 39–40, 164
Fiscal year, 16
Five-channel punched paper tape, A-10
Fixed liabilities, 168
Flexowriter, Friden, A-10; as an output device, A-16
Footing, 19; accounts, 36; the petty cash disbursements record, 56; and ruling the four-column journal, 49; the two-column journal, 31
Footings, in balance, 19
Form 501, 97
Form 941, 99
Form SS-5, 77
Form W-2, 90
Form W-4, 78
Four-column journal, 46–51; footing, 49; illustrated, 47; posting from, 50; proof of journal footings, illustrated, 49; proving, 48; ruling, 49; special columns in, 51, 52
Friden five-channel punched paper tape, A-10
Friden flexowriter, A-10
FUTA tax, employer's 94
FUTA taxes payable, 94

G

General ledger, 31, 115, 135; Mason and Edwards, Physicians and Surgeons, 149–155; Harold R. Stewart, Attorney at Law, 128–131; The Whitman Advertising Agency, 34–35

H

Health insurance for the aged (HIP), 80
High-speed printer, A-8; as an output device, A-16

I

IBM card, A-5; standard, A-6
IBM key punch, A-7
IBM sorter, A-9
IBM verifier, A-8
Identification number, employer's, 90
Imprest method, 58
In balance, 19
Income and expense statement, 164
Income and self-employment taxes, 183
Income statement, 9, 39, 164; form of the, 165; importance of the, 165; Harold R. Stewart, Attorney at Law, 166; The Whitman Advertising Agency (model), 40
Income statement columns, of ten-column work sheet, 162
Income summary, 175
Income tax withholding table, portion of married persons weekly, 79
Income taxes, employees' income taxes payable account, 91; employees' withheld, 77
Increase in asset offset by increase in liability, 7, 14; in asset offset by increase in owner's equity, 7, 14; in asset offset by increase in owner's equity resulting from revenue, 8, 18; in one asset offset by decrease in another asset, 8, 15
Independent contractor, 75
Individual posting, 50
Input, in automated data processing, A-4; magnetic ink symbol numbers as, A-11; magnetic tape as, A-11; punched card as, A-5; punched paper tape as, A-9
Integrated data processing (IDP), A-2; and punched paper tape, A-10
Internal storage, A-14; limitations of, A-15
Internal storage devices, A-14
Internally stored ledgers, A-14
Interpretation, in accounting, 3
Invoice, 120

J

Journal, 22; defined, 21; purpose of, 31
Journal, cash disbursements, 51
Journal, cash payments, 51
Journal, cash receipts, 51
Journal, cashbook, 51
Journal, check register, 51
Journal, combined cash, 51, 114, 135; adjusting entries, 173; closing entries, 176; Mason and Edwards, Physicians and Surgeons, 144–147; special columns in, 51; Harold R. Stewart, Attorney at Law, 124–127
Journal, four-column, 46; footing and ruling, 49; illustrated, 47; journalizing procedure illustrated, 47–48; posting from, 50; proving, 48; special columns in, 51, 52; The Whitman Advertising Agency, 48
Journal, two-column, 22; illustrated, 23; posting from, 32; proving, 31; The Whitman Advertising Agency, 29–30
Journal entries, externally stored, A-13; purpose of, 22
Journalizing, 21, 24, 44; the adjusting entries, 173; the closing entries, 176; compound entry, 58; employers' payroll taxes, 96;

payroll transactions, 92; petty cash disbursements, 58; procedure illustrated, 26, 47; transactions, 21

L

Language of automated accounting systems, A-1
Lawyer's docket, collection, 116, 118; office, 116, 117
Ledger, 22; posting to, 31, 32; patient's, 136; see General ledger
Ledger account with bank, 71
Ledgers, internally stored, A-14
Legal fees income, 113
Liabilities, 4; business, 5; current, 168; fixed, 168; long-term, 168; nonbusiness, 5
Liability, decrease in, 8, 15; increase in, 7, 14
Life insurance premiums payable, 92
Long-lived assets, 168; depreciation of, 111, 173
Long-term liabilities, 168

M

Magnetic ink character recognition (MICR), 66, A-11; equipment, 66
Magnetic ink symbol numbers, bank check with, A-11; as input devices, A-11
Magnetic tape, as an input device, A-11
Mail deposits, 63
Management services, 2
Matching principle, 111
Merit-rating system, 95
Mortgage, 169

N

Narrative of transactions, J. K. Jenkins' petty cash disbursements, 55; Mason and Edwards, Physicians and Surgeons, 136; Harold R. Stewart, Attorney at Law, 119
Nature of business accounting, 1–20
Net income, 6, 16; calculation of, 165
Net loss, 9, 16; calculation of, 165
Net worth, 4
Net profit, 9
Night deposits, 63
Nonbusiness assets, 5
Normal balances of accounts, 19
Normal operating cycle, 167
Notes payable, 4
Notes receivable, 4
NSF check, 62

O

Office docket, lawyer's, 116, 117
Old-age, survivors, and disability insurance (OASDI), 80
Open accounts, balancing and ruling, 180; illustrated, 181
Operating cycle, normal, 167
Operating statement, 9, 164
Original entry, book of, 22, 44
Output phase, in automated accounting, A-16; in electronic data processing, A-5
Output device, A-5; flexowriter, A-16; high-speed printer, A-16; tabulator, A-16

Overdraft, 65
Owner's equity, 4, 169; decrease in, 8, 16, 18; increase in, 7, 8, 14, 15, 17, 18; temporary accounts, 17

P

Paper tape, punched, A-9
Passbook, 61, 73
Patient's account, 136; illustrated, 137
Patients' ledger, 136
Paycheck, machine prepared, 86; manually prepared, 82
Payroll, accounting, 74–101; automated systems, 85; employee's earnings record, 83, 84, 88; employer-operated systems, 86; journalizing transactions, 92; records, 80; service bureaus, 85; types of compensation, 75; withholding allowances, 78; write-it-once principle, 85–87
Payroll register, 81; machine prepared, 89; manually prepared, 80–81
Payroll taxes, 80; application for social security and tax account number, 77; deductions from total earnings, 77; employee's income taxes withheld, 77; Employer's Quarterly Federal Tax Return and Quarterly Report (Form 941), 99; expense of employer, 93; FICA taxes payable, 93; filing returns and paying, 97; FUTA taxes payable, 94; imposed on employer, 93–96; journalizing employer's, 96; state unemployment taxes, 95; state unemployment taxes payable, 96; wage-bracket method of determining, 78; withholding exemption certificate, 78; withholding tax statement, 90
Periodic summary, 158–171
Personal service enterprise, 110–157; adjusting entries, 173; auxiliary records, 115, 136; balancing and ruling open accounts, 181; books of account 114; cash basis of accounting for, 111; chart of accounts, 112, 134; combined cash journal, 114, 124–127, 135, 144–147; financial statements, 164; general ledger, 115, 128–131, 135, 149–155; narrative of transactions, 26, 55, 119, 136; post-closing trial balance, 132, 156; ruling the closed accounts, 177–180; types of, 110; work sheet, 159, 161
Petty cash disbursements record, 54, 115, 136; of J. K. Jenkins, 56–57; proving the, 56
Petty cash disbursements statement, of J. K. Jenkins, 57; of Mason and Edwards, Physicians and Surgeons, 148; of Harold R. Stewart, Attorney at Law, 127
Petty cash fund, 53; imprest method, 58; journalizing disbursements, 58; operating a, 53; writing check for, 65
Petty cash transactions, of J. K. Jenkins, 55
Petty cash voucher, 54
Post-closing trial balance, 182; Harold R. Stewart, Attorney at Law, 183
Postdated checks, 63
Posting, 32, 44; the adjusting entries, 174; automatic, A-14; the closing entries, 176; customer remittance stubs, A-9; from four-column journal, 50; to the ledger, 31; summary, 50

Posting reference column, 12, 23
Practical accounting problems, Chapters 1–4, 102–109; Chapters 5–8, 185–199
Professional enterprises, 110
Professional fees, 134
Profit and loss, 175
Profit and loss statement, 9, 164
Profit and loss summary, 175
Program, in automated data processing, A-5
Programmer, A-5
Proprietorship, 4
Proving, cash, 52, 71; the four-column journal, 48; the petty cash disbursements record, 56; the two-column journal, 31; the work sheet, 163
Public accountants, 2
Punched card, as an input device, A-5; planning the use of, A-6; printing information on, A-8; punching information into, A-7; standard IBM, A-6; statement of account, A-8; verifying the information on, A-8
Punched paper tape, A-9; Friden five-channel, A-10

Q

Quarterly Federal Tax Return and Quarterly Report, Employer's (Form 941), 99

R

Receipts, cash, 45; recording, 46
Reconciling the bank statement, 68, 71
Record, petty cash disbursements, 54, 56–57; daily service, 136, 157
Recording, in accounting, 3; bank transactions, 67; cash receipts and disbursements, 46
Records, auxiliary, 58, 83, 115, 136; of cash receipts and disbursements, 45; employee's earnings, 83, 84, 88; kept by bank, 67; payroll, 80–89
Registered accountants, 2
Remittance stubs, posting customer, A-9, sorting customer, A-8
Report of earnings, 164
Report form, of balance sheet, 167
Restrictive endorsement, 61; illustrated, 62
Revenue, defined, 16; and expense, 15; use of revenue accounts, 17
Revenue and expense statement, 164
Ruling, and balancing open accounts, 181; the closed accounts 178–180; footing the four-column journal, 49

S

Salary, defined, 75
Savings account, 72
Self-employment income, 183, 184
Self-employment taxes, 183, 184
Service bureau, A-17, and payroll accounting, 85
Service charges, 71
Signature card, 59
Social security and tax account number, application for, 77
Sorter, in automated data processing, A-9
Source document, A-2
Standard form of account, 12

State unemployment taxes, 95; merit-rating system, 95; payable, 95
Statement, balance sheet, 9, 41–43, 166; bank, 68; financial, 9, 39–43; income, 9, 39, 40, 164; operating, 9; profit and loss, 9; reconciling the bank, 68; withholding tax, 90
Statement of account, illustrated, A-8; posting remittance stubs, A-9; punched card, A-8; sorting remittance stubs, A-8
Statement of assets and liabilities, 166
Statement of condition, 166
Statement of financial condition, 10, 166
Statement of financial position, 10, 166
Statement of petty cash disbursements, for J. K. Jenkins, 57; for Mason and Edwards, Physicians and Surgeons, 148; for Harold R. Stewart, Attorney at Law, 127
Storage, in automated data processing, A-5, A-13; limitations of internal, A-15
Storage devices, external, A-13; internal, A-14
Structure of accounting systems, A-1
Summarizing, in accounting, 3
Summary account, 17
Summary posting, 50

T

"T" account form, 13
Tabulator, A-8; as an output device, A-16
Tax account number and social security, 77
Taxes, federal income, 77; FICA, 80, 90, 93; filing returns and paying payroll, 97; FUTA, 93, 94; journalizing employers' payroll, 96; merit-rating system, 95; payable, 96; state unemployment, 95; wage-bracket method of withholding, 78; withholding allowances, 78; withholding exemptions, 77
Temporary owner's equity accounts, 17; purpose of, 172
Ticket, deposit, 59, 60
Time deposit, 72
Transactions, 6; analyses of, 14–18; dual effect of, 11; effect of, on the accounting equation, 7; journalizing, 21; journalizing payroll, 92; narrative for Mason and Edwards, Physicians and Surgeons, 136; narrative for Harold R. Stewart, Attorney at Law, 119; narrative for The Whitman Advertising Agency, 26; typical, 6, 7
Transit numbers, American Bankers Association, 61

Trial balance, 19, 31, 36; adjusted, 162; after closing, 182; illustrated, 20; Mason and Edwards, Physicians and Surgeons, 156; model, 38; post-closing, 182, 183; preparing the, 37; purpose of, 36; Harold R. Stewart, Attorney at Law, 132; The Whitman Advertising Agency, 38
Trial balance columns, of ten-column work sheet, 160
Two-column journal, 22; illustrated, 23; posting from, 32; proving, 31; The Whitman Advertising Agency, 29–30

U

Unemployment taxes, federal (FUTA), 94; state, 95
Use of revenue and expense accounts, 17

V

Verifier, A-8
Voucher, petty cash, 54

W

Wage and tax statement, 90
Wage-bracket method, 78
Wage deductions, accounting for, 91
Wage, accounting for, 91; defined, 75; expense account, 91
Wages and hours law, 76
Withdrawals, making, 64
Withholding exemptions, 77
Withholding tax statement, 90
Withholding, FICA taxes, 80; state taxes, 79; table illustrated, 79; wage-bracket method, 78
Withholding allowances, 78
Withholding Exemption Certificate (Form W-4), 78
Work sheet, adjusted trial balance columns, 162; adjustments columns, 160; balance sheet columns, 163; completing the, 163; end-of-period, 159; for Harold R. Stewart, Attorney at Law, 161; income statement columns, 162; proving the, 163; purpose of, 159; ten-column, illustrated, 161; trial balance columns, 160
Write-it-once principle, 85, A-3; as a labor-saving device, A-2

Y

Year, calendar, 16; fiscal, 16